> "Americans believe in tomorrow, and one great reason for this belief is the story of their own yesterdays. ... History is not a dry-as-dust something ... It can be anything at all that shows the American people living and doing and becoming. Whatever it contains, it is part of the world's most fascinating story."
>
> –Bruce Catton

For Barry —
Best Wishes.

[signature]

2004

Voices on the Water

An Oral and Pictorial History of Antrim County's Chain of Lakes by Glenn Ruggles

Susan Scott Galbraith, Editor
Marissa Penrod, Layout and Book Designer
D. James Galbraith, Photographic Consultant

ISBN 0-9662149-2-7

Dedication

To the voices who have been heard
To the voices who will be heard
To the voices who will never be heard

Cover Photo: The steamer Mabel at Alden on Torch Lake, c. 1908.

Contents

Contents, continued

*"Our duty would not have been done
without mention of the Chain of Lakes,
the beauties of which must be seen to be appreciated —
the unsurpassed beauty of the cool shady rivers
on whose surface sports wild fowl,
and in whose pellucid depths
sport pickerel, bass, muskellunge and trout.
The ever-changing panorama —
the grassy banks — the primeval forest
whose mighty trees
cast shadows of their spreading branches
on the mirror-like surface of the water,
makes this trip a pleasure to the tourist
and seeker for pure air and purer water."*

—1900 newspaper reporter

This almost flawless map (c.1940) of the Chain of Lakes was produced by the defunct Chain-O'-Lakes Council, a non-profit organization sponsored by most businesses in the region. Focusing on the unity of the Chain, the Council was not influenced by political boundaries.

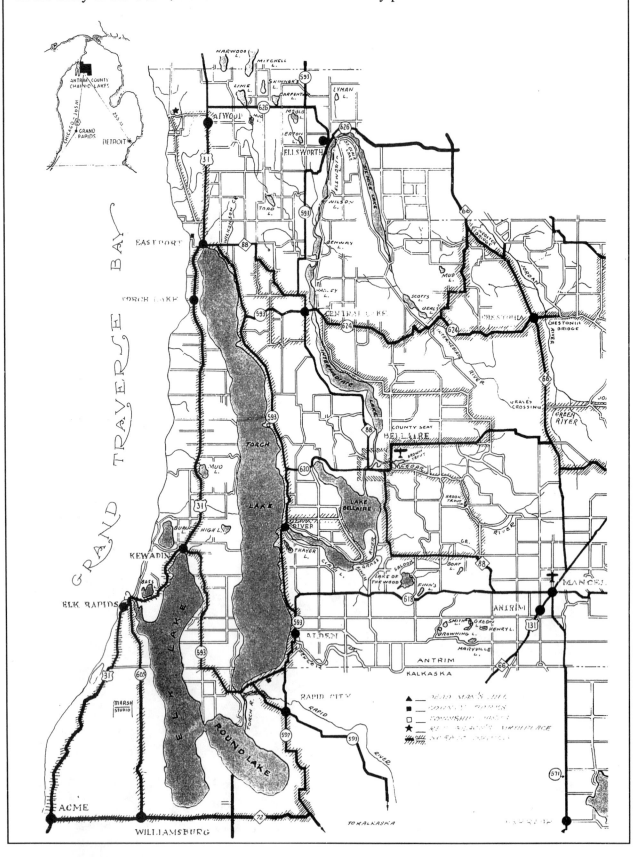

Foreword

by Greg Reisig
Editor, Lake Country Gazette

From its headwaters in north-central Antrim County, the Chain of Lakes runs a serpentine seventy-five miles and touches four counties before it empties into Grand Traverse Bay at Elk Rapids. Nearly every different water form is represented along the way: from small lakes, springs, creeks, wetlands, rivers and streams to the larger, high-profile Torch Lake and into the much shallower Lake Skegemog.

The Chain of Lakes has seldom been written about in its entirety. Most people think of it as only Torch Lake, Torch River and Elk Lake. Few have explored what is known as the upper Chain. **VOICES on the WATER** defines what this fourteen lake chain means to people who have lived on or near the water. Filled with fascinating and essential information, this book is an important twentieth century view of life in northern Michigan.

Using photographs, poems, maps, oral histories and personal reflections, **VOICES on the WATER** tells the story of one of Michigan's unique and valued natural resources.

Author Glenn Ruggles spent twelve years interviewing thirty-eight people who have lived on the Chain. These oral histories tell the story of their relationship to the water and the bonds that have been formed through the generations to this place of spectacular beauty.

Although Ruggles provides the necessary facts and figures about the Chain, it is his oral interviews and personal reflections, combined with the rare historic photographs and maps, that tell the real story.

Once a bustling transportation "highway" for the logging era, the Chain now provides beautiful, clean water for recreational uses. Loved by many, the Chain is watched over by aggressive associations that guard against threats that affect the lakes, properties and lifestyles.

For Ruggles and people on the Chain, this is a place worth caring about.

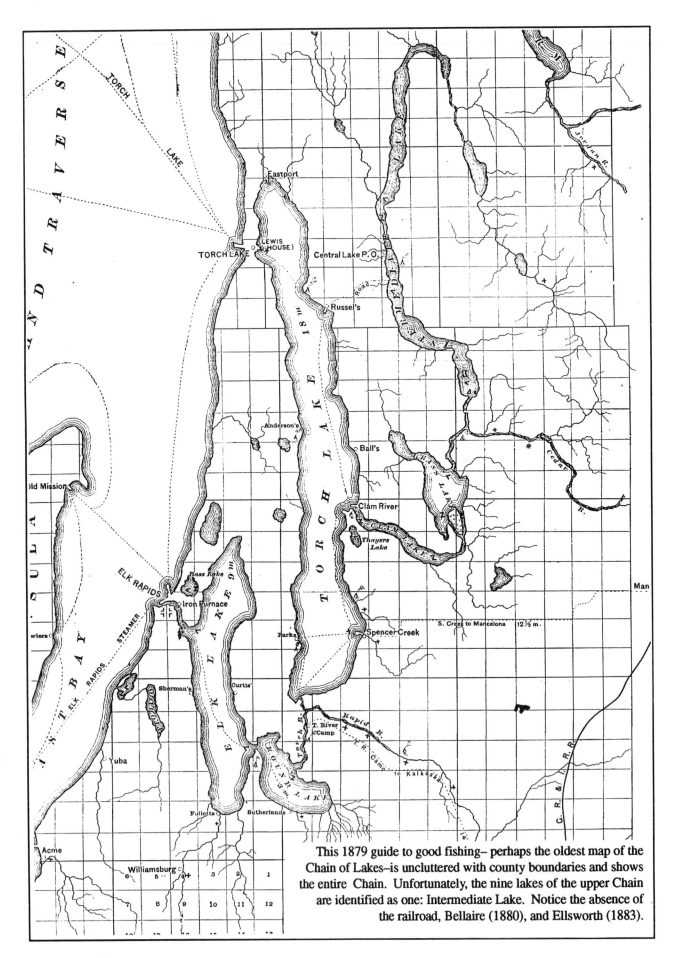

This 1879 guide to good fishing— perhaps the oldest map of the Chain of Lakes—is uncluttered with county boundaries and shows the entire Chain. Unfortunately, the nine lakes of the upper Chain are identified as one: Intermediate Lake. Notice the absence of the railroad, Bellaire (1880), and Ellsworth (1883).

Prologue

Somewhere in the recesses of memory, visual scenes of our past linger expectantly. The photographs and oral histories bring them to the surface offering a strong sense of the past. They are a voice to yesterday as certain as the journal, diary, or the weather-worn 1880 news clipping. Without the itinerant photographer and the spoken word captured on tape, our grasp of yesterday would be seriously lacking.

History is generally written by those who have the luxury to write it; they have the time, the expense and the urge. They are the ones who have created the records and the accounts; they have made the fortunes, held public office and push to preserve their agenda. They are the ones who have built the lumber empires and amassed huge fortunes. But history is lived daily by the unknown and the forgotten. We seldom think they have anything significant to say. They lead their daily lives—often rich and exciting lives—without leaving an account and without being considered by the official chronicler.

Oral history, therefore, is an increasingly popular technique for gathering contemporary history. It involves the tape-recorded interview and the subjects are often people whose views and life experiences have been overlooked. Transcribing a lively and entertaining interview, however, can be difficult, and losing the spoken word to the printed page is a loss that diminishes their lives. The written word fails to depict the laughter, the scowl, the silences that almost speak, and the spontaneity that occurs as the interviewee recalls events of past decades. Nevertheless, to share with others requires that the spoken word appear on paper. My questions have been included so that the reader may enjoy the interaction between the interviewer and interviewee.

The taped and transcribed oral interviews of people who have lived somewhere near the Chain remain the most practical and intimate method for providing a modern-day view of the water.

Many of these individuals have never been interviewed before. Much of what you read here exists in print for the first time. All have a strong sense of the water, though many cannot explain why. All were willing to talk and examine their life experiences with the Chain; that was the chief criteria. There was no hesitation or reluctance; it was as though they understood instantly the importance of the water and the significance of their views.

If the seventy-five mile long Chain is one of the largest spring-fed freshwater chain of lakes in the world—quite a claim—then it deserves a little notice, a bit of attention. Where in the Twentieth Century could one find a book about this magnificent body of water? Bits and pieces appeared in local histories from time to time, but the unity of the Chain was seldom identified.

The obvious void in our local history led to this book. For the proper flavor and historical dimension, I have included much of Antrim County's history as it centered around the Chain: the lumbering, fishing and early settlements of the nineteenth century. Throughout the book, I have chosen to capitalize Chain of Lakes; it is a proper noun.

In writing this book, it was a surprise and a blessing to discover such a candid and highly-qualified group of citizens who were willing to speak of their lives on the Chain. While work on the book took me twelve years, twenty-three of the thirty-eight oral histories were accomplished in the 1990s. There are twenty-five men and thirteen women. There are thirteen interviewees who were older than ninety, and twenty-three who had lived on the Chain since birth or early childhood. With surprising humility, they offered their oral histories for enlightenment and enrichment of the Grand Traverse region.

--Glenn Ruggles

Moving North

The Ruggles family in 1940, a few years before moving north. Left to right: Mary, Charles, Glenn, Margaret, Eugene. Back row: Parents, Beryl and Christena.

It was the summer of 1945 when I first saw Torch Lake. My father and I explored the countryside of Antrim County looking for a farm to buy. At fourteen, I hated the idea of leaving downstate for a permanent move to this God-forsaken place.

We stayed a night or two at Tor-Bay cabins in Torch Lake Village as we explored the area. The rest of the family—two brothers, two sisters, and Mom—stayed behind until a new home was found.

Dad was known as B.D. for Beryl Davis, but he seemed to enjoy it as much for the designation "Black Dirt" Ruggles. During his forty-two years as a landscape architect, he sold a lot of black dirt.

Ever since Dad left farm life in Iowa twenty years earlier, he had yearned to return to the soil. But this is hard country. The land is thin and unforgiving. If a farmer can manage a living here, he can do it anywhere.

"B.D." bought the eighty acre Rosenberg farm, known today as the Cal Bargy farm, on the northeast corner of Campbell Road and old US–31. I thought it was a crazy idea, but Mom and the rest of the kids followed easily.

We had moved frequently during the 1930s and 40s. From Grand Blanc to Hazel Park to Royal Oak and Center Line, landscaping was a bleak business. The Depression had altered or damaged many lives; it was difficult for any family to establish permanence and stability. In time, I came to realize the move north was a good one. Not that I loved farming, but the village of Elk Rapids and the surrounding Chain of Lakes in Antrim County would change my life forever. The rebellious side in me calmed down as I came to love school and learning and everything else about this amazing lakes country.

Our family farm, sandwiched between Torch Lake and Grand Traverse Bay, sat squarely on a thin strip of land in Milton Township, some two and a half miles north of Kewadin.

The sweeping view of Grand Traverse Bay from our front yard was magnificent, offering a daily view of Old Mission and Leelanau peninsulas. We had Torch Lake practically in our back yard. We were happily surrounded by the most unspoiled and attractive water in the world.

Youthful memories are often lost in the passing years. As vivid as my memories seem to be, I know they are elusive like the boundaries of the Chain of Lakes. Years, months, and days blend together. Time and space are difficult places to reach. Our life on the farm is sometimes vague and puzzling to recall. It's amazing how my recollections seem insufficient when compared to another's. Even my younger brother, Eugene, surprised me when he captured our childhood images through the freshness and intimacy of poetry, as he writes in *The Horses*:

THE HORSES

My father's team of horses
a pair of dark roans,
are pulling a huge load of hay
up the last hill toward the barn—

the August heat swarms to them,
its light is buried in the wells
*   of their thighs,*
their legs are rope and bone
and their deep chests nearly measure
the front of the hay wagon,

they stretch out into their strength
until their stomachs are near the ground,
they love their great bodies
and the silent flow between them,

the sun is wet over their backs
it flows along the veins of the harness
and falls from their necks and thighs
into the dry earth where the hoof prints
*   sinking behind them*
have been dusted like bricks by the robes of hay.

Beryl Davis Ruggles, age 18, with his team of horses on an Iowa farm in 1921.

3

Mom left the desolate and isolated fishing village of Whitehead, Nova Scotia twenty-five years before; she had yet to return. It is in *A Harness*, that Eugene captures the loneliness and monotony that farm life had on our Mother, so far from home:

A HARNESS

My mother is churning butter
between her knees
on the porch of the farmhouse,
there is no sound of the steps,
only a small boy dragging a harness
heaped around both shoulders
across the short grass.
She wonders about her brothers,
the ones still setting out
from the fishing village in Nova Scotia
pulling old nets, the boards of their lives,
the holes shining in them.
The harness spreads open behind the boy,
Small bits of darkness fall out of it.
It has hung all winter in the barn
weighing as much as the boy,
older than the horse
who will pull this summer through it.
He listens to the dust behind him
turning over on its back,
its underside burns in the Michigan light.
His shoulder blades unfold in the leather.
And her hands moving above the churn
look to him like two pieces of water
if they could feel pain again,
gathering together
what is left of the morning's milk.
As far as it can come from
the empty road empties into her lap.
The thick sound of the leather begins
as he lays it over the knees
of the old hired man
to rub oil in it.

The shoreline of the Bay from Elk Rapids north looked much the same as the west side of Torch. Few roads led to the water; one could walk for miles without seeing a cottage. In 1945, it would be twenty years before the interstates reached the north country, and those aged two-lane blacktops didn't encourage travel and tourism the way I-75 does today.

US–31, formerly known as M-11, the Dixie Highway, or the West Michigan Pike, was a two-lane blacktop that ran right in front of our farm. It was the main road connecting Traverse City with Charlevoix. In fact, it was the central link between Chicago and Mackinaw City.

It was here, more than fifty years ago, in Milton Township, that our lives became dominated by this unusual natural phenomenon—the Chain of Lakes. Any connection we had to the water around us was defined by the people we knew. It was where we belonged in those last days of the 1940s. World War II had ended. Buss Merillat, Guy Dean, Russ Wheeler, Ralph Nelson, Wally Zupin and so many others had returned home to raise their families and make their mark.

Korea was unknown to most of us and Adlai Stevenson had yet to gamble with Dwight Eisenhower for the '52 presidential election. Viet Nam was still part of French Indochina. It wasn't our world. Ours began and ended somewhere on the water in Antrim County.

Campbell Road didn't go all the way to Torch Lake as it does today. It ran along the south side of our farm, past the Trautman and Montroy farms, to Powell Road. A two-track trail gave "Bunk" Dawson and me a half-mile hike to the shore of the lake. Only a few fish shanties tucked in along the desolate shoreline accented the second-growth cedar, maple and pine. Farm kids found private spots for skinny-dipping along the rocky shore.

Heading to the water became second nature as if there was some curious magnetic pull. While the Bay was much warmer, Torch carried a more dramatic appeal. The water's complexion continually changed from shades of green and blue, always tinged with turquoise. Deep, cold, baffling, mystical. Even as kids we heard the stories of its refusal to give up its dead, creating a mystique that made Torch incomprehensible. It seemed to be challenging us. Should we swim across? Folks could never see both ends at the same time. Its eighteen miles was difficult to fully understand.

In the mid-1940s, the west shore of Torch Lake offered miles of shoreline in its natural pristine state. It resembled those faded nineteenth-century photographs one might find in an attic trunk.

There was minor development where villages touched the shore. On the east side of Torch, a few landmarks defined a changing landscape: DeWitt's Marina at the narrow Clam River, Ethel Higgins' Drug Store, and Fred Aemisegger's Farmers and Merchants Bank in Alden dominate my memory.

If ever this region provided a local hero, the tiny village of Alden had Fred Aemisegger. It was here that Fred earned himself immortality by actually saving his depositors' nest eggs—during the early days of the Great Depression not a penny was lost! Fred paid 100 cents on the dollar. The doors of the bank never closed except for the brief "Bank Holiday" ordered by the government. By the time I went to work for him in the late '40s, it had become the Alden State Bank. Fred was literally worshipped by those who had suffered the trials and tribulations of the 1920s and '30s. Oldtimers still talk of him in reverent tones.

The Alden State Bank.

In those days, lake frontage was affordable for people of modest means. To the north and south of Alden, strips of small cottages interrupted the tranquility of the rocky, natural shoreline. Locals thought those summer folk with simple, frame cottages on the shore of Torch were well-to-do. Many would laugh at that thought today.

At the south end there was Torch River Bridge, known more formally as Persons' Harbor, where Doreen McCrindle outclassed us boys by diving from the highest point of that old swing bridge into the swift-moving current of Torch River.

Summertime at Torch River Bridge, c. 1950.

A cluster of people, mostly swimmers in Torch River, were there to help turn the venerable hand-operated swing bridge when a boat or two wanted to use the river route. There was Elton Rice, George Nichols and Del Hahn; often Barbara and Nancy Guy, Linda and Jo Jo Way would be helping. Turning the bridge by inserting a large wooden key into the gears at the center was one of the few times we could outclass Doreen.

This area of Torch Lake was crowded with small cottages and city folk in the summer months. The shallow sandbar stretching north into the lake for fifteen hundred feet was, and still is, a natural draw.

The new swing bridge at Torch River, c.1905.

The swing bridge at Torch River opens for boats, c.1950.

Harold Wilke's boat marina on the south side of the swing bridge added a colorful touch as boats of all sizes gambled with the stumps of Skegemog to glide up Torch River in order to reach the prize of the county, Torch Lake.

Fifty years later, the feeling—that magnetic pull that I felt as a kid—remains. Naturally, I was a lot smarter and wiser than my Dad, but as I look back to the 1940s, moving north was the best thing he ever did.

Summertime along the Chain, c.1900.

White Gables, an early 20th century resort on Torch Lake.

The Chain

CLAM RIVER, HELENA, MICH.

COPYRIGHT 1912.
E.L.Beeba.

The lake steamer, Ruth, making its daily trip through Clam River from Bellaire to Alden, 1912.

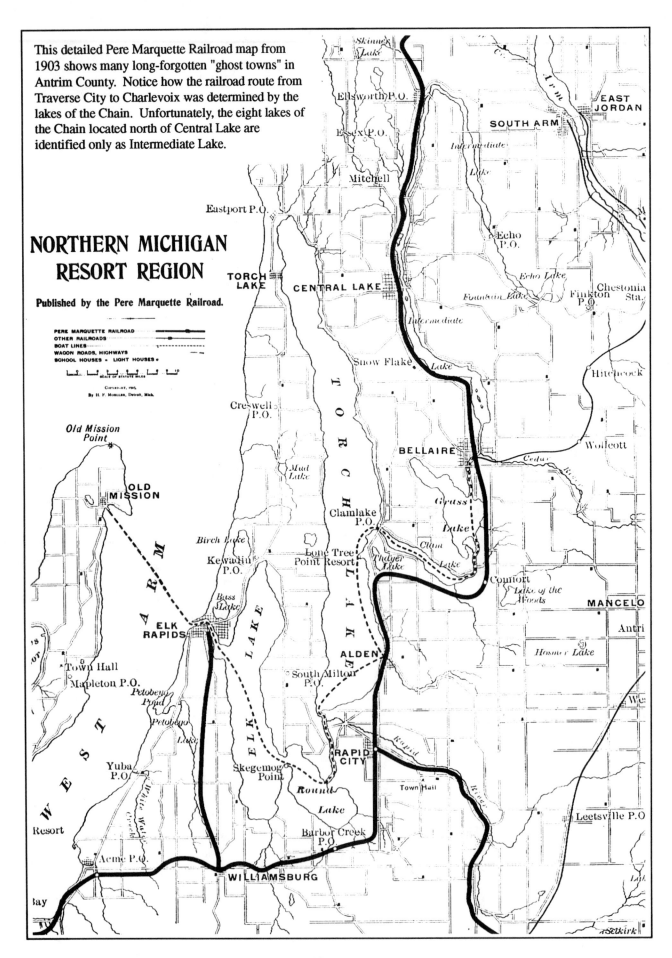

This detailed Pere Marquette Railroad map from 1903 shows many long-forgotten "ghost towns" in Antrim County. Notice how the railroad route from Traverse City to Charlevoix was determined by the lakes of the Chain. Unfortunately, the eight lakes of the Chain located north of Central Lake are identified only as Intermediate Lake.

NORTHERN MICHIGAN RESORT REGION

Published by the Pere Marquette Railroad.

PERE MARQUETTE RAILROAD
OTHER RAILROADS
BOAT LINES
WAGON ROADS, HIGHWAYS
SCHOOL HOUSES ● LIGHT HOUSES ●

SCALE OF STATUTE MILES

COPYRIGHT, 1903,
By H. F. MUELLER, Detroit, Mich.

The Chain of Lakes that runs through western Antrim County is a seventy-five mile long network of fourteen lakes and connecting rivers with countless tributary streams, trickles, and rivers. It is the heart of the vast five-hundred square mile Elk River/Chain of Lakes Watershed which holds a rich history both in human and natural stories.

The fourteen lakes of the Chain gave character to the land of western Antrim County. They shaped its roads, determined the location of its towns, and told the railroads where to lay their tracks. Even the political life of the region was determined by the water. Moving the county seat to Bellaire on the east side of the Chain in 1879 was provoked by the need for a broader geographical base than was offered by the thin spit of land Elk Rapids called home. If political growth and economic expansion were to occur, moving the political center to the broad plains and valleys east of Torch Lake would become irresistible. In 1880, after a legal battle in the State Supreme Court, it became an accomplished fact.

Writers and poets, describing the beauty of the Chain of Lakes, have become ecstatic to the point of exaggeration. But, anything close to exaggeration was, in reality, nearer the truth. Only by seeming to stretch a point can one begin to convey what the water of the Chain really possesses.

An 1874 article from the **Chicago Evening Journal** described the Chain of Lakes. I was amazed how little the landscape had changed in almost a century:

*"The trip around this chain of lakes is one of the pleasantest I know of in the Western country. The water wonderfully clear and pure; the shores are sloping from handsome hills to the water's edge, and covered with heavy timber, except where the improved farms reach the lake. Torch River passes through a cedar swamp, a novelty to most Western people, while Torch Lake is a miniature Lake George. Moreover, there is good fishing for trout, bass, pickerel, and muskellunge, and not simply are there good fish **to be** caught, but good fish **are** caught, and if a man cannot catch a handsome string almost any day he can set it down to his own discredit as a fisherman."*

The Chain of fourteen lakes is unknown to many people who live in the area, let alone those who visit occasionally. The upper Chain, those nine lakes north of the village of Bellaire, are tied together by the Intermediate River and begin somewhere in the quiet corners of Echo and Kearney townships, just a few miles northeast of Bellaire.

To see the birthplace of this chain of water that is so misleading, so innocuous, so dramatic, we could take Montgomery Road east of Bellaire and head toward the sunrise on a two-track known as Bush Road. It is here that tiny streams bubble out of the ground through marsh and cattails in an undramatic fashion. Trickling north for several miles through swamps and fields alongside Skinkle Road, they cross Old State Road near the tiny settlement of Pleasant Valley. It is here that the shape and appearance of a full size stream, known as the Intermediate River, becomes recognizable.

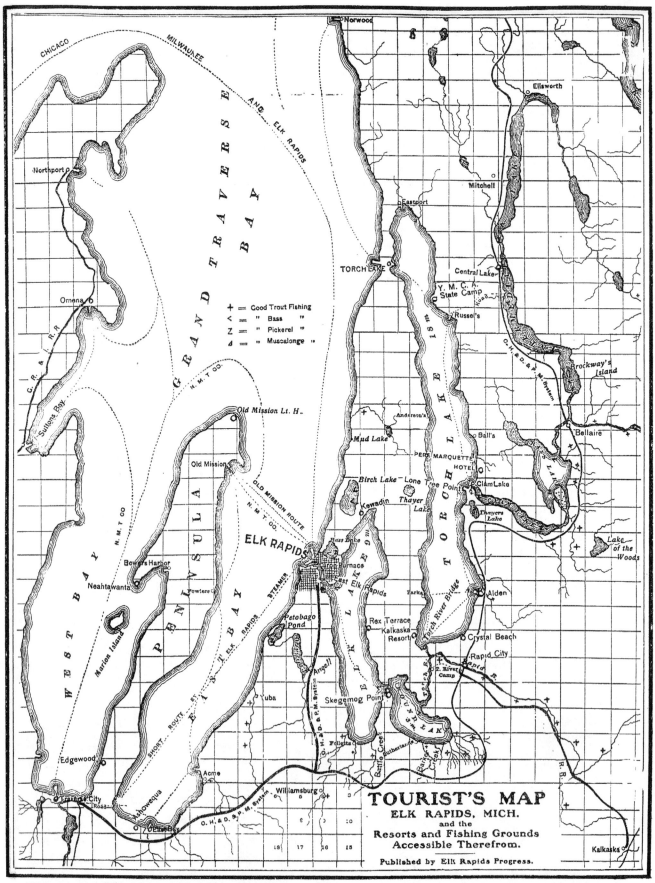

TOURIST'S MAP
ELK RAPIDS, MICH.
and the
Resorts and Fishing Grounds
Accessible Therefrom.

Published by Elk Rapids Progress.

This detailed 1903 fishing guide bears a remarkable resemblance to the 1879 map on page ii. It differs only with the addition of the railroad, Bellaire, and Ellsworth. Spencer Creek's name has been changed to Alden. The errors identifying the lakes of the upper Chain remain.

12

To witness such an inconspicuous beginning for such an outstanding collection of lakes and streams or to think of the swamps and stumps of Skegemog, or the marshes of Grass River, or the shallow, stump-filled Elk River, is to recall John Gray's tribute to swamps and marshes—how he reminds us that we take them for granted, how we scorn them, dismiss them as wasted space, how we want to fill them in and pave them over:

"I am a bedlam of noise. I am dumb with silence. I am life giving. I am murderous. I am home to graceful birds and countless crawling, slithering, swimming creatures. I am cursed by men, and extolled by men. I am repulsive and I am beautiful. Among earthly things I was the beginning. There are those who say I will be the end. . . . I am the marsh."

 A few yards north of Old State Road, Beal Lake, the first and smallest of the upper Chain, is formed. Pull into Murphy Park on the west side of Beal at sunrise to catch a glimpse through the cedars and pines of this tiniest of lakes. At that moment these pearls of the Chain that seem so insignificant, that seldom get the proper respect they deserve, will reward that early dawn excursion.

"One who has never seen those upper lakes," observed Percy Noble in the early 1900s, *"cannot realize the beauty of them at the time; timber right down to the shore with only here and there a clearing ... That region must have been one of God's gifts to the Indians before the white man came along to slaughter the timber."*

The marsh on the Sinclair River.

All of the nine shallow lakes in the upper Chain, except for Intermediate Lake, are each less than one square mile. Many parts of the connecting rivers measure only four feet in depth. The Intermediate, now beginning to look like a respectable-sized river, flows north through Scott Lake.

It is here, between Scott and Six Mile Lake, that the Bauer Nature Preserve, the first of many preservation projects on the Chain, is seen. The two-hundred and forty acre preserve protects a mile of frontage on the Intermediate River and includes an entire watershed which nourishes the headwaters of a small stream. The growth of red oak, maple, basswood and beech trees have been encouraged and the rugged terrain offers refuge to bobcat and bear.

As the river, sometimes known here as Dingman Creek, flows a few yards more, a long and narrow Six Mile Lake, a little more than one-half square mile in size, meanders north out of Antrim County and into the southern portion of Charlevoix County. Here one witnesses the St. Clair Lake/Six Mile Lake Natural Area, one hundred and fifty-six acres and two miles of protected shoreline along the Sinclair River and St. Clair Lake. The primeval sense that is felt in this wilderness river is highlighted by mink, giant turtles, and blue heron.

Six Mile Lake, c.1940.

The unspoiled Sinclair River, only a mile and a half long, connects to St. Clair Lake which makes a hairpin turn known as the "oxbow," pulling the Chain back into Antrim County at the village of Ellsworth. The Chain then continues with the Intermediate River and Ellsworth Lake and begins its southerly journey to Grand Traverse Bay. The tiny, unnoticed Wilson, Ben-Way, and Hanley lakes add to the Upper Chain as it approaches the village of Central Lake.

To an unobservant passerby, this portion of the Chain, from Ellsworth to Central Lake, might appear as a gently flowing river pinched together in several places with

14

bridges to allow access to either side. But each of these tiny gems, Wilson, Ben-Way and Hanley, is a unique body of water, pleased with its separate identity.

The Sinclair River, 1997.

Boating north of Central Lake on the Green River between Hanley and Ben-way Lakes, c.1910.

As it flows casually along the east side of the village of Central Lake, the river widens and introduces Intermediate Lake, more than two-square miles in size, two thousand feet wide, seventy feet deep, and six miles long. Its depth and size make it an intriguing and misleading body of water. Slicing south through Antrim County, the lake's southern tip meets the Intermediate River as it continues through the village of Bellaire and the wooded shores of the Intermediate valley to the head of Lake Bellaire.

The bridge at Central Lake crosses Old State Road, separating Hanley Lake from Intermediate Lake , c.1910.

Here the Cedar River converges with the Intermediate River. The ten mile Cedar River, flowing from the eastern edge of Antrim County, is a major tributary and an essential link that feeds the fourteen lake Chain.

Lake Bellaire, formerly known as Grass Lake, almost three-square miles and with a ninety-five foot depth, is located in the center of the Chain, home to the village of Bellaire, county seat of government. It is here that the Intermediate River comes to an end.

Grass River heading south as it leaves Lake Bellaire, 1997.

Leaving the southeastern shore of Lake Bellaire, Grass River winds for two miles through one of Michigan's finest sanctuaries: the Grass River Natural Area containing more than eleven hundred acres and four and one-half miles of protected shoreline. Taking a gentle turn to the west, Grass River empties into Clam Lake, with the brief Clam River connecting it to Torch Lake.

Now the debate begins. Is Torch the most beautiful lake in the world, or is it the third, or is it ranked at all? An 1878 newspaper reporter, almost delirious in his description, offers:

"Before us lay the wonderful picture of Torch Lake. How can I describe it? It should be done by the brush rather than the pencil, for light and color are its great charms. All the afternoon we sat and watched the scenes shifting and blending like the pictures in a dream—the many-colored water, the darkly, densely-wooded shores with a white line of beach, the long, waving lines of the hills, now standing boldly into the lake, now melting into other lines and dying in the distance; and over all lay a faint, purplish haze full of changing lights and shadows that increased the dream-like effect."

A more modest 1880 newspaper account adds support:

"Torch Lake has been called the Lake George of the west, but we reject the title. Let it stand alone as its own beautiful self, a thing apart, a picture to hold in the memory forever."

Looking north, clockwise from top, Lake Bellaire, Grass River, Clam Lake.

Torch Lake is thirty-square miles of drifting colors, legends, and myths. Eighteen miles long and three hundred feet deep, it is the largest inland lake by water volume in Michigan. It was here that its history took shape as American Indians fished and speared by torch light. Was-wa-gon-ong: Place of the Torches!

Winding south through Torch River is best described by a romantic—one who has fallen in love with the water and feels no need to apologize. An 1878 unidentified newspaper reporter fills this description when he writes:

*"Smooth, still, windless, the river ran between swamps thick set with the dead trunks of pine and hemlock and white cedar fringed with water plants and starred with lilies. I said the river **ran**, but it did nothing so undignified... No, it strolled; it narrowed and widened, it made excursions into the swamp, it curved every half minute and in a last despairing attempt to ground us it took a vicious little turn that brought the bows of the boat crashing along the dead boughs on the banks; then we were free..."*

It is here that the Rapid River, a premier trout stream, ends its thirty-six mile trip through Kalkaska County to converge with Torch River as it flows south to Lake Skegemog. The oak and pine forests provide a basin for the Rapid River, which, like the Cedar, is a major tributary for the Chain. Both outclass the remaining two hundred streams and creeks in size and volume of water that feed the Chain.

Clam Lake heads west into Torch Lake with Grand Traverse Bay in the background.

Torch Lake with Elk Lake and Lake Skegemog in upper left and Grand Traverse Bay and Old Mission Peninsula in upper right.

Looking southwest from Kewadin at the northern tip of Elk Lake. Spencer Bay, Elk River, and Grand Traverse Bay, upper right.

The Chain continues through stump-clogged Lake Skegemog, centered in Antrim, Kalkaska, and Grand Traverse counties. The eastern shore is the site of the seven mile long Lake Skegemog Wildlife Natural Area, three thousand acres of protected wilderness and home to the Massasagua Rattlesnake. Nearby at the north end of the lake is the North Skegemog Preserve offering eleven hundred feet more of protected shoreline. Lake Skegemog, described by some as merely a lobe or extension of Elk Lake, and only twenty-nine feet deep, covers a shallow four square miles.

Heading west, Skegemog connects to Elk Lake at the "narrows," a small channel that gives the two lakes the appearance of being related. Elk Lake, with its southern third in Grand Traverse county, is the second-largest link in the Chain. Heading north from the "narrows," a view of the glistening turquoise of Elk Lake recalls the 1914 musings of long time Wandawood owner, Delos Wilcox:

"I have gazed upon the Lake when its opposite shore was hidden in the mist, and then I stood upon the shore of the boundless sea. I have seen the narrow pathway of the moon stretching across the water, or, if the waves were stirring, it was a broken radiance of diamonds. I have seen the Lake as calm and clear as a crystal river. I have seen it locked in winter's slumber, while the kind north wind spread over its bare bosom the fleecy blankets of the snow. "

Elk is almost nine miles long, covering twelve square miles and one hundred and ninety-two feet in depth. One of the most visible of the Chain, it is bounded on the south by M-72 and U.S. 31 on the west. Partly visible at these two points, the true size of the Chain remains obscure. The Chain offers a greater visual presence only by traveling its veiled and silent seventy-five mile route. Wilcox continues his praise of Elk Lake in an almost prayer-like tone:

Leisure time sailing on the upper Chain, c.1880.

"In the silence of the early hours, while city men are still asleep, and while the rest of the lake is still dark and gloomy, the upper end is adorned to greet the Day. You can watch it while the Dawn is painting it with all the tints of morning until it becomes radiant with glory."

Three more preserves offer protection to the natural beauty of Elk Lake. At the south end is the thirty acre South Elk Lake Wetlands Preserve with seven-hundred and fifty feet of lake frontage. On the southwest edge of the lake, the Palastra Preserve protects 1514 feet of frontage from development. At the north end of Elk Lake, the Kewadin Wetlands Preserve, thirty-eight acres in size, affords another 2600 feet of shoreline protection.

An autumn picnic on the banks of the upper Chain, c. 1880.

Taking on passengers at Skegemog Point, c.1910.

Two-thirds of the way up the west side of Elk, Spencer Bay gives birth to Elk River, a gently flowing mile-long river that ends the Chain as it splits the village of Elk Rapids, flowing over the spillway and under the power plant to empty into Grand Traverse Bay.

The seventy-five mile long Chain begins six hundred and twenty feet above sea level. During its course, it will drop approximately forty feet and, except for a sixteen foot drop at the Bellaire dam and an eleven foot drop at Elk Rapids, the change is hardly noticeable to the human eye. This change in sea level, according to an 1881 account, created a force of three hundred and eighty-seven million gallons in a twenty-four hour period. As it passed over the spillway in Elk Rapids it created enough pressure to generate three hundred horsepower.

Today, both entrances to Grand Traverse Bay, the spillway and the power dam, have a combined force that averages more than four hundred and ninety-two million gallons each day.

The Chain ends as Elk River flows through Elk Rapids, emptying into Grand Traverse Bay, 1892.

ELK RAPIDS, MICH, 1892.

Boeber

Throughout the Chain of Lakes, the pleasures of the water were always found. The late nineteenth century saw a surge of summer resorts as seen by this photo (above) on Torch Lake near Alden, and this early scene at Fisherman's Paradise on Lake Bellaire (below).

The Back Roads of Antrim County

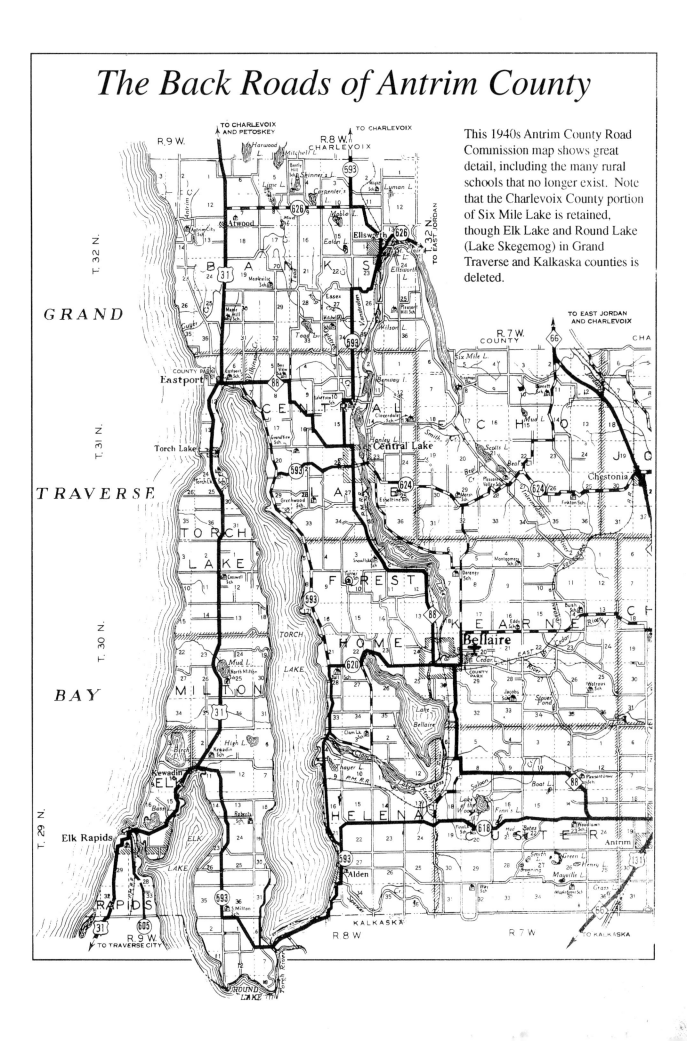

This 1940s Antrim County Road Commission map shows great detail, including the many rural schools that no longer exist. Note that the Charlevoix County portion of Six Mile Lake is retained, though Elk Lake and Round Lake (Lake Skegemog) in Grand Traverse and Kalkaska counties is deleted.

If you don't hit the back roads of Antrim County and see the entire Chain, you will be unable to debate whether or not Torch Lake is the most beautiful of them all. It's on the two-lane blacktops and gravel roads that the true beauty of the Chain, like the rest of America, is to be found. It's refreshing to recall the thoughts of Charles Kuralt in his 1990 *A Life On The Road* as he reflects:

"The interstate system is a wonderful thing. It makes it possible to go from coast to coast without seeing anything or meeting anybody. If the United States interests you, stay off the Interstates."

Miles west of I-75 and somewhat off the beaten track, Antrim County, of Michigan's eighty-three counties, might be one of the least-known throughout most of its history. Sandwiched between the more highly-profiled Grand Traverse to the south, and elite Charlevoix to the north, few famous people came from here, no large cities attracted the weary traveler, and only the inveterate fisherman knew what everyone else was missing. However, even Fisherman's Paradise on Lake Bellaire or the Big Fish Inn at Ellsworth were modest by today's standards and did not measure up to the ambitious and glamorous resorts of the 1990s.

The Chain is outlined by gently curving two-lane blacktop roads that lead one cautiously around the curves at Stevens Point on the western shore of Elk Lake to Kewadin. Here county road 593 heads south hugging the eastern shore of Elk until it cuts straight through the center of south Milton Township before breaking precariously in a double curve approaching Torch River Bridge.

Along the southern shore of Torch Lake the route becomes Crystal Beach Road, where oversized summer homes on undersized lots struggle for a view of Torch Lake as it fades into the northern horizon. As Crystal Beach Road intersects with the Rapid City Road, it heads north to Alden as 593 again, or East Torch Lake Drive. A double ninety-degree turn in Alden takes the road cautiously along the eastern shore of Torch for its entire length before ending at M-88 in Eastport.

The roads surround the upper Chain where M-88 connects Bellaire to Central Lake by following the western shore of Intermediate Lake before it surprises and ends abruptly at US-31 in Eastport. US-31 hurries north to Charlevoix barely noticing the beautiful water.

There are many short links, usually following section lines that lead to the main shoreline routes. Typical are the Hjelte and Indian roads that lead to the winding, strolling West Torch Lake Drive or Cottage Drive that skirts the shores of Clam Lake and Lake Bellaire.

The seemingly endless and rugged Skinkle Road follows the Chain from its origins, suddenly becoming Six Mile Lake Road, cutting into Charlevoix County, then heading south as an unpretentious Rushton Road offering surprising views of Ellsworth, Wilson, Ben-Way, and Hanley lakes on their eastern shores. Continuing south, the shore of Intermediate Lake is outlined by the circuitous Intermediate Lake Road as it winds along the lake's eastern shore.

These are the roads of the Chain, the back roads of Antrim County. They have literally been sculpted by the fourteen lakes of the Chain, just as the Chain was sculpted earlier by the glaciers. They are part of that group of trails that Hamlin Garland identified as the "main-travelled roads" of America. Just as they led others to develop and shape a nation, these rural routes connected the villages of the Chain in a continuous and informal union. Rugged and undeveloped, the roads were hardly more than crude trails in the nineteenth century. Yet they led from the farms to the towns and villages that gave shape and character to an American culture.

The shoreline of Torch Lake, the longest inland lake in Michigan, was privately owned throughout the early decades of the Twentieth Century. Ironically, public access was easy as acres of undeveloped farmland ran to the water's edge. There were no great resorts or land developments that drew the public. The wealthy summer resorter of the nineteenth and early twentieth centuries would relax at the modest and unpretentious inns: Lone Tree Point, Crystal Beach or the Pere Marquette Hotel north of Clam River.

The Beal family in front on their log cabin on Beal Lake, 1886. Left to right: Isabella Beal, Susie Rushton, Becky Barrow, Norman Beal, Asa Beal, Pearl Beal, Lucy Gardner Beal. Descendent Leon Beal with his wife, Shirley, lives today on Old State Road near the original homestead.

So the chain of fourteen lakes remained little known to outsiders. Name changing added to the confusion; many lakes of the upper Chain have been renamed during the last century. An 1880s map shows Beal as Echo, Scott as Fountain, and Wilson, Ben-Way, and Hanley were often known collectively as the Intermediate River. Sometime in the twentieth century, Central Lake became Intermediate. In the lower half of the Chain, Grass Lake became Lake Bellaire, and Round Lake was renamed Lake Skegemog in the 1950s. Many long-time residents are still confused by the size of the Chain; mention those lakes north of Bellaire—the upper Chain—and your remarks may draw a puzzled look. Many do not know that they are connected together in an unimaginable unity, flowing into the lower Chain continuously, forever, through Elk River into Grand Traverse Bay.

In 1882, the *Elk Rapids Progress* added confusion by offering this distorted and misleading description of the Chain:

"We have so far been able to learn the names of the lakes and rivers outflowing at Elk Rapids: The names are Elk River, Elk Lake, The Narrows, Round Lake, Torch River, Torch Lake, Clam River, Clam Lake, Grass River, Grass Lake, Intermediate River and what is known as Intermediate Lake is the chain of lakes and rivers, the names of the rivers being the same as the lakes. They are named Central, Clow, Hanley, Sissons, Wilson, Bowers, Sinclair, Mathers, Wells and Scott. We have heretofore mentioned that there were nineteen, but we believe that we have given them all. Bowers Lake is sometimes given as Gotham and Bowers, but that is really one lake. Fifteen lakes are enough anyway."

Confusion over the Chain is further aggravated by mapmakers who succumb to provincial pressures, if only self-imposed. They describe the land and water according to political boundaries, usually the county lines. When the Antrim County government issues a map, they often delete the portion of Six Mile Lake that flows through Charlevoix County. They do the same with the Kalkaska and Grand Traverse portions of Skegemog and Elk Lakes, and sometimes they do not. Maps of Charlevoix County will show "their portion" of Six Mile, but exclude the rest.

Many maps depict the lakes of the Chain, but without the connecting rivers. Thus, many people are led to believe, because of this faulty or careless cartography, that there is no Chain at all. It is a logical extension of our constantly challenged political and social awareness that the provincialism of county lines does not serve any practical purpose in the settlement of land.

If artificial lines must be used to identify land, the government land survey of 1785 is a logical approach and doesn't compromise the integrity of the Chain. In this survey Kearney Township is identified as T30N, R7W. That is, the 30th township north of the Base Line, and the 7th range west of the Principal Meridian.

T30N, R7W is the result of the Grayson Land Ordinance of 1785 which authorized a survey of all lands in the Northwest Territory which contained the future states of Wisconsin, Ohio, Indiana, Illinois, and Michigan. It wasn't until 1815 that the lower peninsula of Michigan was surveyed, and almost 1840 before the Grand Traverse region was included.

To conduct an orderly survey, a vertical line known as the Principal Meridian was established. Running through the state and crossing the Ohio line about fifty miles west of Toledo, the line terminates on the north at the eastern end of Bois Blanc Island in Lake Huron. Bisecting the Principal Meridian is a horizontal Base Line running along the north side of Wayne, Washtenaw, Jackson, Calhoun, Kalamazoo, and Van Buren counties.

The ranges (vertical rows of townships) are numbered east and west from the Principal Meridian and the townships are numbered north and south from the Base Line. Thus, Kearney Township is Township thirty north or T30N, and it is the 7th range west of the Principal Meridian or R7W.

Antrim County roads, c.1905.

Canoeing at Fisherman's Paradise on Lake Bellaire, c.1910.

Though it lacks the romance and sophistication of a more poetic name, T30N, R7W as a practical and legal description of Kearney Township is appreciated by anyone who has ever purchased property. Each township has thirty-six sections; each section, one square mile in size, contains 640 acres. The imaginary lines that identify the township and all its sections rid property owners of much guesswork and confusion. All property divided and sold is measured from these lines, and lakes and waterways are not chopped off because they are in the wrong township.

The land survey, now two hundred years old, is practical and logical. Its imaginary lines cannot be erased. Boundary disputes can be settled by a survey of property lines; they are not determined by trees, rocks or dried-up river beds. Only the shoreline of the Chain can alter the land mass of a section or township. County lines, however, are confusing and disruptive when they interfere with the natural topography of the land and the flow of the water.

The land survey offered township lines for easy and sensible purchase, but the shores of lakes and rivers were a far greater inducement to settlement than the artificial and needless county boundary. By the twenty-first century, it would seem reasonable to expect maps of our natural resources that are correct and complete.

Thus the identity of the Chain of Lakes, like all land and water, needs protection; its history and topography are riddled with inaccuracies. The Chain, however, faces more subtle threats in the 1990s as oil and gas drilling moves westward from the eastern townships of Antrim County.

Living a safer, quieter lifestyle where solitude is a prized possession has been shattered by the aggressive development tactics of oil and gas companies. Some townships in Antrim County have wells drilled every forty acres with unmuffled processing stations operating on a twenty-four hour basis. Miles and miles of access roads slice through the wilderness where we once enjoyed the memorable silences of these pristine areas.

Canoeing on Torch Lake, c. 1910.

Families bathe at Lone Tree Point on Torch Lake, c.1913.

Susan and Jim Galbraith of rural Antrim County issue an alert as they declare:

"The citizens in Antrim County, and indeed, of Michigan, where mineral rights are separated from property rights, have lost much more than the Michigan Oil & Gas Association can ever make for their investors. Our forests and rivers, our lands and our minerals— which include water, our primary heritage —have long ago been surreptitiously sold out from under us. The numerous intrusions have taken our privacy and the silences we have treasured in Antrim County."

The oil and gas drilling heads west toward the Chain in an uncontrollable fashion. The loud processing stations, powerless politicians and rumors of toxic spills create a threat to the purity of the Chain that is far more insidious than county boundaries or inoperable septic tanks.

Rice's Torch Lake Bus missed a curve on its way to pick up passengers going to resorts on the south end of Torch Lake from Rapid City, c.1915.

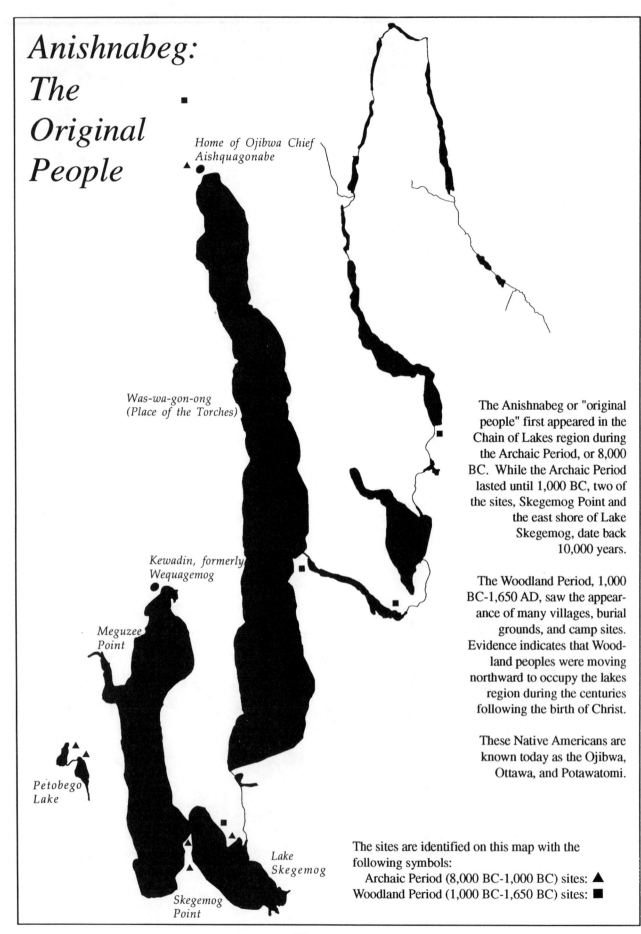

Anishnabeg:
The
Original
People

Home of Ojibwa Chief
Aishquagonabe

Was-wa-gon-ong
(Place of the Torches)

Kewadin, formerly
Wequagemog

Meguzee
Point

Petobego
Lake

Lake
Skegemog

Skegemog
Point

The Anishnabeg or "original people" first appeared in the Chain of Lakes region during the Archaic Period, or 8,000 BC. While the Archaic Period lasted until 1,000 BC, two of the sites, Skegemog Point and the east shore of Lake Skegemog, date back 10,000 years.

The Woodland Period, 1,000 BC-1,650 AD, saw the appearance of many villages, burial grounds, and camp sites. Evidence indicates that Woodland peoples were moving northward to occupy the lakes region during the centuries following the birth of Christ.

These Native Americans are known today as the Ojibwa, Ottawa, and Potawatomi.

The sites are identified on this map with the following symbols:
  Archaic Period (8,000 BC-1,000 BC) sites: ▲
Woodland Period (1,000 BC-1,650 BC) sites: ■

People of the Chain

At 102 years of age, Native American Peter Mark, known as "Old P.M., canoes on the Torch River, c. 1920.

Anishnabeg: The Original People

The Anishnabeg, or "original people," first appeared in the Chain of Lakes region during the Archaic Period, or 8,000 BC. While the Archaic Period lasted until 1,000 BC, two of the sites identified on the accompanying map—Skegemog and the east shore of Lake Skegemog—date back 10,000 years.

The Woodland Period, 1,000 BC–1650 AD, saw the appearance of many villages, burial grounds, and camp sites. Evidence indicates that Woodland peoples were moving northward to occupy the lakes region during the centuries following the birth of Christ. These Americans are known today as the Ojibwa (Chippewa), Ottawa, and Potawatomi.

American Indian names provide a valuable connection to history. It is appropriate and proper to use them to describe places and topography. They glow in comparison to the many European names that were adopted by early settlers with no historical connection to the land. The American Indian names add richness and greater understanding to the places where we live.

The Ojibwa language, **Anishinaabemowin**, is the language of most northern Michigan American Indians. However, there is no complete and accurate account of Indian names in Michigan. Folklore, poor records, careless research and the many tribal or regional languages make it difficult and confusing to identify the correct origin and meaning of many American Indian names. In the art or study of American Indian words, there is no standard shared by all the local varieties of Anishinaabemowin.

The difficulty of identifying and spelling occurs in all languages. The origins, spellings, and meanings of Ojibwa words are no different than the English that most of us speak. Witness the variations, both in pronunciation and spelling, of Michilimackinac. Anglicized from the name of a small tribe, **Mi-she-ne-mackinaw-go**, to Mackinac or Mackinaw, its spelling, pronunciation, and location are still cause today for many heated discussions.

Native American children, Elk Rapids, c.1910.

The Ojibwa word for Chain of Lakes is **Aanikegamaa.** The word torch in Ojibwa is **waaswaagan**, and Torch Lake's Indian name **Was-wa-gon-ong**—Place of the Torches—is more meaningful than a Round or Mud Lake. **Migizi** is the Ojibwa word for "bald eagle." Whether it is spelled **Megezee, Megusee,** or **Meguzee** , as Antrim County's original name it has far more beauty and historical significance than a name taken from a county in Ireland.

Indian names such as **Skegemog, Kewadin** and **Petobego** are more colorful and distinctive than a bland Square Lake or the many Pine and Long Lakes that dot Michigan's landscape. **Agaaming** means "across the lake," and **agamiing** means "at the lakes." Whichever one chooses, both are accurate and unique when compared to other golf courses in the Chain of Lakes region.

Skegemog appears to be an Indian name meaning "meeting of the waters," though like **Copneconic Lake** in Genesee County, **Webinquaw Lake** in Oceana County and many others, there is insufficient evidence to locate its origin and give its correct interpretation.

Confusion concerning the origin of Indian names can be seen in **Kewadin.** Originally known as **Wequagemog**, the small village at the north end of Elk Lake was named for a local Ottawa chief and possibly means "the north wind." In Longfellow's *Hiawatha*, **Keewaydin** is the Northwest wind, and throughout the state it is also spelled **Kiwaten, Keewatin, Keewayden** and **Keewahdin.**

Petobego Lake, a large swamp just inside the Grand Traverse county line a few miles south of Elk Rapids, is a state fish and wildlife area and is closely related to the Ojibwa "bitobig," meaning pond or pool.

Reverend Miller and his wife at the Kewadin Indian Parsonage, c.1900.

Peshaube, a well-known and heroic chief of the Ottawas, gave his name to the Indian village of **Peshabestown** in Leelanau County. This is one of the few place names that is identifiable with any degree of certainty.

In any case, every town carried identifying tribal names and the resident population contained people connected with other tribes. This was the result of marriages and captives from inter-tribal wars. It is not surprising that linguistic confusion exists.

Indian villages were home bases, but were seldom fully occupied during an entire year. Heavily dependent on fishing, they were located on banks of streams, bays, or near springs. For winter hunting grounds the villages split into smaller groups, and by mid-winter the villages were deserted and empty. By the 1830s the use of log cabins made Indian settlements resemble their white counterparts.

The Upper Great Lakes was populated by two closely-related tribes, Ottawa and Ojibwa. Most settlements in the Grand Traverse region were populated by these two groups. **Wequagemog (Kewadin); Ahgosa**, at the tip of Old Mission; **Shabwasons** north of Suttons Bay; and **Chemagohing** near Leland were the main Grand Traverse villages. On the east side of the Grand Traverse Bay at Eastport, the northernmost village was the residence of the leading regional Ojibwa chief, **Aishquagonabe.**

In 1836 only a small reservation, less than thirty-six square miles in size, remained in the Chain of Lakes region. It was located north of Elk Rapids in Milton Township. 1855 records show a similar reservation placed south of Elk Rapids, possibly in or near **Petobego Lake.** Today, there are no signs of either tract of land.

 The Indian people believed that land, like air and water, was available to all on the basis of need. Personal ownership was rare, usually involving individual crafts, crops, or the results of hunting and fishing endeavors. Expressed by the memorable nineteenth-century Indian leader, Tecumseh, it was a plea that would echo into the twentieth century: *"No tribe has the right to sell, even to each other, much less strangers ... Sell a country! Why not sell the air, the great sea, as well as the earth! Did not the Great Spirit make them all for the use of his children?"*

In 1830, there were fourteen thousand American Indians in the lower peninsula. The 1860 census listed only 6,172 in Michigan.

The Villages of the Chain

Throughout the Antrim County region, small villages sprouted at the mouths of rivers to cut and saw the logs that were floated downstream from the rich inland forests. There the boards were loaded on ships for Chicago, Buffalo, Detroit, and points throughout the Midwest. It was the same throughout the rest of Michigan. Small temporary communities had been founded for the sole purpose of harvesting the forests. Little thought was given to long-range planning. As the pine and hard-

Elk River/Chain of Lakes Watershed Map
with Villages of the Chain

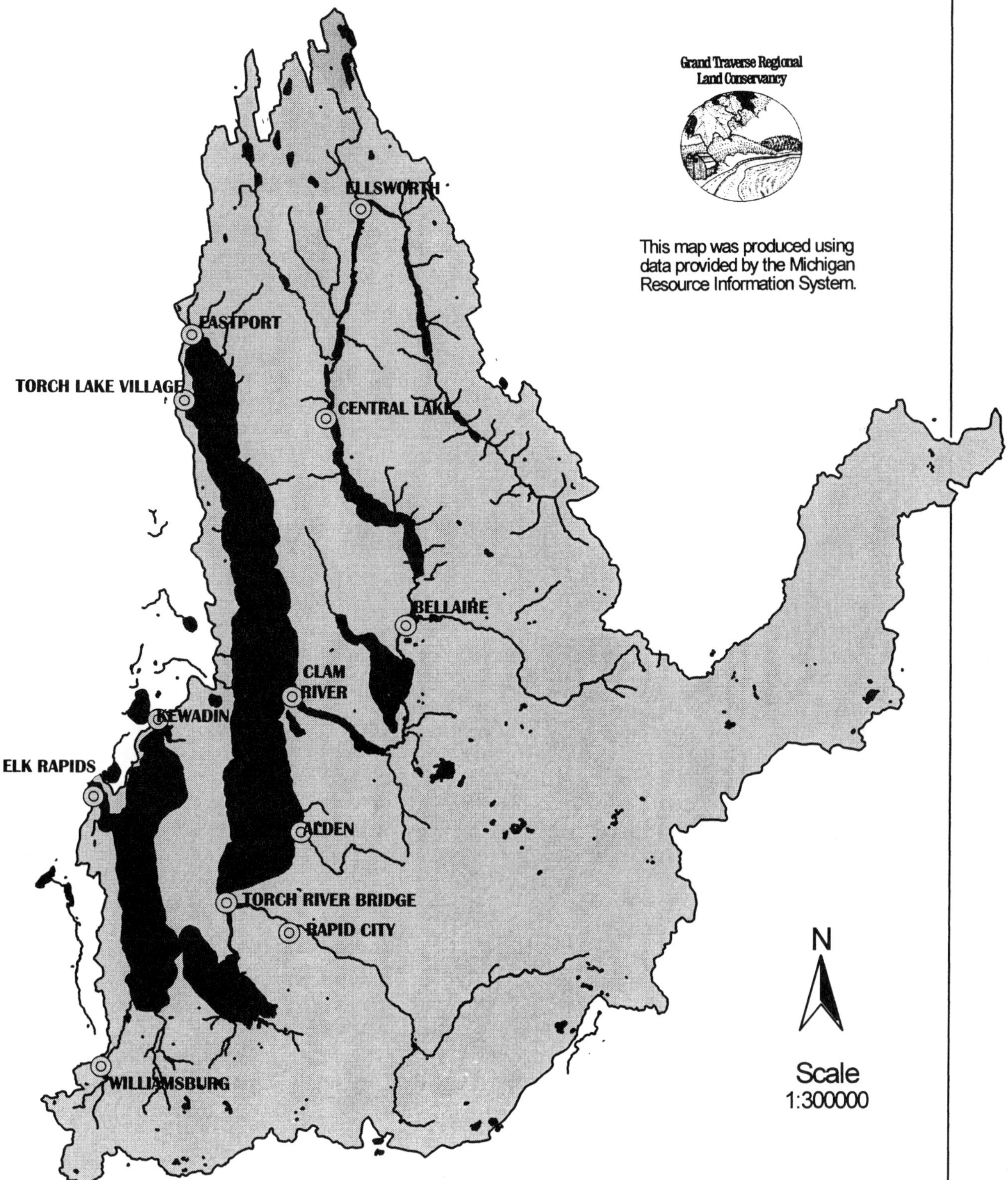

Grand Traverse Regional Land Conservancy

This map was produced using data provided by the Michigan Resource Information System.

ELLSWORTH

EASTPORT

TORCH LAKE VILLAGE

CENTRAL LAKE

BELLAIRE

CLAM RIVER

KEWADIN

ELK RAPIDS

ALDEN

TORCH RIVER BRIDGE

RAPID CITY

WILLIAMSBURG

N

Scale
1:300000

wood were cut, the supply diminished and the economic life of the villages began to weaken. By the time the railroads had entered the scene in the 1890s, lumbering had reached its prime. An economic slide began and by World War I, most of the timber was gone.

Dominating the economic life of the county for almost sixty years (1850-1910) were large, monopolistic companies such as the Cameron Brothers at Torch Lake Village, Richardi and Bechtold in Bellaire, Wood, Pearl & Company at Eastport, and the Dexter-Noble firm in Elk Rapids. These firms owned most of the hotels, ran the steamboat lines, built large sawmills, flour mills, and company stores. They purchased thousands of acres of heavily wooded land along miles of lake shore. Their many lumber camps covered most of Antrim County and stretched into parts of Kalkaska and Grand Traverse counties as well.

Kewadin, c.1925.

In 1882, a reporter for the *Louisville Courier-Journal* describes the Antrim County region and it's Chain of Lakes:

"Fine steamers run daily from Petoskey and Mackinac. Taking one of these steamers, you are in two or three hours landed at Elk Rapids, the very paradise of the fisherman, and one of the most delightful spots for a summer residence. ... Elk Rapids is a busy and stirring little place, with the largest iron furnace in the State, flouring-mills, saw-mills, etc. The sportsman will find excellent fishing in Elk River and Traverse bay. Elk Lake, Round Lake, Torch Lake, and a dozen other lakes can be reached in an hour or two, in all of which black bass and pickerel may be found in abundance; while those fond of brook trout can find this splendid fish in Rapid River, Battle Creek and half a dozen other streams.

"The sojourner at this favored spot has the opportunity during the sultry months of July and August to enjoy at any time an excursion full of delight by taking the Queen of the Lakes, a beautiful steamer, and running up through Elk River, Elk Lake, Round Lake, Torch River and Torch Lake. Nothing can exceed the beauty of these streams and lakes, and a trip through them is a notable event in one's life."

While the beauty of the Chain of Lakes remained, by the end of the nineteenth century, the county's heyday had passed.

The following villages survived in one fashion or another; their chief asset today is their location somewhere on the Chain of Lakes:

Kewadin: Possibly the oldest community in Antrim County, this Ojibwa community was originally known as Wequagemog and was identified by locals as Indian Town. George Wyckoff became its first postmaster in 1883. The 1884 *The Traverse Region* describes it:

"A small settlement of Indians own lands in the western part of the town[ship]. They live in a little village at the north end of Elk Lake, and farm only on a very small scale, the Indians spending their time mostly in fishing and hunting, or in working for the whites, while the squaws do nearly all the planting, hoeing and harvesting. This is the only Indian settlement in the county."

Elk Rapids: First settled in 1848 by Abram Wadsworth, the first sawmill was built in 1850 and the lake levels of the Chain began their many changes. A village began to take shape. Platted as a village in 1852, Wadsworth named it for the elk horns and rapids found near the mouth of the river. Most everything east of Torch Lake was still wilderness. When the young firm of Dexter-Noble took over the sawmill operation in 1853, a hint of things to come was revealed in Wirt Dexter's advice to a friend:

"It would be well for you to see that country—for if you would look upon its prospects as I do you would take some of its broad acres of which there is plenty heavily timbered and well-watered for ten shillings."

By the 1870s Wirt Dexter, Henry Noble, and Edwin Noble had developed a lumber and blast furnace company known as the Elk Rapids Iron Company. Newspapers described the firm as the "principality" for they were "in short, monarchs of all they survey." Excluding the Dexter-Noble Company store in Elk Rapids and the thousands of acres of land they owned, the Iron Company's assets totalled $1,059,179.74 in 1886.

Through many economic rises and declines, Elk Rapids' population grew to 1800 in 1905, dropping to 600 by 1930. By 1990, with a rising tourist industry, its citizenry stood at 1626.

Williamsburg: This small village in Grand Traverse County was known as Mill Creek in 1856. It became Williamsburg in 1860 and when the Chicago and West Michigan Railroad was built in 1892, the village thrived as a center for travellers heading north along the Bay.

Torch Lake Village: Captain John W. Brown first settled here in 1858 and called it Brownstown. Major Cicero Newell became its first postmaster in 1866 and the name Brownstown was discontinued; it has been known as Torch Lake Village since then. Silkman and Hart, a Milwaukee firm, established a mill and store. In 1883, the Cameron Brothers purchased Silkman and Hart and became the dominant industrial firm of the area.

Williamsburg, c.1900.

Alden: In 1868, F.J. Lewis built a store and called the small village Noble in honor of H. H. Noble of the Dexter-Noble firm. John B. Spencer, later named the creek and village after himself. When the Chicago and West Michigan Railroad came through in 1892, the village of Spencer Creek became Alden in honor of William Alden Smith, a prominent railroad official and United States Senator. Its mills, "sportin' houses," and saloons made it a minor commercial center by the 1890s.

Eastport: Murdock Andress, a one-armed man, built the first log cabin and a man named Phillips built a hotel in 1869. The place was called Wilson. Andrew Mudge opened a wagon shop and became postmaster in 1872. When Newell & Wilcox built a mill and dock on Grand Traverse Bay directly east of Northport the name of the village became Eastport. When the bayshore project was abandoned, the village was established at the head of Torch Lake and Eastport remained as its name. Moses

Lumbermen gather in Elk Rapids with their big wheels, c.1905.

The Cameron Brothers sawmill at Torch Lake Village, c.1890.

Alden dresses up for its annual regatta, c. 1908.

Ellsworth: a pioneer town of the 1880s.

Central Lake, looking northeast toward Hanley Lake, c. 1910.

Anderson's store in Clam River, c.1905.

Haddock's general store flourished and John W. Pearl began business as a merchant in that same year. Pearl's wife, Adda, described the confusion surrounding the town's name. In an 1876 letter to her mother, Eliza Harris, she wrote:

"I can see the Queen of the Lakes coming into the dock from my window. Eastport is the name of the place, but some call it Torch Lake and others Head-of-the-Lake. It's hardly ever called Eastport."

Adda bore two children, Norton and Ethel. Today, Norton's daughters, Betty Beeby, Dorothy Pearl, Ann Bretz, and granddaughter, Katherine Lambert, still reside in the small village where M-88 meets US–31.

Ellsworth: Situated at the northern end of the Chain of Lakes, Erwin Dean and his nephew, August Dean, founded the town in 1881. Lewis A. DeLine was the first postmaster (1884-1891), and had served under Colonel Ephraim Elmer Ellsworth, the first Union Officer killed in Civil War. DeLine named the town in honor of his former commanding officer. The village included the nearby settlements of Needmore and Oxbow. Ellsworth was incorporated in 1938; its 1990 population was 418.

Eastport, c. 1920.

Central Lake: Local folklore claims, correctly no doubt, that the village takes its name from its central, or intermediate, location between Ellsworth and Bellaire. In 1869 Stephen B. Davis became Central Lake's first postmaster, and in 1872 James Wadsworth built the first store. The Chicago and West Michigan Railroad, following the western shore of Intermediate Lake, entered the village in 1892 and incorporation followed three years later.

Again, the 1882 *Louisville Courier-Journal* pays homage to the beauty of the Chain and the Intermediate Valley in which Central Lake [Intermediate Lake] lies:

"Leaving the Torch Lake House [at Torch Lake Village] after an early breakfast, a five-mile ride on this great lake will take you to Russell's where a carriage will convey you four miles

Bellaire on the Intermediate River, c.1910.

Rapid City, c. 1910.

Torch River Bridge welcomes the Mabel, c.1916.

through a grand and romantic country to Central Lake. Central Lake is famous for the large and game black bass found in it, and it is an enjoyable spot for ladies, for they will find keen sport in catching sunfish and small bass, which are found there in surprising numbers."

"No visitors to Northern Michigan should fail to go to Central Lake [Intermediate Lake today]. It is worth a journey of a thousand miles to see. It is the central one of a series of six or seven lakes connected by small rivers from one hundred yards to one or two miles in length, this one being the largest of the series of lakes, and is about seven miles long and from one to three miles wide. These lakes are all of surpassing beauty and loveliness, and have been pronounced as far excelling the most noted lakes that attract the tourist in Europe. Before the sun goes down the reflection of objects on the adjacent hills and shores is so intensely vivid and beautiful that it would compel exclamations of wonder and delight from the most unromantic and matter-of-fact people."

Clam River: Four miles north of Alden, where Clam River enters Torch Lake, sits the small village of Clam River. Known originally as Clam Lake, Solomon Dewey was its first postmaster. It became Helena in 1911 and its name was changed to Clam River in 1925. Its post office continued until 1944. Today it serves as the waterway entrance to Bellaire and the upper Chain.

Bellaire: Bellaire was a stagecoach stop known as Keno in 1879. The name was changed to Bellaire in that year after a disputed election which moved the county seat from Elk Rapids to this more central location. Three years later, in 1882, its population was 232, and Ambrose Palmer had developed the plan for a new community. John Cook opened his hotel: the Bellaire House; Dempster Stebbins was postmaster, and Henry Stewart was maintaining law and order as the new sheriff. Richardi and Bechtold had begun their woodenware factory and would become an economic force in the county. Two sawmills, a planing mill, a shingle mill, three general stores and another hotel gave Bellaire the appearance of a "boom town." The Chicago and West Michigan Railroad gave Bellaire an added pinch of legitimacy when it ran its tracks through the new seat of government in 1892.

Rapid City: Known as Van Buren until 1891, Rapid City is located in the northwest corner of Kalkaska County. Situated on the Rapid River, a major tributary of the Chain of Lakes, the village and surrounding area were often known as a fisherman's paradise. Like many other communities on the Chain of Lakes and its tributaries, Rapid City flourished when the tracks of the Chicago and West Michigan railroad cut through the village in 1892.

Persons Harbor (Torch River Bridge) : This small community was a point where early travellers crossed Torch River in order to get around the southern end of Torch Lake. Generally known as Torch River Bridge, it gave these early travellers their first glimpse of Torch Lake as they cruised the river north from Skegemog. Today, though it is a small unincorporated village, the attraction of the water makes it an overpopulated and traffic-clogged summer resort.

Were they Ghost Towns?

Many villages in the Chain of Lakes region never made it into the Twentieth Century. A few crept in, stayed a few years, fizzled and disappeared. Some were not towns, nor were they intended to be permanent settlements. To search the record and read old maps is misleading. Appearing as permanent settlements they were often a mail drop, a lumber camp, or a watering station along the railroad route. A few were farm communities that declined as the economic forces pulled in another direction. Often company-owned camps or railroad stations, they didn't die because of dire economic conditions; they were simply dismantled when business was done. While Antrim County's population had peaked at 12,427 in 1894, most of these "ghost towns" would not be part of it.

SNOWFLAKE, a spiritualist camp that once had a post office, continues today as a summer camp on the west shore of Intermediate Lake. Located in Forest Home Township, Snowflake was a stop on the Chicago & West Michigan railroad.

In Grand Traverse County, the village of **ANGELL** recorded a 1905 population of seventy-five. Located in Whitewater Township, it was just four miles south of Elk Rapids on the Pere Marquette spur from Williamsburg.

Busy traffic along M-72 today hardly notices **BATES** in Acme Township, except for the mild bump in the highway caused by the aging railroad tracks. In 1918 it had a population of twenty-five. Today, the remarkable restoration of a small country church may bring it some well-deserved attention.

The church at Bates today.

46

BARKER CREEK and **MABEL,** east of Bates on the M-72 route to Kalkaska, are non-existent today. Both were railroad stops during the latter decades of the nineteenth century. For a few bustling and hustling years, they serviced the lumber camps and farmers. By World War I, population of both had declined to a handful.

Local myth surrounds the village of **FRANCE** (also known as **FRENCH LAND-ING)**. Located on the east end of Lake Skegemog on the Pere Marquette Railroad in Kalkaska County, it was an elaborate lumber camp. Mr. McNulty of Chicago built the first home and Link Simmons built a sawmill in 1900. The French Lumber Company of Battle Creek, from which the settlement takes its name, built a steam-powered sawmill. When the lumber was gone, the town was gone. Today, old-timers recall its heyday, and tourists walk the railroad bed looking for souvenirs.

In 1900, Andrew Stebbins was appointed postmaster of **LULL.** Nine years earlier it had been established as a flag station on the Pere Marquette Railroad in Helena Township; there is no indication that a permanent settlement was ever intended.

ELGIN was a brief settlement seven miles south of Kewadin in Milton Township. Both **STOVER,** on the Cedar River in Kearney Township, and **ARKONA** near Grass River in Custer Township, were as short-lived in the 1880s.

Remnants of **FINKTON** remain visible today. Located at the corner of Finkton and Old State Roads, two weather-worn buildings are all that exist of this 1890 village in Echo Township.

Finkton, 1997.

GREEN RIVER was a railroad stop in Chestonia Township eight miles east of Bellaire. For a few short years, while the lumber camps flourished, Green River had a promising life.

From 1902 until 1909, **HITCHCOCK**, six miles east of Bellaire, was a center of activity for East Jordan Lumber Company sawmills.

CASCADE, established in 1877 in Forest Home Township, was hardly more than a flag station on the Grand Rapids and Indiana Railroad.

KEARNEY, LAKE SHORE, ROOTVILLE, SIMONS, WETZEL, MOUNT BLISS and **COMFORT** were all short-lived items on the map of Antrim County, most dying a natural death somewhere near the turn of the Twentieth Century.

CRESWELL was founded in 1877 in Milton Township just eight miles north of Elk Rapids. Arch Cameron Sr. was the first postmaster, and until the 1960s, a small schoolhouse reminded longtime residents of an earlier and simpler time. Today, the small community is identified by McLachlan Road as it meets U.S. 31, offering an entrance to Ag-A-Ming Golf Course.

ECHO was a post office on Intermediate Lake and listed Eber Dingman as its postmaster in 1905.

AARWOOD in Kalkaska County, located where Rapid River meets Torch River, was a small lumber town in 1887, and storekeeper Allan Little became its first postmaster in that year. Aarwood gained attention by spelling its name with a double "A' so that it would appear first in state directories. Its founders failed to anticipate the same device used by settlers of Aabec in Antrim County .

Greater notoriety fell on Aarwood when the world's oldest profession came to town. When the "sportin' house" opened for business, lumberjacks followed in large numbers. While typical of most lumber towns, such business was never listed in the directories.

Though the population reached two hundred in 1882, by the early twentieth century, most of Aarwood was gone. Only a few oldtimers could recall "the sportin' house" that attracted so many shanty boys.

ANTRIM CITY, in Banks Township south of Norwood, was possibly the most ambitious of early settlements in the region. It was also the most disappointing and its origins are poorly recorded. While one source lists James Sickles as its first postmaster in 1863, another claims that the village was founded in 1861 by the lumber company of Wood, Pearl & Company. In either case, it was promoted heavily by the Dexter-Noble lumber firm of Elk Rapids in an attempt to establish a port at the north edge of Grand Traverse Bay. A store was built, churches were established, and sawmills flourished temporarily. But in 1865, Henry Graves wrote to his wife, Elzada, in Battle Creek:

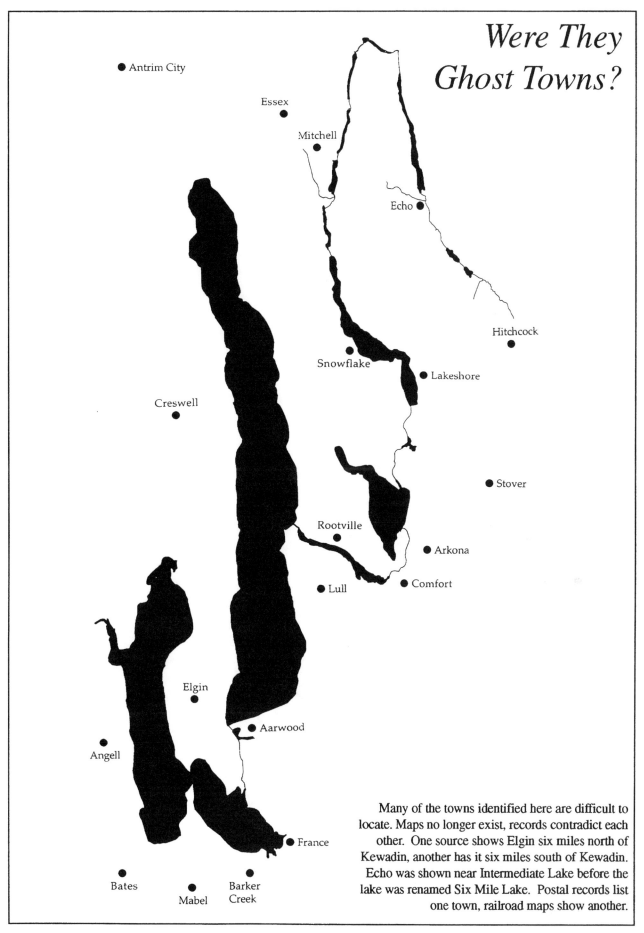

Were They Ghost Towns?

● Antrim City

Essex ●

Mitchell ●

Echo ●

Hitchcock ●

Snowflake ●

● Lakeshore

Creswell ●

● Stover

Rootville ●

● Arkona

● Lull

● Comfort

Elgin ●

● Aarwood

Angell ●

France ●

Bates ●

Mabel ●

Barker Creek ●

Many of the towns identified here are difficult to locate. Maps no longer exist, records contradict each other. One source shows Elgin six miles north of Kewadin, another has it six miles south of Kewadin. Echo was shown near Intermediate Lake before the lake was renamed Six Mile Lake. Postal records list one town, railroad maps show another.

*Antrim City as portrayed by illustrator Betty Beeby in **Whistle Up the Bay.***

"Everything is as usual in this city in the woods. Someone is coming in here almost every-day to find their everlasting fortune or get sick and go out again."

With no natural harbor, the village disappeared. By 1884 all signs of civilization were gone. Today Antrim City is memorialized by Betty Beeby's illustrations and Nancy Stone's narrative in **Whistle Up The Bay.**

Throughout Michigan and the nation, small communities struggled to survive the tumultuous upheavals of the nineteenth century. As the villages and sawmills faded, the men and women who stayed ruined their backs clearing stump farms and getting to know hard-scrabble farming at its worst. In this sense, the Chain of Lakes region in Antrim County was typical of a rural America. Today third-generation family members glance nostalgically at musty scrapbooks and savor the memories found in aged and yellowed letters.

A roadside remnant of the past on the upper Chain, c.1985.

The Voices on the Water

The Lumberjack
Jess Letherby

The Resort Owner
Bill DeFauw
Chet Maltby
Ted Miller
Pat Rode
Carolyn Shah

The Fisherman
Gertie Barber
Mike Huntly
Roger Marker
Thale Yettaw

The Homemaker
Mae Fitzpatrick
Helen Larsen
Dorothy Pearl
Amy Smith

The Scientist
Richmond Brown
LaVerne Curry
Bill Weiss

The Poet
Terry Wooten

The Businessman
Guy Dean
Lyle Paradise
Harold Wilke
Joe Yuchasz

The Summer Resident
Warren Daane
Ellen Moore Poulson

The Preservationist
JoAnne Beemon
Harry Janis
June Janis
Walter Kirkpatrick
Warren Studley

The Farmer
Ben Samels
Bob Samels
Byrnece White
Versil White
Doyle Willson

The Teacher
Floyd Gregory
Beulah Morrison
Lena Stalker

The Historian
Mary Kay McDuffie

Lumber camps appeared throughout the Chain of Lakes in large numbers, along every stream, lakeshore, and river. Even without water, the big wheels and narrow gauge railroads enabled lumber operations to be less affected by weather, seasons, and geography.

By 1875, there were 1600 sawmills in Michigan. During the peak years of 1840-1890, Michigan lumber companies cut 161 billion board feet of pine, and 50 billion feet of cedar, hemlock, and hardwoods.

1. *Jess Letherby*

1

"If you didn't get out and make a livin'
some way or other, you didn't eat too good."

——Jess Letherby

" . . . practically the only thing we had to make a living at was working in the woods 'n the timber 'n one thing another." —Jess Letherby

The Oddfellow, renamed the Ruth, carries passengers and freight on its daily trip from Elk Rapids to Alden. By World War I, good roads and automobiles ended the era of the lake steamers.

54

Jess Letherby

Jess Letherby was born to "dirt poor" farmers in Kalkaska County during the summer of 1896. Kalkaska County was being lumbered bare as Jess grew to manhood. Fatherless at fifteen, he took to the lumber camps and became the family's sole supporter. In 1987, I interviewed Jess on the family farm on the southeast corner of Lake Skegemog. In 1992, Jess died at the age of ninety-six. He talks here of life near the "swamp" and the struggle to keep the family together:

We lived here in the days when practically the only thing we had to make a living at was working in the woods 'n the timber 'n one thing another. My father worked in the woods and did a little farming in the summertime—it was the wintertime we had to make our money.

When you were a young boy on the farm, describe a typical work day.

We didn't have any well. We had to carry our water from the swamp [Lake Skegemog] which was about forty rods away [660 feet]—summer and winter. In the wintertime, for water for bathing and water 'round the house, outside a drinkin' water, they melted snow on a big copper boiler on the stove. It was pretty rough going.

He died when I was fifteen years old and I was the only source of income for the rest of the family. Then I took care of my mother and my sister till I was twenty-one.

When your dad died and you started supporting your mother, what kind of work did you do?

We were so poor—he was sick three years before he died—working out in the woods in the winter in the wet. He had the flu and that turned into different things; it finally got 'im in the end, ya know.

I got a job in a lumber camp 'bout a mile and a half away from home as a chore boy. The camp was up on the Morrison hill—it's about half a mile up the hill from what is now the Crossroads Bar.

My job was to get up in the morning and build a fire in the office where the foreman and his wife slept and lived. Then there was the men's shanty that housed about sixty men, 'n then they had a cook shanty there that fed the men and they worked from daylight till dark in the woods. My job was to get up and call the teamsters out of the camp so they could take care of their horses. Then I'd get in wood 'n water.

In those days you didn't have much accommodations. There was no electricity, so everything was lamps that we had to go by. They had a big stove in the men's shanty that took four foot wood—that never went out—always put wood in there to keep the shanty warm.

During the day there was always some farmers around that had a piece of timber and they was puttin' logs down on the bankin' ground. My job was to take the horse and cutter 'n scale the logs for these farmers on a certain skidway, see? Then I'd come back 'n get things ready for the night—wood, water. There was always a few chores out around the barn there. They had a few horses that wasn't being used so ya had to see that they got fed, watered, and bedded down.

Worked till about eight o'clock at night. So from five o'clock in the morning I was busy till eight o'clock at night. I lived there. My check was sixteen dollars a month, fifty cents a day from five o'clock till eight o'clock at night.

Did you bring that sixteen dollars home to your mother?

I give that to my mother because I had my board and room at the camp. If you didn't get out and make a livin' some way or other, you didn't eat too good. There was no social aid, no welfare. The only thing the people had—there was a poor house east of Kalkaska.

There was a lotta' loggin' goin' on in those days because that was the only occupation there was around.

There was a bankin' ground about four miles south of Rapid City where the railroad was, so there's where all this timber was going. That was right on the fringe edge of the swamp, that was Round Lake at the time. Later on, they changed it over to Lake Skegemog.

There was a big lumber company come in from Battle Creek, the French Lumber Company. Looked this country over and brought in all their equipment in down by the railroad and called this little town France. They had a big mill—steam outfit. They could cut one hundred thousand feet of lumber a day down there. They were in there for years until all the timber got taken care of.

What did the men do for entertainment?

There was no saloons down there in Barker Creek. Prior to this time, over in Rapid City, there was five to seven saloons.

Outta' Rapid City towards Torch River there was a place they called Aarwood. There was a sportin' house [whorehouse] in there—I don't know how many gals they had there. That was legal at that time, to have a sportin' house. Everybody go just like you go to the theater or anything else. Also, at that time, Traverse City was thriving with lumber. There was no cars at that time, but Rapid City had a livery stable— that was the transportation at that time. The

Jess Letherby in 1987

fellas—was a lot of activity around there for the lumberjacks in those days. Some fights goin' on—nothin' serious.

A lot of the lumberjacks would get on the train and go to Traverse City and booze it up and there was a couple of sportin' houses that was across from the insane asylum there, what they called the "swamp house." It was all wooded out there—there's where the sportin' houses was. That was for the lumberjacks and the rougher class of people.

Did you ever get a chance to ride on those boats to Elk Rapids and Alden—the Ruth and Mabel?

Those boats were going back and forth. There was no cars in those days. The rail-road track went through and there was a spur went into Elk Rapids from Williamsburg. They had two passenger boats running from Elk Rapids to Bellaire. That was the only way you had to get to the summer resorts. Skegemog Point—they built a hotel, people come from Chicago, ride the boat and resort at this hotel.

From the hill where we lived, we could look across the swamp [Lake Skegemog] and see these boats going back and forth, comin' out of Torch Lake and going into Torch River. After cars came in, it took that business out.

Let's talk about Skegemog and the nature preserve. You've lived here for ninety years; are you bothered by the fact that so many people are moving in and there's a threat to polluting the water?

As time goes on, the whole world is changing, see? The environment is changing. The older people—there's such a contrast with the younger generations today. Every generation, every ten years it changes a little bit, see.

So as the time went by, it has changed a lot, and the younger generations wasn't raised up in hard times, see. They were raised up in luxury, money was more available, and the entertainment was different. They live in a different world, so they're taking over the world that they like to live in.

Jess Letherby ponders the future.

Do you think we should save some of the water and the land?

Well, I tell ya. I think they're takin' over too fast, everything is premature. That's what bankrupt this country today.

"The Swamp." A view of Lake Skegemog from the Letherby farm.

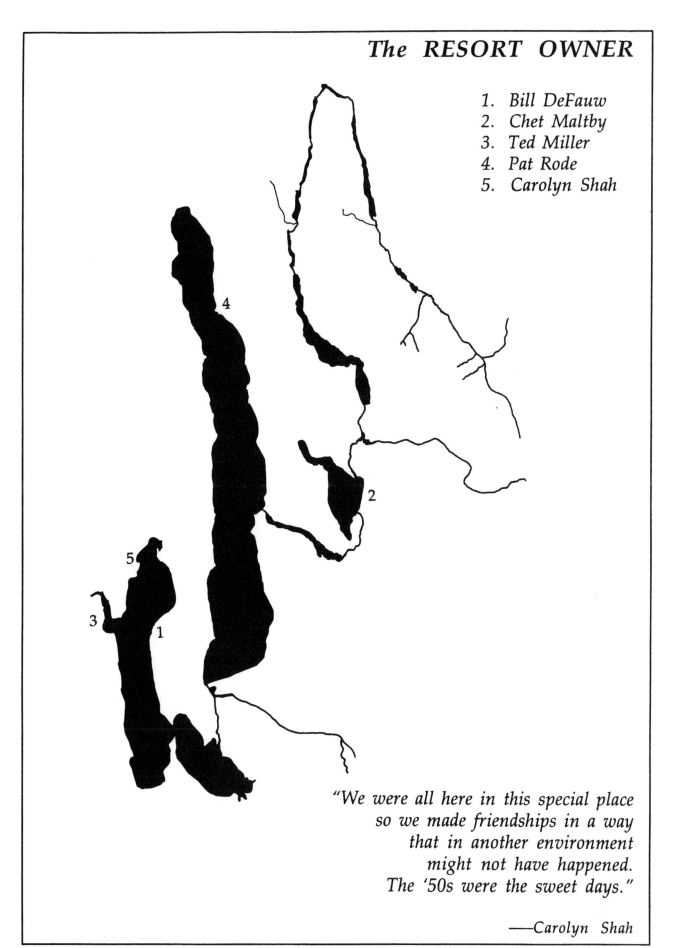

The RESORT OWNER

1. Bill DeFauw
2. Chet Maltby
3. Ted Miller
4. Pat Rode
5. Carolyn Shah

"We were all here in this special place
so we made friendships in a way
that in another environment
might not have happened.
The '50s were the sweet days."

——Carolyn Shah

Bill DeFauw

Bill's parents, Emil DeFauw and Julia Martin, came from Belgium shortly after the turn of the century. Bill was one of eleven children and he worked constantly on the family truck farm at Harper and Conners in Detroit. In 1945 Bill, with his wife, Bertha, and two children, Judy and Bob, discovered Elk Lake. In 1955, Bill retired from the Detroit Fire Department and the move north became permanent. Rambling Hills Resort, on the east side of Elk Lake, has been home for the last half-century. He became a vice-president of the Elk-Skegemog Association in the early '50s when there were only forty members. Bill does not mince words nor engage in subtleties that mislead you; he enjoys frank and blunt conversation. I first interviewed Bill in 1993 when he was eighty-six, and again in 1997. At ninety-one, he still operates one of the few remaining family resorts on the Chain. This is his story.

You have an unusual work ethic. What makes Bill DeFauw keep going at eighty-six?

I was born working. I started to work as long as I can remember. If you could tell the difference, on a produce farm, between a carrot and a weed, you were on your knees pullin' those weeds out. You better do it right with my dad 'cause he'd only tell ya' once. Second time you'd get a boot—then you remember, real good. We had our chores—eleven kids—everybody had something to do. There wasn't no such thing as one sittin' here, one sittin' there, twirling their thumbs.

My dad died when I was twelve years old. We tried to run the farm for two years, but none of the kids liked it, so we sold out and went our different ways. I started to learn the mason trade and was a brick mason for ten years. In 1929, the building business went in to a slump and I joined the fire department in 1930, and retired from there in 1955.

When I was in the fire department, I enjoyed a busy house—we were twenty-four on, twenty-four off. We had maybe thirty-five runs a month. When I got transferred to Alexandrine and Cass where they knock off 157 runs a month, the day was gone, it just flew.

Let's talk about the end of World War II and the way you came in contact with the north country. How did you bump into this property?

In 1938, we spent our first vacation on Higgins Lake. We rented a cottage for thirty-five dollars a week, shared by my brother-in-law and his family. They were the crummiest cottages; it was so dirty, it took us two hours to clean before we moved in.

I said to my wife, "This would be something nice when I retire from the fire department—get a piece of land somewhere on a lake, build a few cottages which would give me something to do and a little extra income."

So we drifted around and [in 1945] we come to look over here. The Hirt place was in the paper, we come to look at that; it had been sold the week before. It was listed by Archie Valleau—he lived in Alden. I said, "Isn't there anything else on this lake for sale?" He said, "I don't think so—wait a minute. Paul Hesley told me he'd sell his lake property, it's right next to this." It was all sumac and broken down barbed wire fences—cows used to come down here to drink. I walked down to the lake, took off my shoes, rolled up my pants and walked out there. It was all rocky and I saw there was no drop-off. I said, "What would he want for this property?" He said, " I don't know, let's go and see him."

We stopped in to see Paul who was as poor as a church mouse at the time. He was driving a Model A Ford with the doors wired shut. Archie asked him, "What do you want for your property?" He says, "I'll take $4,000." He wanted $1500 down, the rest on land contract. We paid with an option to pay it off whenever we wanted to.

With that $1500, he could buy some fertilizer and put a little boost in his cherry orchard which was right in its prime. At that time they were selling their cherries to the government at $300 a ton and he had eighty-five ton the first year. Well, he soon stopped being a poor man and he blossomed up in a Lincoln Zephyr. He was livin' high off the hog.

So the following year we came down here, put up a tent, and we started to work. First, I had to have a road put in so we could get down to the lake. I asked Hesley who I could get to do the job. He suggested Allie Burch in Kewadin. I contacted him and he did the job. So, later, I called him asking if the road was complete, he said yes. I had the roof pre-cut, doors pre-hung, and windows pre-hung. I put everything on a trailer and hauled them up here from Detroit—it took me nine hours. Then I got stuck coming down my road. I was alone and carried all this material on my back, piece by piece to where cottage #1 is. I slept in the car that night and got Hesley to pull me out in the morning. I then got Burch to fix the road so we could get in and out; he did. Allie hauled block, gravel and cement for me.

When I got my furlough—nineteen days—we came up, pitched a tent, and went to work. I dug the trench and started mixing concrete by hand. Bertie and Bob—he was only ten—hauled water from the lake. I mixed cement in a wheelbarrow one at a time. What a job. No one had a mixer up here. Things were hard to get—World War II was just getting over. If you think puttin' a wheelbarrow of cement in that trench isn't like puttin' a drop of water in a five-gallon bucket, you're crazy [Laughs].

Sometimes I wonder how we got the strength to do all this hard work. I thank God for that. In nineteen days we had the building up, no partitions, but we moved in from the tent.

We had no power for six years; didn't get power until 1951. I brought the power in from the Ringler Road and they charged me fifty cents a foot to bring it in and Fred Vermeersch took it from there to his house.

It sounds as though it was kind of lonely up here; there weren't many people?

There wasn't anybody, not until Vermeersch came in there in '50 and then Bensons came in '52. That was it for a long, long time.

I didn't buy this to make money on it; it's not for sale. That's what I tried to tell Bargy [Lon Bargy, Milton Township Supervisor]. He says, "You're under-ap-praised." I says, "Look, Lon, my place isn't worth that much money until I sell it—and it's not for sale. All my place is worth to me is what I've got in it. It's just like putting money in the bank." My kids are gonna have this. Hopefully, they can enjoy it for awhile before the tax collectors come along and take it away from 'em.

Do you think they're taking advantage of the lake owners?

They're taking advantage of the riparian owners, you bet your life they are. Now they raise my taxes forty-three percent—cross the lake in Elk Rapids Township they raise ten percent. Same school district, same lake—why? Milton Township has more lake property than Elk Rapids Township has. Look it, we're on a peninsula here. They got the whole west shore of Torch Lake as far north as the Township goes. They've got this here [Elk Lake] around to Williams Road. The taxes here have gone up more than Elk Rapids Township and I can't see why.

When the lake property only had a few buildings on it and the cows would come down to drink, the property was low in value; the taxes were low; the township was poor. Then in the '60s, '70s, '80s, and '90s, everyone started to buy lake frontage. The property went up in price and became scarce. Now the cost of property is out of sight, and as the lake property is being developed there is more revenue coming in.

The taxes are going sky high, and we get nothing for them but the air you breath. Something's wrong. Like I said, the horses are all gone, but there's still a lot of horse manure runnin' around here [Chuckles].

Let's talk about some of the changes up here, especially the water. You've been sitting on the edge of Elk Lake for close to fifty years. What's the biggest single change that you can think of?

It's getting better now. When we first came here, we did drink the water out of the lake. You could go out there with a boat and look down thirty feet and see logs layin' at the bottom. You can't see down half that

Bill DeFauw speaks his piece.

now. But they're getting after these people that were in here first. They didn't care––they just run their septic tanks right into the lakes. I've seen raw sewage come right into the lake. My septic tanks are far away from the lake. I've seen and raised hell about it; they put 'em fifty feet from the water's edge. Your drain field should be at least one hundred feet from the lake.

There wasn't any policing or restriction when we started here. But now it's getting better—they're tearing out a lot of these old septic tanks.

Where's the limit, Bill, to all the people heading up here? Everyone complains that the people who were here first want to keep other people out.

It's just about reached its limit. There's very little vacant property that's suitable to build on anymore in this Chain of Lakes. We have the cleanest chain of waterways in the state of Michigan because it's all spring-fed. You can stand in one spot, you got that spring action coming up all the time.

When we first came here there wasn't any silt in the bottom of the lake at all; now there's silt. The tests the Elk-Skegemog Association takes is proving that it's getting clearer, little clearer each year. It's coming back.

About five years ago, they had these houseboats—remember them? They rented 'em over here at Kewadin. I see a houseboat going real slow—and I thought, "By god, there's something real nice on this Chain of Lakes. You can anchor here awhile and then go on, fish if you want to." A woman came out of the boat cabin with a peck bag and threw it into the water—her rubbish. Well, that cured my thoughts right away. I grabbed the phone and I got the sheriff. He bawled her out, but the evidence was at the bottom of the lake.

The people that don't own property on the lakes, they have no respect for the lakes. Even the ice-fishermen, they go out with bottles, junk—down the hole it goes. All that stuff comes up on the shore—broken bottles, tin cans.

You mentioned that the Elk-Skegemog Association should be more of a taxpayers' protective association.

In every respect. Right now, they're pickin' on the riparian owner. There's only so much lake property and property is very, very high and that's what they go by. I blame the real estate people—suppose I want to sell this piece of land. They're gonna come and tell me they can get more than they can actually get for it, just to entice me to put up a for sale sign and give them an option on it. Imagine, they're gettin' ten per cent.

The first thing they throw at me when I go down to complain to the Board of Review—"Well, you don't have a complaint at all, look at so-and-so sold his place for $450,000 and he had nothing compared to what you have. With today's market, you know your place is worth more than that." What're you gonna do? You don't say anything because it doesn't do you any good anyway.

When you first settled here, do you recall what your first taxes were?

When I bought the property from Hesley, I asked Paul how much was the tax on his lake property? He said $7. Well, the first year we had it, we paid $35 and it has gone up ever since. Now in 1996, I paid $8,791.66. After I pay my tax, utility bills, rubbish removal—$56 a month—and maintenance, I work for the privilege of living here. They cut the taxes when Proposal A passed. Thank God for that; I was paying up in the teens. They'll get it all back by raising the valuation a little each year.

Bill DeFauw (standing), Bob DeFauw (center),
and cousin Joey DeMaire, c. 1947.

64

Aside from the fact that you're a property owner, you spend your entire year here—you've never left it. The water here must have some attraction for you?

It does—it's so peaceful. I have relatives and many friends in Florida and they say, "Come on down. Jump in a plane. Why do you put up with this snow and ice?" Why should I go there? I can see more of Florida right here on the tube than if I drove around down there. I got plenty of room to move around; down there it's congested. Everybody goes to Florida. When they leave, I've got more room. The driving is pleasant; you can relax. To me, this is heaven.

Although I've had to work real hard, my wife too, I've enjoyed every minute that I've been here.

As you wander around your property, Bill, through all the seasons, what's your favorite spot? Or your favorite view?

Well, I used to get up on top of the hill—from there I can see [Old] Mission Point right over the top of Elk Rapids. I can see East Bay. The lake really looks beautiful from up there. I like to sit up there, sit quiet, wait for a deer to go by, a wild turkey––or even watch a squirrel. It's a good pastime.

I just hope the tax assessor leaves me here and I can afford to stay here for the rest of my days.

Five of the six Ruggles children at DeFauw's resort in 1968.
Bottom: Suzy; Middle: Scott, Angela, Julie; Back: Tim.

Bill, you've led a rather long and hardworking life. Looking back, if you could change anything, would you do anything differently?

I wouldn't put up any cottages [Laughs]. That's one of the mistakes I made in my life. They're payin' my taxes now, yes, but it's a lot of hard work for me in the spring of the year. I don't leave the work pile up on me if I can help it. I keep 'em in pretty good shape. The hard cleaning, the waxing and scrubbin' of the floors and painting and fixin' this and fixin' that, I do. That's why I'm eighty-six years old [1993]—I've never seen anybody get killed by hard work. Look at me. I've heard of a lot of people dyin' from doin' nothin'—sit around and drink a twelve-pack of beer and smoke a couple packs of cigarettes. You're not gonna last long doin' that.

We were pioneers. Talk about the covered wagon—it's the only thing we didn't have. It makes you feel good, you did it yourself. I have never received one cent from anybody that I didn't have comin' to me.

You ever hear of the American dream? That's a myth. There is no more American dream. When you work all your life for your dream home and you can't afford to live in it anymore, there's something wrong with this country. This is my dream if I can hang on to it—they're crowdin' me pretty doggone close. And that's the way it is, 1997, fifty two years later.

Chet Maltby

Chet Maltby was born in 1898, five miles west of Bellaire to Edward and Theresa Maltby. Chet attended the University of Michigan during World War I, returned home to teach, and eventually bought a resort on Lake Bellaire which he operated for fifty-one years. He married Agnes Mohrmann in 1926. During the lean years of the 1930s, teaching gave him an income that enabled him to hang on to his favorite occupation: the resort. With their two daughters, Laura and Camilla, the Maltbys spent most summers on Lake Bellaire. I interviewed Chet in his Bellaire home in 1986; he died September 3, 1988. These are his memories of the water and his life on the Chain:

Dad tried farming for awhile, he was really a horse man—a teamster. He had a chance to buy a dray line—the one horse dray line in Bellaire. From then on we were in the dray business and the livery business for quite a number of years—we grew up in it. It was a matter of serving the people who wanted that. In the early days of the dray business Dad had the contract with the government to handle the mail; he handled freight for the merchants.

The livery and dray service was in close touch with the resort business, so we knew what they wanted—we handled their baggage. In addition to resort hotels, there were a lot of cottagers. They had work for us because there wasn't a profusion of automobiles. However, we did go from horses—we went through the transition from horsepower to automobile. By that time we had a Model T Ford.

We would meet the trains; I remember—we could listen for the Resort Special, or the Flyer. It came about six o'clock in the morning. We could hear it coming across the lake. If we hurried we could get across the railroad tracks in time to be on the right side [Chuckles]. A surprising number of people came to Bellaire looking for a resort or hotel—they didn't have any reservations.

When I was in high school, I was planning on going to the University of Michigan. Through happenstance, I made it. I graduated from Bellaire in 1916; it was during the war years. We weren't in the war then; we were busy with it, supplies. I knew that I was going to be drafted when I was twenty-one, so I made preparation with that in mind. At the University I joined the Reserve Officer Training School. That summer, after my freshman year, I went to a training camp in Fort Sheridan.

When I went back for my sophomore year, we were in the war then. The University campus with all the sororities and dorms—they were taken over by the government for barracks.

I went to Detroit for a job—was there two or three days when I got a call from my dad—they needed a school teacher. I came back on the Flyer, the Resort Special. That was my introduction to school teaching. District #5 near Chestonia, eight grades and kindergarten.

During the logging days, I was teaching school and the fact was the boys, along in their early teens, in the summertime they would work in the woods, decking the logs for the winter sleighing. When they hauled them into Bellaire, then these kids would come back to school. One boy, fifteen years old, came in the fourth grade [Chuckles]. I had one youngster in the eighth grade for the third year. He knew all the books by heart. But he wouldn't come in to Bellaire to take the eighth grade exam; he didn't have the money; he didn't have the clothes.

The Maltbys. Front: Pete, Chet. Back: Edward, Bill, Theresa.

Let's talk about the resort. How did it grow from two little cottages?

My brother and his wife and I came up on vacation by boat to Mackinaw. When we got here, this property on Lake Bellaire was for sale. It was a two cottage deal, two-story cottages with a breeze way porch in between—ideal set-up for a resort. We bought it. Partially furnished—beds, the slop jars and pitchers, wash basins. Extremely primitive. My dad co-signed the notes.

There was just the main building with a couple of outhouses. The first thing we did was put running water in the kitchen. There was no plumbing. It was called Northlakes Resort.

What did you offer people at Northlakes Resort?

It was a fishing resort. The trout season opened the first of May—that was practically a holiday in the area. Trout fishing was very strong. We were open for lake fishing too. Fishermen started coming in as soon as bass season was open, about June fifteenth.

Let's talk about the different kinds of fishing. Where would you go for trout fishing from your resort?

Bellaire pond. Very soon resort people started calling it "electric pond" because there was an electric power plant on it that serviced Bellaire. That was a very good trout pond, and there was the Cedar River which furnished the water for that pond. There was brook trout there. All of the streams had trout in them and the lakes all had fish [Chuckles]. Fishing was good.

The Maltby livery and dray business in Bellaire, c. 1910.

We started with the slogan "Fun for the fishermen and their families" and we ended up with the slogan "Fun for families and their fishermen." So it was a gradual transition from the kind of demand.

It was all American Plan. If you invited resorters in, you had to feed 'em because I think the local restaurants in Bellaire would handle a capacity of twelve. You had to take care of 'em completely.

We were able to accommodate thirty people the first year. We introduced one thing that hadn't been available previously. All the hotels had their heavy meal, dinner, in the middle of the day. We changed the schedule and had dinner at night and lunch at noon. Also we served breakfast for at least three hours—seven to ten.

Northlakes Resort in the late 1920s. From right: Chet Maltby (standing),
Agnes Maltby, Marian Burt, and two unidentified guests.

Children at Northlakes Resort in the mid-1920s. Dorothy Ann Maltby, center.

How much could a person spend in those early days at Northlakes Resort?

Eighteen dollars a week with all your meals, half-rate for children under ten. A few dollars was quite a bit of money then.

By 1970, when you closed, how much had that changed?

Depending on the type of accommodations, it was over one hundred dollars per person. My cook was worth the rate for one week. They all seemed satisfied with it. When we finished, we could accommodate seventy-five people regularly and we could feed about one hundred. We had twenty-four cottages.

You mentioned that you used to take some of your customers through the Chain over to Six Mile Lake for fishing.

In the early days, I used to go fishing with some of the devoted fishermen. We would drive over there and rent a boat and fish. It was lake fishing, mostly casting for largemouth bass and smallmouth. You could fish with night crawlers for small-mouth. There was all kinds of fishin' around here. They'd catch lake trout outta Lake Bellaire even.

One thing we had to sell, after the fishing petered out, was the washed shore here on the east side of Lake Bellaire. We invited people with families and we hired a couple of counselors; they entertained the children while the adults played golf, went fishing.

When did the fishing peter out?

Before the Second World War. Gas was rationed [during the war] and people were lucky if they could get up here. One surprising thing that kept us in business was in Lake Bellaire—the walleye and lake trout and brown trout started biting. You could troll for them and they would run five, seven to eight, with the maximum of ten pounds. So that kept us in business. They would get them occasionally before the war, and they still get fish out of Lake Bellaire, but you have to work for them. You used to be able to catch smallmouth bass on a fly-rod which was pretty good sport. I never could think like a fish.

These old-fashioned resorts like Northlakes and Fisherman's Paradise seem to be all gone. Are there any left?

The demand for them petered out; it changed. As more people got automobiles, the demand for types of accommodations changed from cabin camps to motels. Then the hotels that were serving American Plan changed over to housekeeping cottages and let the people do their own cooking. People were making more money.

Lets' talk about water quality. Did you have some thoughts on the water quality of the Chain?

I've been aware of the quality of the water. Bellaire first got its water out of the Intermediate River. The band mill toilet—they called it the band mill because they used a band saw rather than a circular saw—was a two by four shelter. It was an outdoor toilet just built out over the Cedar River. It dropped its sewage into the Chain of Lakes—raw sewage. There was no problem of disposing of the sewage; it just went down the river—raw [Chuckles]—from the turn of the century on for several years. Anything you didn't want, throw it in the river, that'd take it. It'd go somewhere.

People today are more or less water conscious. Bellaire water comes out of deep wells now—good water, cold water.

You've spent most of your life on these lakes. Has it affected the way you see the world around you?

I was always happy living in Bellaire—years, good years. I had a rather pleasant life. I've enjoyed it greatly. I wouldn't know how to change it. My aim in life was to be in business—maybe because of the Horatio Alger stories I read at that time. I wanted to amount to something, finally decided I didn't have the brains for it, too much hard work anyway, so I settled down to teaching and running a summer resort. The summer resort, most of the time, made more than school teaching.

You've had your resort for fifty years—1920 to 1970. That's a long time to be in business.

Well, fifty-one, I'll have you know! The first year was 1920, the last year was 1970. That's fifty-one summers [Chuckles].

Northlakes Resort in the mid-1930s.

72

Laura (Maltby) Sexton (left) and Camilla (Maltby) Fisher with a "catch" of smallmouth bass, c. 1947.

Agnes Maltby with a string of smallmouth bass.

A new mode of transportation arrives at Lake Bellaire, c. 1935.

Ted Miller

*Ted Miller's father started Miller's Park on Elk River on the south edge of Elk Rapids in 1914. Ted, born a few years later, has spent most of his life here. He has the pleasant memory of spending every summer on this portion of the Chain. An outstanding citizen and former mayor of Elk Rapids, Ted died in 1997. This interview was made in 1986. Ted's memories were first published in my 1993 book, **Voices from River Street.** Ted fondly recalls:*

My father loved to fish and hunt. He used to come up to Fisherman's Paradise in Bellaire to fish. One time he came up to Meguzee Point, which is now White Birch Lodge, and saw the property across the river.

In August, 1914, he purchased what was to become Miller's Park from Agnes and Gertrude Love. Came up fishing, built a cottage—now Sunnyside—in 1914. Built without a kitchen, clapboard siding dining hall was put up. The next year several people, who were friends from Sydney, Ohio, came up and tented. Dad told 'em he was gonna sell off lots, and platted it. They put up the dining hall 'cause they wanted to give the vacationers a full vacation.

My first recollection is when I was five or six years old—they're all good. We always went back to Indiana the first of November. I started school here in Elk Rapids—all my good recollections are here, and my bad ones, I hated it, are down in Indiana.

Here I could swim, I could run a motor, I could be anything—and it was a family-type operation completely. The people weren't oriented to drive long distances. They used to drive around the lake, pack a picnic lunch, drive around the lake and back over on the south end of Skegemog—that hill—you used to get out and push to get up over the hill. Some time you'd have to take a fence rail and pry the car outta the sand—we'd get stuck. But we all had a good time.

It used to take us three days to get up here from Kokomo, Indiana. We'd leave early one morning, and we might make it to Hart, Michigan. But it was all square corners and southern Michigan was bad. The roads didn't go straight through; you'd detour around the farmer's lot if he didn't let you go through. Not all section lines were open for roads—go a mile one way, there'd be a square corner, you'd have to turn and go a mile the other way and then a mile north, a mile east and go a mile north again. Could make it to Hart.

Second night we might make it to Frankfort, usually the third day we'd be, oh, about two o'clock in the afternoon, we'd be coming down old M-ll, called it Dixie Highway in them days, and come in through the campgrounds.

It wouldn't be but about three hours later, we'd see ol' Ed Anderson coming down the railroad track with a freshly-speared whitefish or trout for my dad. How he knew we were here—Bert Wilson, Lloyd Crisp, Asa Maxwell, no one knew we were in town—none of 'em knew—but old Ed would be there.

What type of clientele would be attracted to Miller's Park?

They were all types, professionals, plumbers, schoolteachers. My recollection of the price of cottages was twenty dollars a week and, so later, it got to be $37.50 and on up. We had wooden boats that had to be caulked every year.

I was taking people out for hire during the Depression—trout fishing, and I'd get five dollars in the morning and five dollars in the afternoon—and you guarantee 'em the fish or they don't pay you. All my expenses were less than a dollar 'cause gas was about fifteen cents a gallon. The thing was if they broke the tackle and it was their fault, they had to replace it. If it wasn't their fault, I had to replace it. I had good experiences—but ten dollars a day for a fourteen year old boy was out of this world! My dad let me keep it all; I had to buy my own gas out of it. However, in the fall of the year, my dad suggested I buy my street clothes and things like that. I still had enough spending money.

Describe a typical summer day for a young boy in Miller's Park.

Ted Miller

75

Usually I would go swimming until I got old enough to run a boat and take people out for hire.

Most meals were fish, homemade dinners. They had an oven right in the stack, they would bake biscuits in there for morning breakfast. Ella would bake bread in there. My god, people today with all their automatic ovens—we had old kerosene stoves too—kerosene stoves and well water. We had well water up until 1934.

Then every night there'd be an old swing set out in front of Pine Lodge cottage and they called it the Liar's Bench and the first liar didn't have a chance. They'd tell fish stories—I just wish they had recorders in those days 'cause I could have written several books. They were all fish stories, all made up. When I was a kid I used to sit there in awe; I believed everyone of 'em.

My grandfather and William Hensler's uncle drowned out here. I took my grandfather Shaw, who was seventy-five at the time, and William Hensler. At the last minute, I asked Bill if he wanted to come along, so he did. It was the third of July, 1934. I made a swing and swung out toward the center of the lake instead of swinging towards the shore—it was a little bit rough and we were shifting a little water. There were four of us in the boat. I told 'em just sit still and I was bailin' water. All of a sudden, we shifted a pretty good one, put up four inches of water in the boat and grandfather and Clarence Hamler stood up and they upset the boat.

Grandfather and Clarence drowned. I didn't see 'em go down, but my cousin had on my jacket which was a horsehide jacket and when it hit that water it shrunk and he could hardly move, but he still could swim. He literally threw me up on top of the boat, told me to hang on. When they finally got rid of it, my fingernails were still in the bottom of that boat. He turned around to pick up grandfather and Clarence and they were gone. They never did recover the bodies, so my grandfather and his uncle are buried out there in the deepest part of Elk Lake.

Bill Hensler and Ted Miller recall childhood memories at Miller's Park.

There was a trolling thing from just off Meguzee Point, little bit east of Meguzee Point, line up with Hildreth's barn and the sand bar down at the south end of the lake—troll in that area with copper wire. We'd have the copper wire marked at certain feet and we'd raise and lower. Now with the advent of depth finders, you can follow that course very easy. Well known trolling spot for those days. There was Ivan Ketchum, later on Floyd Kline used to take people out there.

Describe the changes in the water that have occurred over the years.

We used to—when I was a kid—we could see twenty, twenty-five feet with no problem, looking down. Tumidity—that's the amount of algae and plankton that's caused by phosphate that's growing in the water. It's terrific. Now in the winter, you can see down through the ice twenty-five, thirty feet 'cause it kills that stuff off. By the time August comes around, you can't even find the old intake out here off Mert Schuler's—and it's only about six and a half feet down.

Unless they get sewers all around the lakes, they'll find it'll take quite awhile for 'em to end up like Bass Lake 'cause Elk and Torch are large cold water, but eventually they will. It'll kill 'em and it's the phosphate and nutrients that kill the lake. It's gonna grow plants whether in or out of the water.

Describe your favorite view for us.

Favorite view? From down in front, looking out across the lake, across Meguzee Point. I've been all over the world, and I've never seen the view that you can see right from here. It's soothin'.

Elk Rapids where Ted spent his boyhood days, c. 1930s.

Meguzee Point Hotel, now White Birch Lodge. Looking south to Spencer Bay and Elk Rapids, c. 1930s.

Ted Miller's favorite view across Spencer Bay.

Pat Rode

Pat Rode is Director of Camp Hayo-Went-Ha, the YMCA [Young Mens Christian Association] camp on the east shore of Torch Lake. He was born in Grand Rapids and began his college education at Grand Rapids Community College. He became a history teacher. His career was interrupted by the Korean War where he spent two years in the 11th Airborne Division in the Ranger Battalion of the Special Forces. After the war, his teaching career continued and he eventually acquired his Ph.D. at Michigan State University. In 1995, I interviewed Pat as he discussed the history and philosophy of this unique place on the Chain of Lakes:

In 1903, the Executive Secretary of the State YMCA was a man named Lincoln E. Buell. He visited Camp Dudley in Massachusetts, the oldest YMCA camp in the country. He had been impressed with what it had been able to do for boys and came back to Michigan with the idea that he wanted to start a summer camp in Michigan for boys.

He got together with two businessmen who were involved with the YMCA— Charles Wagner and William H. Gay. The three of them decided, in the summer of 1903, to take the train to Alden and start walking the shore of Torch Lake. The land had been lumbered; there were very few trees, if any, left. They came up to what is now called Hayo-Went-Ha Point—it was called then Tyler Point. They decided this was the place they would start this camp. In the summer of 1904, they brought the first boys to camp on that property. Through the next few years, the camping just grew.

It started with a gift of some land and some money from the Central Lake merchants—$350 to buy some land. Today it probably wouldn't buy much land on Torch Lake.

The idea was to get the kids in the wilderness, away from civilization, which we are still concerned about. It's just a little harder to get away from civilization today. The YMCA at that time was clearly a Christian organization. In the early days, their first period in the morning was Bible study and meditation. It was an extension of the YMCA mission which started with George Williams in England in the late 1800s. It was aimed at working with young boys particularly the homeless kids, although it translated into normal kids, to reinforce the Christian message—the whole idea of building character. The YMCA motto is "Spirit, Mind, and Body."

You used Christian in the past tense.

The YMCA started out as a very evangelical organization aimed at conversion and had a much narrower focus. As the YMCA evolved, it still has in its mission the idea of building Christian families and Christian people, but not in an evangelization way. It emphasizes those things that are common to most of the religions, aimed really at reinforcing the Judaeo-Christian values. We get boys now that are Jewish, agnostics, a variety of things. It is not as much evangelistic as it is reinforcing.

Years ago Jewish kids never came into the "Y." Even Catholic boys were discouraged from joining because they had the CYO [Catholic Youth Organization]—and they saw it as a watering-down of things. Today, there is no YMCA in the country that is anything but non-discriminatory. At our place, we have Jewish Board members, Jewish campers; we have a range of belief systems. Our goal is to reinforce those things that they have that are common to all of us.

That you have a mile and a half of frontage on Torch Lake in 1995 is amazing. What problems do you incur in maintaining the natural wilderness, the uncluttered look that it has?

Don't have any real problems with it. Historically, we've just made sure that we leave the vast majority of the property in its natural state. We lumbered under advice from the State to be sure we take the right trees down; we manage it as a forest. We watch erosion so we don't do things near the waterfront. We keep snowmobilers out as much as possible or on the trails. Because we've been doing it that way for so long, we don't seem to have a problem with it.

Can you give me a physical description of the overall size of the camp?

Pat Rode

80

It's a little over 640 acres, irregularly shaped, obviously. Mostly trees, paths—we cross-country ski in the wintertime. On the lake side of the road there're only three places visible from the lake. One is the meadow on the south end which is a natural open spot that we use for overnight campouts, and the kids swim down there. At the north end there is another area where you can get at the water but there's nothing visible. Then there's the center of the camp with our waterfront with the boathouse built in 1908—the cement pier where we keep all the boats—that's the landmark. That's what people see when they come up and down the lake in boats. At Hayo-Went-Ha Point, which is the early settlement, there's nothing there except a large cross that was built there years ago by a group of boys. We use it for campfires.

What kind of trees are found on this side of the lake?

Lots of red pine. Lots of scrub pine. Some years ago, L.E. Buell and a lot of others planted literally tens of thousands of trees. All the trees here came as a result of reforestation. We now take out a lot of trees to open up the area. We've got a lot of hardwood, white pine, basswood, birch trees—although they're disappearing. Birch trees are having some disease problems. It's really amazing, the whole variety we've had. The University of Michigan School of Natural Resources has been up here; they're helping us develop our campsite in to an outdoor laboratory for high school science classes. They think it's just amazing—the different variety of trees on the property. It's more accident than design. I don't think there's a virgin tree on the property; if there is, it's very well hidden. This whole area was lumbered. At Eastport you can still see the pilings in the Bay—it was nothing more than a place to pick-up lumber to take to Chicago.

To the environment in general, are you concerned about any environmental problems, water quality, for instance? Have you seen it change over thirty year's time?

There's been a little change in the lake. The lake is not as clear as it used to be. There's more seaweed growing. Probably from the phenomenon of more cottagers on the lake now who put fertilizer on their lawns. We all wish they wouldn't, but they do. The lake association really monitors the water and makes sure, with the health department, that sewage—they're really tough about septic systems. They do check the water so that we can swim in it; they've not found anything that's dangerous in that sense. But I'd be a little cautious about using the lake for drinking.

We've had no problem with our water except that we've had to soften it. So we've not seen any real change. We're very careful about how we deal with things here. When I first came here thirty years ago, people'd take soap down to the lake and shampoo. We just don't allow it at all anymore. The kids are very cooperative. Erosion is a problem, but we work at keeping the kids on the trails and on the paths and steps down the hill.

Let's talk about some of the people connected with the history of the camp. We've talked about Cap Drury. Tell me about him and some of the other people who made this such a memorable place.

Cap is the one that is at the center of developing our summer camp philosophy and program for what it is. I see myself as a caretaker of that which has been established. He was a phenomenal man. He came to the State YMCA in 1929, discharged out of the service. There's a story that he rode his horse from Fort Riley [Kansas] to Michigan. He just laughed when I mentioned it, so I don't know if it's apocryphal or not.

In 1931, he became the first real Camp Director—a person who was solely responsible for the operation of the camp—and he stayed until '64. So the program and the out in the wilderness, the values of developing friendship, the motto of "Each for all, and all for each," the foundation of our program came out of that period of time. Obviously, he didn't do it alone because he had good support from business, the Board, the staff and campers, but he was certainly the leader.

Carl Bonbright was a camper here in 1905, the second year we had a regular camp— '05, '06, '07, '08. He was associated with Hayo-Went-Ha from that time on; it had such a strong influence on him. He became a prominent businessman in Flint with the auto business. In 1930, he gave fifty thousand dollars to the camp. He built the seawall, the first pier, Bonbright Lodge—which is a remarkable log building, and the original twelve cabins and a bathroom building. That was the first time living quarters were in buildings.

There were no cabins until the early '30s? It was a rather primitive camp.

It still is. None of the cabins have electricity. None of the cabins have water or bathrooms; they walk up the trail.

The boathouse was the first building—1908. It's got an aluminum tin roof; we paint it silver; it just shines with a big sign. That was the only building on the property until 1915 when they built a camp office and store. There were no other real buildings until 1930. We had a bandstand with cement slab and a canvas roof, eventually a wooden roof—it's where they cooked. In 1978—the 75th anniversary—we built other cabins and this office building. But there's still no electricity in the cabins; kids do not bring radios; there's no television, no Coke machines. It's a rustic camp and we keep it that way. There are showers to wash 'em off occasionally.

Over the years, a lot of other camps have opened up along Torch Lake. They're all gone.

Four-Way Lodge and Camp Fairwood on Torch Lake closed in the 1970s. They were private camps, they sold off their property. Camp Maplehurst is still in operation— they have one hundred feet of frontage on the lake. But that property has been for sale for some time.

That gives Hayo-Went-Ha even a little more character; it's about the only camp left.

Camps like ours have disappeared. Private camps—every year there are fewer camps. It's the changing times in demographics. There are certainly fewer kids, changes in what kids do. Universities now offer sports camps, computer camps. All are commendable. There are just fewer and fewer people.

How do you compete with that? What do you offer?

With difficulty [Laughs]. It's a problem to convince kids to be in the wilderness, to carry a canoe on their back, to walk one hundred miles on Isle Royale with a back-

At Hayo-Went-Ha dock on Torch Lake, 1931.

pack, in a single gender camp with only boys—or at our girls' camp with only girls. But we have a niche in camping. There are people who are looking for this type of thing. There are boys and girls who are looking for the opportunity to test themselves. The growth of Outward Bound in this country is an indication that there's a strong need for that. It's just that it's a little harder to find them now; you have to search farther and farther. Recruitment is a little more difficult than it used to be.

I noticed a few accents here this summer. How international have you become?

Camp Hayo-Went-Ha has always been international. There was a Chinese counselor in 1908, the summer the boathouse was dedicated. He was going to school at the University of Michigan. He later became Vice-President of China under Sun Yat-sen. He was the leader of the YMCA in China. There were camps in China that were started because Chinese students went from here to China. Cap Drury, when he retired, spent the next twenty years in Japan; we have a daughter camp on Hokkaido.

At both our boys' camp here and our girls' camp—Camp Arbutus / Hayo-Went-Ha, south of Traverse City—the boys and girls live in a cabin with an American counselor and also a counselor from another country. Last summer [1994] we had twelve to fourteen different countries represented from Japan, Russia, England, Spain, the Netherlands, Sweden—we're older than the UN and we don't have as many troubles [Laughs].

Could Hayo-Went-Ha be considered a home school?

Everything is aimed at building relationships, strengthening kids' self-esteem and their ability to stand on their own two feet. We organize with eight boys and two leaders—that's a family and they do things as a cabin group. Even our out-of-camp

Girls from Four Way Lodge on Torch Lake, c. 1940.

84

trips—we've done everything from sailing the Mediterranean, the English Channel; we've climbed Mt. Ranier; we've hiked the Phillip Smith Mountains north of the Arctic Circle in Alaska. We've canoed all the way to the Bering Sea out of Denali National Park. We do Isle Royale backpacking. Those are exciting; they're real challenges. The idea is to give kids a chance to see if, together, we can do these things. There's strength in community.

Take me on a day, if you can, in the camp. What would a typical boy be doing?

The bell rings at eight o'clock in the morning—that's the wake-up call. When you hear the waterfront person yell at the top of their voice, "Polar bear!" That's the time that the kids that want to, go down to the lake and jump in and wake up—and, of course, Torch Lake will wake you up. Most of the kids go down and take off their pajamas—bathing suits are not needed.

After Polar bear, we raise the flag and go to breakfast. After breakfast is cabin clean-up time. Then the morning is divided into two activity periods; the boys do this as a cabin group and each cabin plans their week's activity. They have a wide range of activities available from which to choose.

At one o'clock we have the big meal of the day, dinner. After that, rest period—they have to lay on their bunks and take off their shoes. They can talk quietly. We encourage them to write letters, read, sleep.

Every other day they can get a candy bar—that's during rest period. Then there's a period called instruction. A boy signs up for that individually—it's multi-aged—

"Everything is aimed at building relationships, strengthening kids' self-esteem." --Pat Rode

85

and he may be the only boy from his cabin taking sailing or whatever it is. They do that Monday through Friday. So we're teaching particular skills. From 4:15 to 5:30 is a free time; craft shop is open; riflery and archery are open everyday. Every other day they can sail, boat, swim, table tennis; there's always a roof ball game going. Some of the kids bring their guitars and play together.

At 5:45 the bell rings again. We meet at the flagpole, take down the flag, come to supper. After supper until bedtime, during the week, it's different every day: it might be a campfire; it might be another cabin activity; there's never the same thing every night. Then we put 'em to bed at dark. Counselors stay in the cabins; they have a little story time, talk about how the day has gone.

I, periodically, tell the kids that I'll be on the porch of the boathouse—anyone who wants to come and listen to me read. This past summer I read *The Lion, The Witch, and the Wardrobe* to them over the course of a week and a half. It's a time for me to talk with the kids.

After taps and lights out, counselors walk around the cabins—we call that "rat patrol"—to be sure that everything's fine. They go to bed by midnight. Then the next day we start all over again.

What do you do with a kid—the fat, roly-poly kid that nobody ever chooses to play with, or no one chooses him as a buddy, the lonely, shy kid?

The counselors job is to try to build that kid into the cabin group; it's not easy. There are some kids that Will Rogers never met, that are difficult. Kids come with a lot of baggage sometimes. But it's amazing, we don't have a terrible problem with that. We have some homesickness, and we have some kids that don't fit in. We have a remarkable group of campers that really go out of their way to be friendly and deal with kids. It tends to work out. Obviously, some kids have a better time than others.

I was impressed with the price structure.

It's about $300 a week. It's $595 for two weeks. That's fairly standard; we're a little above the median in agency camps, YMCA and things of that nature. Private camps are probably twice as much. But, again, they have to pay taxes and we don't. I'd hate to think of what the taxes would be for a mile and a half of shoreline on Torch Lake.

We raise money all year round for camperships. If you were to call me and say, "I've got this little boy, he comes from a single-parent home, really needs to be at camp and they don't have the money." I would say, "OK, let's get him enrolled in camp and we'll find the money to pay his way." This is not a rich kid's camp. A lot of people think it is; some people around here feel that way, but it really isn't. Last summer, we had 330 to 340 kids; over one hundred got some kind of financial help.

We're very fortunate here; everybody gets some because, through the gifts of Stanley Kresge and others, we have an endowment. That endowment helps keep the costs down.

How does the camp fit in with the surrounding community?

We run programs; we teach astronomy—we take it around to schools. Bob Thurston, one of our staff, plays the violin, sings old sea shanties, uses music to teach history. He goes around and puts on assemblies. The alternative schools in the area that deal with kids at risk come out and use our ropes course and use our camp; they cross-country ski on our property. We provide scholarships through the Antrim County Probate Court and through the schools. We also put on a Thanksgiving dinner for the community; we fill the dining room with 150 people. The problem is, for the average guy in the street, that impact is not visible.

Any thoughts about the future of the camp; is it going to roll on the same?

We're positioned well. We have a school-based program. Almost five thousand school children went through here last year on either one day, two days, three days, a week. We run an outdoor education program. Teachers bring the kids; we provide the program. We have a relationship with the Inland Seas program—the big boat out in the Bay.

We're involved with the University of Michigan School of Natural Resources. Out of it is going to come: how can we use this site to reinforce the science teaching in the public schools in the area? Some can use it as an outdoor lab.

Hayo-Went-Ha swim team, c. 1930.

The Mabel brings the YMCA to Elk Rapids, 1916.

This 1930 view of Hayo-Went-Ha's shoreline looks much the same today.

Let's talk about your personal life. How did you happen to wind up at Hayo-Went-Ha?

My summers were always as a counselor. This is one of those things: I was standing on the corner of Division and Monroe in Grand Rapids, outside Peck's drugstore. Roger Blood, who had taken over Camp Hayo-Went-Ha from Cap Drury, came up. We talked and he said, "How would you like to come to Hayo-Went-Ha?" "That sounds good." I was here in '66 as Assistant Camp Director. In '81 I became Camp Director. In '89 I became Executive Director of the State YMCA full time as well as Camp Director.

The boathouse: the first building at Hayo-Went-Ha, 1908.

Let me ask a spiritual or philosophical question: How has the water affected your own life?

Obviously it's had a tremendous effect on camp programs and thus on me. It's a marvelous sailing lake, swimming, boating and all of that. The thing it does for me––we have here, with the water, the whole environment. From a religious as well as philosophical point, God created the water and the land for man to enjoy. One of the Psalms says, "As the deer pants for the water, so pants my soul for you, O Lord." That fills a spot in one's life. I have a hard time imagining living in the inner-city or the center of New York City and never being in the woods. The silence, the serenity, just the physical enjoyment of the views. There are other beautiful places that don't have water or don't have the other, but the combination has made this just an ideal spot. The people who started this couldn't have picked a better place.

Since you mentioned views, what is your favorite view?

My favorite view is standing on the porch of the boathouse, looking out on the lake about four-thirty in the afternoon on a sunny day in the summer. You look out on the lake and see our sailboats—white sails going up and down. You see kids swimming. You see kids playing cricket on the beach. You look out to the Point; you see the cross built there, sticking up above the trees—a reminder of the place where the first people camped. It is an incredibly beautiful view, but when you hear the voices, it reinforces everything this place stands for.

My wish is that everybody has a place like this. The world is so hurly-burly. It's so unfortunate that so many people don't understand and see the value of what it can do for children. It is not a vacation; it is an experience.

Carolyn Shah

Carolyn Shah is the owner and operator of Wandawood Resort on the northwest shore of Elk Lake. The resort is the last one hundred acres of a six hundred acre family farm that was settled in 1864 by her great, great grandfather, Moses Fish Gates. The resort stretched west to Grand Traverse Bay and Carolyn's parents, Carlos and Emily Palmer, donated two thousand feet of Bay frontage to the Nature Conservancy in the mid-1970s. This area is now known as the Palmer-Wilcox-Gates Preserve (PWG). Her preservation of two significant historic buildings in Elk Rapids plus her recent contribution of the PWG Preserve rank Carolyn as a leading preservationist and conservationist in the Grand Traverse region. My first interview in 1993 was followed by a second one in 1995, and updated in 1997. Carolyn recalls fondly the innocence of the 1950s and her childhood on Elk Lake.

Carolyn, we're sitting in a house almost one hundred years old on land that your family settled in the 1860s. Let's talk about your grandparents, Delos and Mina Wilcox.

My grandfather, Delos Franklin Wilcox, was an extraordinary personality in addition to his being somewhat of a public figure. He became somewhat of a gentleman farmer here at Wandawood. He was very creative in his thinking and he experimented with grafting several different kinds of apples. He also had an art shop—he got interested in photography and took numerous pictures of the area, which he sold at this shop in the 1920s.

Describe the size of the farm.

It's a short section running between Elk Lake and Grand Traverse Bay—it was around six hundred acres. Currently I own, with my brother David, around one hundred acres.

The major change in the amount of land occurred in 1948 when my grandmother died. The farm was sold and the resort was retained. There was major acreage there—on the farm. During her lifetime, after my grandfather died, she did both— ran the farm and ran the resort.

Let's go back to your childhood experiences as far as you can. What are your earliest memories of Wandawood?

I only have vague memories of my grandmother Mina, since she died when I was four. Mina was a stern lady with very white hair. She was called "the general" and she really ran the show. To a young child she was pretty intimidating. She was around the resort some in the summer, but most of her time was spent at the farm. Between her being very busy at the farm and with my parents being very busy running Wandawood, family visiting didn't occur.

I remember some scenes—they were happy times in my memory. The Wandawood office up until 1948 was in Brownie which is a now a cottage. I can remember we had an enclosure in the yard to keep my brother David and me from running further away. We had family help because of the resort which was a full time job for my parents. Various girls came in to help. We had our favorites and disfavorites among these caretakers. I can remember our cookies at that time were graham crackers with frosting—it was a real treat to have these cookies.

The McLeans—Kate and Jim—were a couple that helped here at Wandawood. They were a wonderful couple and contributed a great deal to Wandawood. He did the yard and she did the cleaning. They were the answer to the Wandawood problem— they came off the road and landed and stayed. In the summers Kate and Jim stayed in the orchard, in a unit which is now called Hideaway. Those were wonderful years. It never seemed possible to find anyone like them again. Kate took in the resorters' wash; she did it all on a wringer washer. She also made bread, which we called "Kate" bread. It was just plain white bread most of us wouldn't eat today. But at that time, it was just the "cat's meow". When she was baking, we'd all smell it. You could smell it all through the orchard and everyone placed their orders. She made loaf after loaf. To this day, people from that era talk about Kate bread– –it was the most sensational bread.

One time when I was around four, David and I had been collecting caterpillars and we had a number of cocoons that were ready to hatch. A resorter was intrigued by these monarchs and said that if we had another hatch by the next day, we would each get a quarter which seemed like a tremendous amount of money at that time and caused all kinds of excitement.

Delos Franklin Wilcox

91

Who were some of those memorable characters—those resorters that you ran around with?

Many of the families that came year after year, had children the same ages as David and myself. Most of what we did was pretty innocent by today's standards. But at the time, the parents had some concerns about what we would be up to. There was Steven and Bruce Redman, Betsy and John Ebert, Roger and Herb Gustaltder and Phyllis and Billy Conn. Also, some families with older children who were significant in our lives, such as the McGees, with their daughter, Barbara, who we all adored.

Why does Wandawood mean so much? It was just a summer resort and its over with now.

At the time, it was a special place for the resorters who came from all over the United States. We had one family from Florida for several summers. Some came from the East Coast and other parts of the United States.

If we had been kids growing up during the summer in Ann Arbor where our home was, would it have had the same feeling? I don't think so. This is a vacation spot. When we're all here, we're just a stone's throw away—literally, we used stones against the windows to attract each other's attention [Laughs].

We were all here in this special place so we made friendships in a way that in another environment might not have happened. The '50s were the sweet days.

Autumn at Wandawood on Elk Lake, 1925.

You've seen a lot of changes over the years. What is the most significant change?

When we were growing up here during the 1950s, the resort had primarily repeaters and many of the units were occupied by seasonal renters. The turnover was smaller then. It was a different kind of a place.

What are you running into now?

I have no seasonal renters. We stopped having seasonal renters at the end of the '50s. They would come in June and stay till Labor Day. They opened and closed the cottage. There was nobody else in that unit.

If the season-long resorter ended in the late '50s, do you know why that change occurred?

It's reflective of societal change. During that period, it was more common for families to take the entire summer—not always the father, but the mother and the children. But the father was here most of the time. We had doctors, significant people— they took the summer off with their families. Those that were left without their husbands were known as "merry widows."

Describe the current shoreline and the cottages you have.

The shoreline on Elk Lake is about one thousand feet. We have cottages at Wandawood that are both on the Elk Lake shoreline and across the road in the orchard. The main house that we're sitting in now was built in 1899. Wandawood Hall was built in the 1920s for my grandparents. It was built as a family residence and when grandfather died, it became part of the resort.

One of the great contributions your parents have made to the community is The Nature Conservancy property (PWG) on the Bay. That is such a big chunk of land that there must have been a lot of decision-making or discussion in the family. Tell me how that came about— —that they would literally give away such a valuable piece of property.

We started doing estate planning for Wandawood in the 1960s. I became very involved in Wandawood as a young adult and I began to get concerned when it became apparent that we had a lot of value here and my parents were aging.

One of the things that was done was that they started a gift plan to us, to move the property to the next generation. Then we began to fret over the Bay. We had all wanted it to remain undeveloped. We realized it may not be possible to keep that amount of property undeveloped in family ownership. Its value would necessitate sale upon somebody's death.

I was very instrumental in looking into alternatives. We explored the State of Michigan, we explored Elk Rapids Township, but we ultimately settled on The Nature Conservancy. The original donation was made in 1974. I think it was unusual that we all agreed. Our family didn't really see the big bucks in it, but saw more the need and desire to keep it natural. It's two thousand feet and it was pretty clear that protecting that land was paramount. The way to do it was to get it out of my parents' estate and make a gift. David and I were not interested in capitalizing on the land. There was no urgency to have a windfall.

One of the most notable concerns I hear from people up here are the tremendous taxes they pay. Can you comment on the property tax dilemma?

Taxes are a burden. The taxation problem has been felt more by owners of smaller parcels who have been taxed at a higher rate per foot then I have been with the large parcel. I also think I've been spared some increases because of its use—rather than it being taken at its highest and best use which might be a different type of development than the resort.

Let's talk about the changes today that could threaten or alter the land here. What's your greatest concern?

I have a lot of anxiety about the property. I've been concerned about how we can continue to run the resort and how we can protect it into the future. The increasing traffic and hazard of the road is a major threat. The possibility of sewer and water and the cost that would come with it is also a threat.

Right now, Wandawood is in demand and I'm at one hundred percent [occupancy] for the key weeks during the season. It's a shoe-string operation and it's sustained on one hundred percent occupancy. That's asking a lot. Six to eight weeks is a very short season.

What do you see for the future of Wandawood; what do you hope for it?

What we're working on now is ways of protecting as natural land more than what is protected by The Nature Conservancy. The other thing we're working on is how to accept in our estate planning what Wandawood is as a resort. My desire is to main-

Wandawood Hall, c. 1925, is a mainstay of Wandawood resort today.

tain Wandawood as a resort and to make that possible for my children.

I've two major concerns related to governmental decisions. One is the road which could become worse than it is—if it were to be widened, the speed limit raised or if it were to be used more as a major truck route. It's number one on the complaint list of the resorters. I do have people who leave because of it.

The road to the water, how much depth do you have?

It's under one hundred feet at some sections of the frontage. It's a pretty narrow strip. The impact is substantial because of noise, speed, passing.

The other concern is the sewer.

The only fishing costume allowed during mosquito time, c. 1920.

I'm hoping that the township board will continue to be aware, as some of them are now, about what happens when you do sewer extension along a major roadway— what the consequences are in terms of development. But that is an educational process. It's almost certain that if a sewer were to come down Cairn Highway to Kewadin that it would force a change in a lot of development patterns along the highway.

What about water concerns, problems with water quality?

The lake is in good shape. The tests that have been made show that it has shown improvement over some other years. There are some hot spots [year round homes with outdated septic systems], but the hot spots aren't necessarily getting worse. It's not paramount on my list of concerns unless the Wetland Control Act loses all of its guts and people are able to build wherever they want and have septics drain directly into the water. The lake is almost completely built up now and so what we see today is what there will be.

You're one of the last family-owned resorts on the Chain of Lakes. All of the summer resorts seem to be disappearing. Why do you think that might be happening and what do you predict for Wandawood?

Running a resort, certainly because of the family life-style changes, became a different sort of a business. More stressful, more time-consuming because of the frequent turnover and having more new people rather than repeaters. The other thing that has happened to a lot of these family resorts is that death has occurred and the heirs, for a variety of reasons, have not been able to, or wanted to, keep things intact, so they've been sold.

My intention is to continue to run Wandawood as a resort. I have no interest in profiting from the sale. That's like blood money to me. If I hadn't stepped in when my parents died, the resort would have been sold.

Looking southeast, a view of the Palmer-Wilcox-Gates Preserve (left) on the shore of Grand Traverse Bay. Elk Lake and Elk River are at the top.

Time out on the farm for a family picnic, c. 1900.

96

Scenes from Wandawood Farm: The Early Years

Farmhands with Don, Molly, and Popsy.

The boy, the birch tree and the butterfly.

The road to town.

Leisure time on a Sunday afternoon.

Picking apples at Wandawood.

A group of friends gather at Wandawood, 1902.

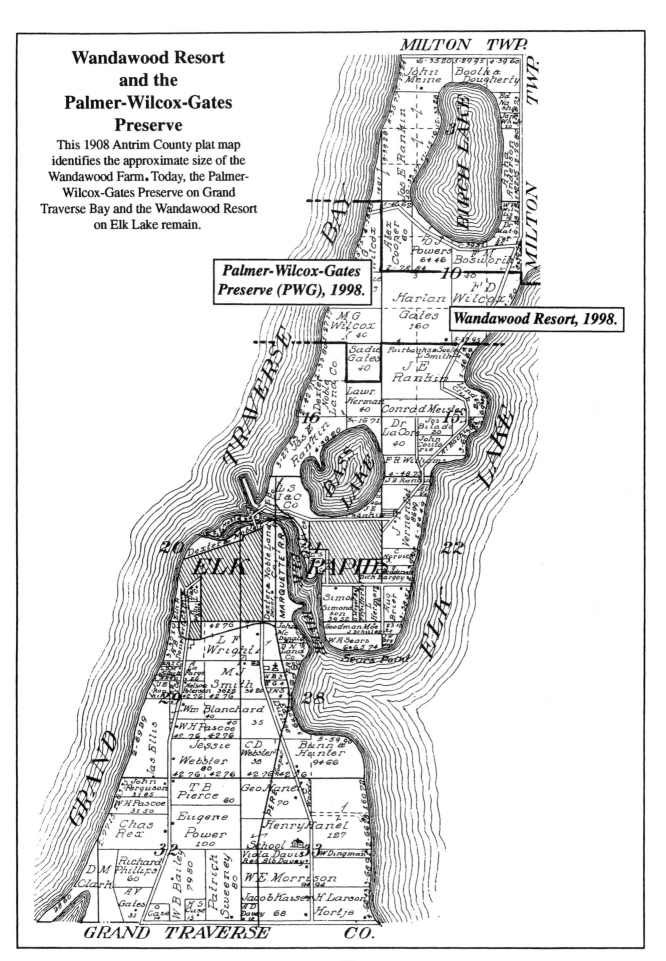

Wandawood Resort and the Palmer-Wilcox-Gates Preserve

This 1908 Antrim County plat map identifies the approximate size of the Wandawood Farm. Today, the Palmer-Wilcox-Gates Preserve on Grand Traverse Bay and the Wandawood Resort on Elk Lake remain.

Palmer-Wilcox-Gates Preserve (PWG), 1998.

Wandawood Resort, 1998.

Whether casting for brook trout (above) or spearing muskies (below), the excitement of fishing on the Chain has always presented a challenge.

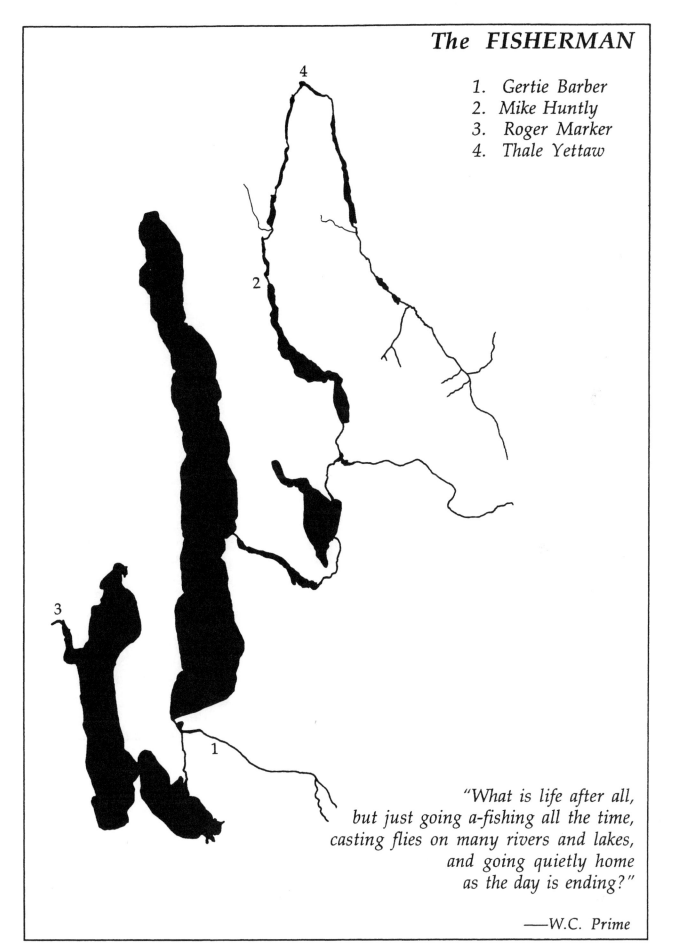

The *FISHERMAN*

1. *Gertie Barber*
2. *Mike Huntly*
3. *Roger Marker*
4. *Thale Yettaw*

*"What is life after all,
but just going a-fishing all the time,
casting flies on many rivers and lakes,
and going quietly home
as the day is ending?"*

—W.C. Prime

Gertie Barber

Born at Central Lake in 1902, Gertie was one of ten children. Struggling to keep the family together, her father, Theodore Mosher, operated a sawmill in Rapid City where Gertie worked as a planer. She started trout fishing at four years of age. One of Michigan's first women trout fishing guides, Gertie was highly sought after because of her knowledge of the lakes and streams on the Chain of Lakes. Her name has become legendary in fishing circles. Still sassy and spry when this interview occurred in 1990, she showed no sign of quitting. One of my old friends, Gertie Barber, died in 1997. This is her story:

I'm gonna' tell you something that's crazy. Nine times outta ten, I had dreams before I'd get a fish. Everytime I would go out to the lake—lotta times before I'd get a fish, I'd dream about getting a fish and then I'd get up and tell my husband I was gonna get the fish. I'd go out to the lake 'n never see one. So I told myself, "Keep your mouth shut 'n maybe you'll get a fish." That was kinda hard work [Laughs].

When I got that big one [forty-four pounds], I dreamed I saw him in the hole. I had a sucker on for a decoy and that big ole spear. I never said "boo" to my husband about getting this fish. So I waited, here he came right under the stove [in the shanty] towards my spear. I got 'im. Then I had to get my husband [Forrest] to help me get it out of the hole. I was fishing in about sixteen feet of water and that fish took that spear and went all around down there. I had to lay the rope right down on the bottom, so he couldn't carry the spear too far.

It's a good idea to put a couple of spears in those muskies, because they can fight. All you gotta' do is get the spear over him before he sees you. That's quite a little trick. Keep the sucker wiggling so he can watch the sucker instead of your spear. You have a live sucker just about two feet below your spear. It's sixteen feet long and you leave maybe four or five feet above the hole in the shanty.

I didn't get excited. You could miss it if you got excited. I thought, "If I don't get you today, I'll get you another day."

What is there to like about fishing?

Well, you get all the good exercise and when you're fishing you don't think about anything else. You only fish. It's good for you.

I haven't got a favorite fishing spot. I have fished Spencer Creek, I've been fishing Rapid River—I've got a lot of fish out of Rapid River—not lately. Lately there's no fish any place—here or in Finch Crik. I don't know why and I'd like to know.

Have you seen changes over the years that might answer that question?

No, but somebody, I don't know who, cleaned out a lot of the cover in Rapid River. Fish have to have places to hide. From Rapid City down there's not hardly anything in the river to hide under—and I don't know who authorized them to do that. I understood they cleaned it out so they could run skis up there with motors on.

Do you think there are too many people up here?

No. I don't think the people's got anything to do with it because people have been coming here all these years. There's been lots of fish there. You didn't have to fish very long and you had your limit. You could look down and see fish all over, and now you can't see nothing. There's gotta be something wrong.

There's a lotta people, but trout fishing's hard work. Unless they know when and where to go, it's no big deal. You don't have very many people fishing on the rivers any more. It's a little hard getting along these streams, ya know. You gotta know where to go 'n what

Gertie and her forty-four pound Muskie, 1972.

103

time to go. A lotta people, they'd rather boat fish, if you know what I mean, instead of walking through the woods 'n over logs 'n all that. There's a time for everything.

Has the water had an effect on your life, living near rivers and lakes in the Chain of Lakes area?

The water has especially. When I was taking people out fishing, I would go bare-legged. I wouldn't wear waders in the summertime. Some of the doctors that came up here and fished with me, they told me, "when you're fifty years old, you won't be able to walk because you'll have arthiritis so bad." But I'm still walking now—yet—good. I probably outlived most of those people 'cause I haven't heard from any of 'em, so I think they're all gone.

I got paid for taking 'em out. They'd always pay us. You can show 'em how, you can tell 'em how, but you can't make the fish bite their hook. There are days like that.

When you fish one river all the time, you know just about every hole you're gonna catch fish in. There used to be lotsa fish in Rapid River, now there's not hardly any there at all. You look for holes and fish under logs. You just don't fish one hole, you go from one hole to the other and fish. Nine times outta ten there'll be fish in each hole. It isn't that way anymore. There's not any there!

We used muddlers most of the time; we used to sell muddlers here. A muddler is a fish bait—they grow in the river. They look like a little bullhead only they're not smooth like a bullhead. It's a type of fish. They're wonderful bait. They got a little teeny horn on 'em.

The weather has a lot to do with your fishin' too. You can go fishin' in a rain storm, but not thunder 'n lightning.

I got one hole we used to go fishing in. I was fishing down here on Rapid River one night. See, it was cloudy and it was muggy. I said to my husband, "Lets go up to that one hole fishing." Ten o'clock at night. He got a rainbow—it must've been three or four pounds and then I got four that night. The smallest one was three pounds, and the rest was all four pounds a piece—all outta one hole.

I went another time—I was fishin' down by Rapid City with a fly rod 'n grasshoppers. It was a real muggy night and I said to my husband, "Let's go up the crik and fish that big hole." That night I got an eight and a half pound brown—and don't think I didn't have fun landin' it!

Do you think the mugginess had something to do with it?

Yes, it did. Yep. See, those browns don't bite when it's just any ordinary day. They have to have certain times when they bite. And I've caught down here good sized browns and brookies. I've got brookies down here nineteen and a half inches long.

But that's not lately.

When I lake fished—speared out on the lakes, I'd look at the barometer before I went. If the barometer was rising, nine times outta ten, you'd see fish. You gotta catch these fish when the moon's filling up, they fill up too. You'll have days after the moon's full that they'll bite, but it won't be easy.

Are there any other signs that we should look for when we're fishing besides the full moon?

Yeah. There's gotta be fish there, too [Laughs]. I didn't catch ten fish all last summer and I went fishing ever night in good water. It's a big mystery.

I fished Skegemog and Elk in the winter. That's where I got my forty-four pound muskie and all those other big fish I got.

I got a box 'bout three feet long, about a foot deep down at Nichols' Hardware. George Nichols said,"I'm goin' out with you, Gertie." Before I could drink a cup of coffee and eat that sandwich, I had that box full of fish—whitefish and lake trout. I pulled up one right after the other. That line never went to the bottom. That's the best time I ever had fishing on Elk Lake.

I've went fishing over to Deep Water Point—it goes into 150 feet of water.   Before I'd get there, they'd be guys come from Kalkaska and they'd be setting right up agin my shanty with a hole cut right there—fishin'. They're not supposed to do that. My spot where I fish is just right inside the shanty—and those lines'd be just a couple feet apart.

Rapid River in the early 1900s.

I did have a good spot too. I told 'em to move. They moved. They said they didn't think I'd be out there that day. That's something I wouldn't do.

I've had these guys come from Traverse City and they'd have lines all away around my shanty in a big circle. I said, "Why didn't you guys just move my shanty off and fish right in the hole?" I let 'em have it.

How can a person your age [Eighty-eight] get out there and hunt and fish. What have you done right with your life?

Gertie in 1995.

Well, I can tell you what I've done right more than I can tell you what I've done wrong. I've done all the things I've wanted to do, like hunting and fishing—and I'm still doing what I wanta do at my age. I walked about two miles the other day and ... my legs felt better than they ever had before. I guess you just gotta keep movin', doin' the things you like to do. As far as a living's concerned, you just keep on living. One thing is live and let live.

Gertie, do you feel like you're part of history?

Are you supposed to feel important? A person should take time off to do things they like to do.

Ben Marsh, long-time Elk Rapids summer resident, tries his luck in Gertie Barber's favorite fishing spot, the Rapid River, c. 1925.

"Fly-fishing may well be considered the most beautiful of all rural sports." --Frank Forester

Mike Huntly

Mike was born Charles Gordon Huntly Jr. in Eaton County, but moved north as a young eleven year old boy. His father, Charles Gordon Huntly Sr., was a pharmacist in Central Lake and Mike grew up in the small village. He spent a lot of time on the water fishing. He graduated from Central Lake High School in 1940. He is a member of the Lion's Club, the VFW, and served as county commissioner for ten years. He married Betty Cahill and they raised three children: Nancy, Michael, and David. Today, Mike and Betty still reside in Central Lake. Here is Mike's story as he recalled it for this interview in 1996:

Back in the Depression, in that pharmacy, we sold bait, rented boats and motors, and furnished motors. I picked up night crawlers till you couldn't count 'em. I seined literally tens of thousands of minnows that we sold out of there. We sold hunting supplies and both hunting and fishing licenses.

During the Depression, there was good money in bait. We'd sell three dozen minnows for one dollar. The bigger minnows for walleye—three or four inch—ninety cents a dozen. That was good bait. We were selling to well-heeled summer residents or parties of fishermen.

I can remember taking bait up to Big Fish Inn on St. Clair Lake when they were short. The owner's name was Henry VanderArk. Marvin Elzinga, he did some guiding out of there. I knew Thale Yettaw.

It seems like a sporting goods store; it was more than a pharmacy?

Yes, we sold guns, ammunition, and we sold a lot of fishing tackle. Back then we did a lot more business in sporting goods and souvenirs than we did in pharmacy.

Let's go back to your childhood on the Chain of Lakes. You referred to your dad as your buddy. Describe your dad.

We fished and hunted together all the time. He was a workaholic—I knew he worked hard as it seems that everyone did that had a job in the Depression. I think he worked himself to death. He died at the age of fifty-three about seven weeks after I enlisted in the Navy on September 30, 1942 at the age of twenty.

How do you recall those Depression years in Central Lake?

We moved here in 1934 from Oakland County. I was young; I'm sure my parents and older people had a tougher time than I realized. Everyone worked—I worked the creeks three days a week getting bait. I ferried boats around. The YMCA camp or Four-Way Lodge or Camp Fairwood would come in and want to rent maybe ten boats. We didn't have that many boats on any one lake. We had twenty-four boats all together—on Six Mile, Wilson, Ben-Way, Hanley and Intermediate. I could move the boats around. At Six Mile Lake, we took those by trailer—the other I'd tow them up through the river to Wilson or Ben-Way. That was simpler than taking them one at a time.

Let's talk about fishing. What is your favorite or best fishing story?

I had so many with my brother-in-law, George "Tubby" Washburn. He loved to play—he never grew old. He was the main guide; he was always busy, in great demand. He was an excellent fisherman. He had a tremendous amount of stories; he could entertain them even if they didn't catch fish. But they always caught fish. Anybody could catch fish back then—they didn't need a guide, unless they wanted walleye or smallmouth bass.

All through the '30s and '40s, the people who came up here fishing were wealthy. The president of Wolverine Shoe Company, fella named Grossjean. Wonderful person. After he'd been here a few summers, he gave my brother-in-law a beautiful Clinker boat and the nicest outboard motor. He drove a Cord; he wasn't exactly poor. There was the president of Marion Light and Power of Ohio—named Roberts; he was regular. He came every year; money was not an object.

Charles Huntly, Mike's dad, shows off a thirty-pound Muskie, late 1930s.

We always controlled the anchor. Ya know, people set there and they catch fish until they run over the sides of the boat. You can't allow that—you give 'em a nice mess of fish, but when you figure they have enough, you ease up the anchor and you drift out of the hole. They didn't even know you drifted out of the hole. There were pretty definite holes, there weren't just fish everywhere. You had to know the lake.

We fished the island out from Fisk Lodge [Intermediate Lake] for walleyes a lot right at daylight. This was the best time, we'd just drift around. Used chub minnows. There might be other fishermen now and then, but they didn't have good bait. They were using miserable dead shiners that wouldn't live long enough to catch anything. We always had good bait because we got the bait, sold the bait.

About day light, in July and August, the fog was pretty apt to roll in, you could see it coming, it'd get just thicker than thick. We shut the motor off and rowed the last hundred yards so they, the fishermen, wouldn't know where we were. We could hear 'em talking around there—they couldn't find us. That was the fun of it. [Chuckles] We knew all of 'em, they were from town.

The other fishermen weren't aware of good bait as opposed to bad bait?

No, they weren't. No, no. They never found out either. If they got too close we eased 'em out of there. Always had an extra rod or two—we'd put a couple of plugs on them and cast over that way. We weren't fishin' there, but it kept them away. We'd cast right at 'em. That's the way it was done.

Excellent walleye fishing then. Good size—two and a half pounds to seven pounds. Great eating fish.

LOOKIN SOUTH FROM MILE POINT

Mile Point on Intermediate Lake, c. 1900

A logging drive is slowed by the Devil's Elbow, a 90-degree turn on the Green River (Intermediate River) between Hanley and Ben-Way Lakes, c. 1900.

If anyone wanted to fish crappies, he could almost let them run over the side of the boat 'cause there were so many; a prolific fish. It's a member of the sunfish family. They were good eating, but there's nothing better than walleye. Smallmouth bass were good, the largemouth weren't so hot. They could catch pike, too, if they wanted pike. There was nothing to it. Pike is an underrated fish, he's really a pretty good fish—the knock on 'em is the bones 'cause they got a bunch of Y bones. But they're flaky meat; it's a good eating fish.

What's the most difficult fish to catch?

Probably as good a fighter is the smallmouth. He isn't the most difficult, but he's one of the best fighters. Of course, the muskie is—you can't just go out and catch a muskellunge. Per number of days, you might get a hit, but ninety-nine out of one hundred people have never caught a muskie and never will. Excellent eating.

If you took somebody out there today to these favorite fishing holes, what might we run into?

We'd run into a lot of bad fishermen and a lot of people without any manners on the lake. To start with, the motors are too big—we never used anything, or saw anything, over five or ten horse; now they're two-hundred twenty-five horse—pulling water skiers and they don't care how close they come. You sit there and rock for five minutes.

These ski-doos—I think they're terrible. There are a lot of accidents and they're gonna have more trouble with ski-doos.

Let's talk about good manners in your childhood days. Was there an unwritten code of behavior?

You might fish all day on Ben-Way or Wilson, never see another boat. If you did, it'd maybe be one or two. There's probably fifty people fish now to one then. But they didn't crowd you. If you're both going along the shoreline, one would go out around, give you room.

They didn't keep every little thing they caught. They wanted a decent size fish—legal fish. Walleyes had to be thirteen inches. Perch, bluegill, crappies, rock bass had to be at least six inches. Twenty-five a day total, but not more than fifteen blue-gills—they had to be six inches. Trout, seven inches, fifteen in one day and not more than ten pounds in one fish. Large and smallmouth bass, the limit was five in a day and they had to be ten inches long. This was back in the '30s and '40s. Pike were fourteen inches long and you were allowed five in one day. You didn't have any trouble getting five or any of those other limits.

Aside from bad manners today, how has the quality and quantity of the fish changed today?

Both are way down. The quantity doesn't even come close to what it was in the '30s and '40s—and '50s too.

Do you recall the Helin flatfish lure? Charlie Helin made that. He was working in Ford's paint department, so he knew his finishes. This was in the middle '30s—he came up and he stayed down at the park. He didn't have two nickels to rub together, same as everyone else. He perfected the artificial flatfish lure and became a millionaire. Built a plant in Detroit and another in Finland. They were a big seller, excellent finish on 'em, excellent action. It was a curved bait—like a crescent—it caught the water at the front of it and gave it fast action. He whittled the first one out of white pine down in the park. We would go through eight or ten gross a summer just in this one store. Almost every fisherman who walked in bought one.

As a fishing guide, what was your preference, artificial or live bait?

Live bait–you're pretty sure of getting fish for one thing. Back then we used both. Depended on what we were fishing for and what time of day. If it was bass and pike, you used mostly artificial. For the walleyes, definitely live bait. Although we did troll some; if it was a good choppy day, you got a lot of action out of your artificial. Early morning when it was just as flat as it could be, real quiet, use live bait and you controlled your speed with the oars—very, very slow down around the sunken island out from Fisk Lodge.

Could you tell me how the water of the Chain of Lakes has affected your life?

I did a lot of hunting and fishing up here. There were a couple of small liveries. One of 'em, Charlie Briggs, then there was Cluett, 'nother one was a fella named John Barry. A couple of teachers, Paul Shattuck and Harry Smith, came up and bought the properties there—it became S & S Harbor. They eventually retired up here.

Having the drug store, as a young kid I was downtown a lot. I swept out, helped out here and there. I knew all those people sixty, seventy years old.

I hunted over east of Mancelona with my dad. There were no deer on this side of the county; they just hadn't got here. It wasn't even open for hunting. The explosion of deer was in the middle '30s—just exploded because of the lumbering, then they burned everything. There was a lot of open country. Pretty barren compared to today. A few years later everything just boomed and they had food and cover. They had the habitat.

Fishing has been described as a very private experience. Is there a value to that?

Sure, it's relaxing. That's why I said the quality is deteriorating because people don't act right on the lakes anymore. It takes away that relaxing; you can't relax if someone comes zooming by you.

Intermediate Lake is different from the lakes further on up. They're weedier, shallower, some sand, but mostly mud bottom. Intermediate is deeper; it gets pretty deep around Snowflake and Deep Water Point—eighty, ninety feet. On the upper lakes, I don't think you'd find anything more than thirty feet.

The lakes have deteriorated—the reason is the water quality. The turtles, the water snakes, crayfish and clams, there were lots of 'em. There isn't ten per cent of what there was. The Ogletree Creek at the south end of Ben-Way used to have a big sucker run. You don't get that anymore.

It may be obvious, but tell me about water quality changing.

People, it's that simple. There were so few—there were some awful long stretches, no cottages on 'em—maybe find one or two. Not any more, that's prime property. If you could start all over again, no one on the lakes—if I were emperor, no one would build on the lakes. They wouldn't like that idea. Today, they run stuff in the lakes; there're too many boats and motors. You've never seen a motorboat—outboard or inboard—at the dock that there wasn't an oil slick on the water. When you don't have the turtles and water snakes and clams, that water is not the same as it was.

Is there anything unique about the lakes of the Chain?

I think they're terrific. Without the Chain of Lakes, Antrim County would not have two nickels to rub together. That's where the taxes come from.

Do you think the lake property owner—the riparian—is treated fairly?

They may not be; I hear them complaining. However, the natives here had a place on the lake. They wanted to live there the rest of their lives. They got forced out because people came in and paid more and taxes boomed until the natives couldn't afford to be there anymore. It was desirable and they bought the land. Now it's doctors, attorneys, and industrialists, or those with large pensions.

You know what's happened to the property on Torch, on any of 'em? When we came here, it might have been twenty-five dollars a foot. That'd be top price. Now you can't buy any for two thousand, twenty-five hundred a foot. When they pay a quarter million, they're not gonna put a shack on it. Those are beautiful places.

How has the resort business changed from the time you were a boy?

They're individually owned places now. Back then, person might have owned three, four cottages. Take Recreation Point or Gorham's Beach—they had half a dozen cottages. Fisk Lodge, across the lake, had a lodge and cottages—beautiful land and beach. They're all singles now.

Thinking of the Chain of Lakes, can you describe your favorite view?

The south end of Ben-Way. That had sandy beach too. You can see the whole length of Ben-Way Lake. I spent a lot of time there with boats.

Torch Lake—there's a place on Meggison Road looking across there, nothing's as pretty as that. You can see the Bay, too. It's quite a high piece out there. Torch catches the colors of the water, sunrise and sunset. It's a terrific view.

Boating on the Green River north of Central Lake, c. 1900.

A quiet day on Central Lake (Intermediate Lake), c. 1880.

By 1900, private motor launches were becoming popular on the Chain of Lakes. This scene is taken at the village of Central Lake looking south on Intermediate Lake.

Roger Marker

Roger was born in Elk Rapids. He was a 1946 graduate of Elk Rapids High School and served his country during the Korean War. He lived most of his life down on the west end of River Street where he and his wife, Maxine, raised six children. Roger was a friendly and lovable fisherman and hunter. He enjoyed the simple life offered by the woods and water on the Chain and Grand Traverse Bay. This interview was made on December 30, 1988, six months before Roger died of cancer.

Roger, tell me—where are the great fishing spots? What's your favorite?

[Loud laughter] They keep changing. Depends on what species you're after and what body of water you're on. It's hard to have a favorite. This last year hasn't been the best on record. I did very little fishing this last year. Couple years before— our perch have been excellent in the Bay out here, what you call the yellow-bellied jumbo perch—and we did real good. And this past fall, they ran much smaller; you just couldn't find the big ones. Every now and then you'd get a big one and do a lot of fishin' and sortin' to come in with a few.

What are your feelings about the water quality issue?

Take Elk River—coming out of our Chain of Lakes and draining into the Bay, the water quality is definitely different than it was twenty years ago 'cause when I'd haul fish parties there, I just kept a glass there. If I was thirsty out on Elk Lake, I'd reach over the side and scoop up a glass of good, pure water and drink it. Today, you scoop 'er up and you can't see through it as good as you used to, which tells you there's gotta be something in it.

116

It's simply an influx of people that live on the lakes and all the way through the whole Chain as far as I'm concerned—when you get a lotta people, you're gonna get pollution. It does change the quality of it somewhat.

What's the biggest change that has occurred?

Not too many years ago, you could jump in your boat and go out on Elk Lake and fish. If you wanted to pull in to shore and build a little fire and cook a hot dog, you could do it. Today, you better stay out on the lake because you are not gonna get on shore except on the south end where the swamp is and nobody can build. Or pull into Whitewater Park or unless you know somebody, you're not gonna get ashore anymore. You used to come in, swim, build a fire, have a lot of fun. To me, there's not enough public land left for the local people that don't own property right on the lake. That's the main thing that bothers me the most.

Where was the favorite spot when you took people out?

Elk Lake. Of course, it was handy and we didn't have lake trout in the Great Lakes at that time; they had been depleted by over-netting and the lamprey eel. The only place you could catch lake trout was in Elk or Torch.

Everybody has their pet spots, but there were a few that always produced better than others—and there were herring in the lake at that time and, of course, the fish go where the herring are. So you might have a spot that was doing good for three, four days and all of a sudden you couldn't hardly catch a fish there. But the herring'd move somewhere else. You simply kept right on fishing until you had another strike or caught another fish.

Off the mouth of the narrows in deep water, it was one of my favorites. Off Rex Terrace, from Rex Terrace a little bit north where Paint's Point comes out was always a productive spot—-and, for awhile, off the mouth of our river, only, of course, out in deep water. Of course, for lake trout, you're fishing down 100-120 feet. But when you weren't catching fish, you simply drag your baits along, changed a few baits, changed your speed till you caught one.

Have you always been a fisherman?

My dad, 'course, fished a lot, but he wasn't here much, so you learned by yourself. First fish I ever caught was a great big ol' rock bass right through the middle of the spillway. Got if off the hook . . . had my mother run down, put it in a bucket of water so it wouldn't die. Then we took it back and threw it back in the river later.

You watched what the old Indians did, and if they were fishing for bass, you scrounged around and came up with something that looked like what they were using and you went and did the same thing.

To me, I would say minnows are one of the most effective live baits. I use a lot of artificials now—it's kind of a game. If you can fool a fish on artificial, I think—if I was really hungry for fish, want to be assured of a fish dinner, I go right back to my natural baits; minnows are the number one choice. 'Course, certain times of the year, wigglers, crawlers—but a natural food for fish in this area are minnows. That would be my number one choice.

What caused the loss or decline of the commercial fisherman.

Bert Bratschi—I used to row out in my little dinghy and watch him raise his spawn net. He was a good ol' boy. He'd tell you himself, which he has to me, he said if I coulda had nets like they got today and you give me enough of 'em and enough time, he says, I could've cleaned that Bay completely out where there wouldn't have been a fish left. That shows you what nets can do.

This 40 1/2-pound muskie gets some attention on Elk Rapids' main street, February 19, 1925.

They [commercial fishermen] actually depleted the big lakes down to the point where the lamprey could move in, then take control and virtually wiped lake trout right out. A truthful one'll tell you that, as Bert did because he was a truthful man. So that was back in the late '30s and '40s when the big lakes just lost their fish supply. It had nothing to do with the Indians—we did that ourselves.

Let's discuss myths and tall fish tales.

'Course I always figured anything I heard was true, maybe that's why they're not myths. My dad measured the one hole in the Bay at one time with a cable—uh— big hole where the whiskey boat is out here. He got roughly 620 feet which is what the Coast Guard has come up with.

Take a look at growth and development. Is there too much?

There isn't any way to stop it as long as people got money. No matter what you charge for a piece of property on Elk or Torch or the Bay, there's somebody that's gonna pay for it because they make that kinda money today and they want to get out of the damn city. So, I can't blame

118

Carl Merillat poses with his twelve pound lake trout caught in Elk Lake, February, 1960.

Charles Butler and a string of large-mouth bass, 1920.

BEFORE . . . . *AFTER*
Fishing for rainbow trout in Elk River, c. 1910

Two of Elk Rapids' merchants get a fine catch of small-mouth bass, c.1910.

'em for it. I don't like to see 'em move up and build their places, but I certainly don't blame 'em at all. If I had the same choice and I lived down there, I would too.

But, I don't think I'd preach, really they're pretty much gonna do what they want. There definitely is a difference in the area somewhat and plus water quality. Far as tryin' to tell someone to do it different, they're not gonna. I'd just stick with how it was, how it is—there's a lotta beauty left out in those lakes. Who said the river's the same? Huh?

Roger, can you describe your favorite view?

[Chuckle] Well, I suppose because of where we live, I guess it's watchin' the sun go down over Old Mission—I'd have to have that as number one. Wake up in the morning, she's there. In the evening, you watch the sun go down. When my wife looks up and says "They stole the peninsula again," that means there's either a rain squall or a snow storm comin' across the Bay 'cause it just disappears. That's her favorite: "Damn it, they stole the peninsula again." I say "Oh, oh, here comes more snow, Ma—hold on."

Thale Yettaw

Thale Yettaw was born in 1908 to Lena and Henry Yettaw. One of seven children and grow-ing up in Ellsworth, Thale worked in his father's blacksmith shop and spent most of his life on the small lakes of the upper Chain. He grew up as the lumber era was coming to a close, the railroads were in their prime, and resort hotels were attracting large numbers of fisher-men. Beginning in the eighth grade, Thale spent a large portion of his life as a fishing guide. This interview was first made in 1986 and updated in 1997. Today, with his wife, Wilma, he resides on the shore of St. Clair Lake near his birthplace. This is his story:

I remember the mill at the north end of Ellsworth Lake. They used to have a tug; they'd pull the logs from upper Six Mile Lake through the rivers and get 'em to Ellsworth. There would be—floating way out in the lakes, we used to run those logs barefooted as a kid—have fun and like a that—on top of 'em, spin 'em, keep 'em afloat and jump from one to the other.

Wasn't that dangerous?

Oh, no. Not when you swim like a fish like we could. We didn't live on shore; we lived out in the middle most of the time [Laughs]. That was our sport, get out away from the shore, get out into the middle of the lake and swim all the time. There's Maynard Alward, there was Ed Kinner and there was George Klooster—but most of them are gone now.

You've spent most of ninety years on the water. Let's go back to the age of nine or ten and take a look at summer time for a young boy growing up in Ellsworth.

I can go back to the age of six. The railroad was working at that time. 'Course it was quite a treat to watch all the trains come in—see the mail come up. There was the Pere Marquette—they had a freight train, a passenger train and they also had a Flyer. It got people from Detroit and Chicago to the hotels in this northern area.

Thale becomes a fishing guide at age 15, 1923.

I used to go down to the hotel and sit around and talk to the fishermen. God, I met a lot of good people. There the fishermen came from all over and fished these lakes. It was very good fishing at that time.

How good?

[Laughs] Compared to now, it was much better. The fish were a lot bigger. I imagine you could go out most any day and get ten, fifteen bass per person. I remember back when they had ten the limit. Then, of course, it was five. They used to catch big muskies and pike. Those are shallow waterfish.

In Ellsworth Lake there's probably fifty foot a water in some places. The lakes aren't that shallow. St. Clair that we're on, there's about thirty to thirty-five feet in some places, but most of it's twelve to ten feet. Of course, it's silted up.

Did you have chores around the house or in the blacksmith shop?

Well, after I got older, I helped Dad in the blacksmith shop. I shod horses when I was about fourteen or fifteen and helped him put spokes in wheels and set tires and put things together. He used to make some sleighs for the farmers and the lumber mill and whittle 'em out.

This was about the time the horse and buggy was being replaced by the automobile.

Oh, yes—I can remember the first car. It was an old Brush. Dad used to weld some of the chains together. Those were the days of the nickel beer—you take a pail—I can remember many times when I was a small child—a tin pail with a cover on it. Take it down to the beer garden with ten cents and a penny. The ten cents bought two quarts of beer and I'd take it back to the blacksmith shop for the men [Laughs] and the penny was mine. I usually bought a bunch of candy.

You eventually went to work as a fishing guide at the Big Fish Inn.

There was Rock Miller and Albert Parsons, two of the main fishing guides. My older brother, Dales, was guidin', that's how I happened to get my first job—they needed an extra guide. I was in the eighth grade

122

I came down to the hotel [Big Fish Inn] and I can remember Rock sayin',
"I don't know if this kid'll be much of a guide, but he's on the lake fishin' all the
time so he certainly oughta be worth somethin'.

Man's name was Harmon, a wealthy lumberman. Harmon says,
"That's all right. I'll take him for my guide."

So we started out that evening. We were going to Six Mile Lake at Gonyea's Landing for a shore dinner. At that time, they used to take the dinner up by car and
they'd meet us at the landing at the head of Six Mile Lake. We started out; Harmon
asked me "Where we gonna fish?" "Gosh," I says, "everybody else is going to Six

Thale shows off a good string of pike and large-mouth bass, c. 1940.

123

Mile Lake, we gotta go there." He says, "No, not necessarily. We're just gonna catch fish until we get there—now, where'll we start?" I says, "If we wanta catch fish, this lake right here. I know where to catch 'em here, but I don't know too much about Six Mile Lake 'cause that's an awful long row up there." Harmon had a Kalie outboard motor—two cycle—and we decided to start out here.

He said, "We'll see just exactly what we can do." I went to the head of St. Clair Lake, I knew exactly where I could catch bass one right after another. Well, we caught five bass, then I said "We better get up there, won't be long before dinner." I knew Rock'd be madder 'n a wet hen; he'd be just stormin' if I didn't get up there on time.

We went through the river and got on the other side—I knew that purty well. We caught about a six pound pike there, another bass and we went down to where we were gonna have dinner. Looked like a pretty good catch to me and Harmon was well pleased. We started the motor, and he did all the drivin'. When we got up there, we had dinner. There was four different guides, only two of 'em had fish— they only had two or three fish a piece. I was a big shot. [Laughs] I had the fish and, boy, that didn't do me no harm with Harmon, I'll tell ya.

After dinner, they had their drinks—'course I had to join in. I didn't really want it, had a little sip of this and a little sip of that—you know, good fellowship. I was 'bout ten foot tall—I caught all those fish and you know how a kid'd be.

That was quite an eventful day for me. Ol' Rock, he was tickled when he got in. He says, "Come on, Thale, come up to the room."—Al Hicks' room—he took a big shot of liquor and he poured me one. I says, "I hadn't better take it." You don't say no to Rock. "You gonna fish like a man, you gotta drink like a man." Half-scared, I downed it. I tell you that was the powerfullest drink I ever had.

Harmon was there for 'bout a week 'n I fished with him all week. I settled down a bit, I wasn't so tall [Laughs].

It they asked you for the good fishing spots in those days, what would you have told people?

Those days—just along the shoreline, that's all. There's no difference in these lakes– –never has been—just a matter of knowin' where the fish are and have patience. 'Course we used to—day after day, you get so you know where they are—and they're there because there's feed there. We always fished with live bait then—it was chub minnows or leopard frogs. Very few worms at that time. They had the big ol' Bass-a-reno—that's the first lure I had. That was a good one and still is today.

Tell me about Rock Miller. What kind of a guide was he?

He was a very good guide. He was very knowledgeable. He could talk about any subject. He was quite politically-minded. He fished with Senators and congress-men—they're people that are somebody or they can't pay the fee. He was hard as a rock; he was tough. But he could talk so nice to judges and factory owners. He read the Grand Rapids Press about every day. One look at 'im, and he's a character—you don't find people like that—they stand out—very gruff.

What makes a guide a good guide?

Ah-h-h, [Thoughtfully] it isn't all catchin' fish. It's holdin' people's attention and when the fishin' gets tough, bein' able to tell a story or gettin' people back on the track of fishin'. I think you have to catch fish, of course. If you don't catch fish, you ain't gonna be guidin' long. You won't get no customers. You gotta come in with a certain amount of fish.

There's the old companionship in the boat because you fish too, ya see. You row the boat 'n fish and keep the boat parallel with the shore as much as you can 'n go slow where the fish are. Keep your eyes open and look for new spots.

When you're drawin' the bait across the bottom, notice what kinda vegetation you pick up because there's a certain kinda vegetation attracts those crawfish and they naturally attract bass. Bass fishin' is what people come up for.

I guided two men from New York—they came here to fish bass. They owned hotels in New York. They were happy. I guided for the Purple Gang and didn't even know it—Bernstein and the others.

I think I was a good guide because a doctor in Chicago used to send his people who were havin' nervous break-downs up to me and I would guide for 'em. I was able to hold 'em.

There was a guy—he'd lost a lot of money in the stock market and he also had a grainery—very wealthy man. You can imagine me. He said, "I've got three days—where we goin'?—when do the fish bite?" I says, "I don't know when the fish bite. I don't think they give a damn whether you're here and they'd prefer that they didn't get caught." Boy, was he rough.

Why would you keep the boat parallel to shore?

So people could cast the shoreline. You're workin' the shoreline, you work the lily pads along. Well, if you got [the

Fred and Anne Vermeersch honeymooning at Big Fish Inn, 1928.

125

boat] out there the right distance, so you don't disturb the fish, so they're able to throw their bait right out and let it sink down. Keep it workin' along so that you can work the shoreline real well. Casting towards the shore.

Did you ever have the occasion where the fishing wasn't so good and you did have to tell some good stories to hold their interest?

Oh, yeah. [Chuckles] Lots of times. I'll tell you a story. I was fishin' with a lady from Chicago. At that time, the one that got the least fish had to buy the beer when they come in. So I'd been out two days with her and, of course, I wasn't gettin' no fish because she wouldn't fish. She'd sit there 'n talk 'n talk 'n talk. I'd make her put the bait over the back of the boat and I'd keep jerking the boat a little bit to give it a little action. But the only fish that was being caught is what I's catchin'.

Thale in 1997

So finally I said to her, "God, you're payin me good money for this guide and you've been here two days. Now, you haven't caught any fish and all you seem to wanta do is just sit here and talk." I says, "This is gettin' serious. I've had to buy the beer in town every day for two days. You gotta help me out on this."

She says, "Oh, is that right? I'll go down and buy the beer for 'em."

I says, "Well, what really brings you here?"

Just about that time, the train was comin' along the shore of the lake and she was lookin' up there and she says, "Thale, bein' with you is a pleasure and everytime I blink my eyes, there's a different picture. Just look at that train."

I says, "By god, I guess you were right—there is. I never thought of it that way." So that day she come to the beer garden with us and she bought the beer.

If the fish weren't bitin', you'd usually start tellin' a story or relatin' something. All at once you'd give a jerk on the pole and "Oops! God, I lost 'em." That'd kinda pick 'em up a little bit. That was a common thing to do.

Why would people living down in the lower end of the Chain—Torch, Skegemog and Elk— come all the way up here to the upper Chain to fish?

Well, different kinds of fish. You don't get the action—I think that you look for the head of a stream for real action in the lakes. They don't have the bluegills, you know, the small pan fish that we do up here. A lot of people don't want to sit 'n wait for a big fish to bite. Patience is what you have to have. Different type of fishin' here.

Eighty-five feet is the ideal depth for lake trout. The ideal depth for bass fishin' is in the weeds.

What's the most satisfying fishing experience you had as a guide?

Oh, boy. I think it was fishin' with Maurice Spitalny—that's the brother of Phil Spitalny of the All-Girl Orchestra.* We fished for a week and we got about four six-pound bass—that's big bass for these lakes. I only saw one seven-pounder in my life. We got a bunch of big pike. We used to go up in Six Mile Lake in the afternoon and turn and fish for big pike.

I remember the last day, he wanted me to take a picture of him and we had a little dock out here. We got about a dozen of these big pike on the stringer. He got out to the end of the dock there and he held 'em up and said, "Now take a picture of 'em." One of 'em flopped and he fell off the dock and into the water. We never did get that string of fish. They swam out in the lake and that's all there was. Poor Maurice.

Has fishing changed any on the lakes?

Oh, I wouldn't say these are fishing lakes anymore. But it's as good as anything there is in the country. Man is his own worst enemy—greed has a lot to do with it. If the fish were bitin' out there, he'd sit right there until he caught every one and take 'em home and throw 'em away.

What did he do wrong in his greed?

I think just the last few years—we used to have the bass season come in around June twentieth. Now it comes Decoration Day. The bass don't get a chance to get up on the shores and spawn. Each year I usually get in a boat before bass season and go up along the shore—see how many I can count in a certain area. Well, this year I counted ten bass in a little section. The next morning, here was about ten people tryin' to catch those bass—it just doesn't give 'em a chance. I don't think we have the fishermen on these lakes that we used to. Some of 'em are good fishermen, but not many.

I think the DNR is wrong in their thinkin'. They seem to want to put more game wardens on, try to protect what they got. They haven't got anything they're protecting anymore. Oh, you get a certain amount—I don't think you'll ever be able to fish the lakes out. But, I'll tell you, you can fish 'em down till there's a long time between strikes.

I haven't kept a fish this year and I do notice those bass boats—the good bass fishermen—they're throwin' almost all of 'em back. Fishin' for the sport of it. But there's some of 'em that come up that first day of bass season, they're just right after 'em.

127

But I try to talk to 'em. I say, "You got eight, ten thousand dollars in that boat of yours. If you keep bringin' these bass in, what're you gonna fish with it?" I think it's catchin' on. I've seen some five pound bass thrown back this year. Normally, that same person'd be eatin' it.

What other problems exist here on the water?

They should keep these channels open for—not big boats—but cruise boats, twenty-five, thirty-five horsepower motors. Let the people through. They got these little tubes ties it up [culverts that connect several small lakes in the upper Chain]. If you're gonna keep these channels open, you've got to have a bigger boat go through there with a little larger propeller, so it digs down. It would make a better channel through here. Fish, they move between these lakes. I don't know that it would do anything for the fishin' in them, but it sure would make 'em more usable. You're not going to get back where you were years ago unless people quit catchin' and keepin' 'em.

Thale surveys his "shangri-la" in 1986.

We've covered just about everything except for taking a boat trip up the lake.

Each foot of that ground, I've walked it all. I used to run a trap line from Ellsworth to down below the clay pit and back home. The next day I would take the trip up to the head of Six Mile Lake and back to Ellsworth—in the winter, trapping.

You start up the lakes, you go slow enough and you're reminiscing. I think that's the way to do it, really.

[*Maurice Spitalny was a symphony conductor in California. Phil Spitalny and his All-Girl Orchestra played the big dance band circuit from 1934 until 1950. From 1935 to 1948 the orchestra had its own radio show, the *"Hour of Charm."*]

One of Thale's favorite fishing spots, the Sinclair River, 1997

Boating on St. Clair Lake, c. 1880.

Fish stories have always been a mainstay of the Chain of Lakes lore. "The one that got away" was a standard around the campfire. This prehistoric-looking sturgeon (below), however, was a genuine point of pride as these two fisherman pose in front of Elk River near the spillway in Elk Rapids, c. 1905.

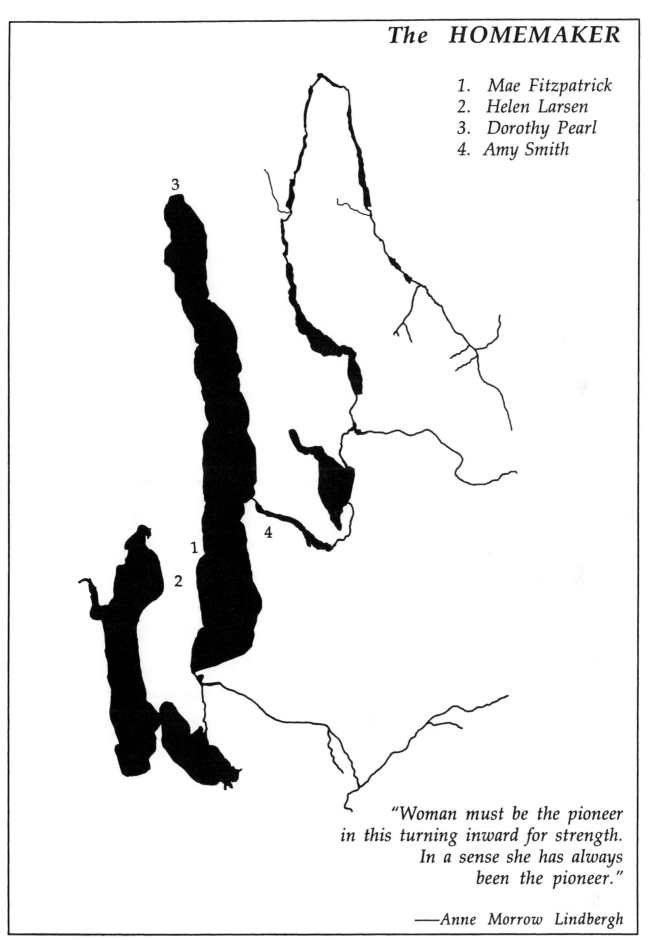

The HOMEMAKER

1. Mae Fitzpatrick
2. Helen Larsen
3. Dorothy Pearl
4. Amy Smith

*"Woman must be the pioneer
in this turning inward for strength.
In a sense she has always
been the pioneer."*

——Anne Morrow Lindbergh

The tug Torch Lake on Grass River. Fifty-seven feet long, this tug plied the Chain for the Elk Rapids Iron Company for almost forty years. "The logs would come down the Grass River...we could see those logs. They would drift 'em clear down to Torch Lake, down the lakes, clear to Elk Rapids." —Amy Smith

Frank Adams, bold Bellaire photographer, takes another risk to capture scenes of logging in Antrim County, c. 1900.

Mae Fitzpatrick

Mae Fitzpatrick left Pennsylvania as a young girl. She came to the farm on the west side of Torch Lake in 1919 to marry Leo Bussa. Widowed with six small children, she stayed and survived. In a recent letter, Mae's daughter, Marie Veliquette, tells why her mother is such an admirable person:

"In 1930, when she and my father were expecting their sixth child, my father died of pnuemonia. ...she resolved to keep and raise all of us kids. So, with the help of only a hired hand and her small children, she took over the farm. ... We felt well-cared for. We picked wild berries and had our own eggs and meat. ... She made our clothes from feed sacks and we had kerosene lamps. Although we had outdoor "facilities," we had water piped into the house from a spring on the hill. ... These were the hard lean years of the 1930s. But Mother succeeded in raising us, even making it possible for most of us to go to high school eight miles away, getting an education that she had never had. ... Her principles of family unity, value on education, self-reliance, and faith brought, not only a long healthy life for her, but stood as an example and role model for her children and all those who have known her."

Today Mae Fitzpatrick remains on the Bussa Road farm. With Torch Lake as her front yard, she reflects on the past ninety years in this 1995 interview:

They worked the farm with oxen and cleared it. When I came here, they had horses to work the land. We would get up at five in the morning. My husband done the work in the fields. He'd go to the barn and feed the horses. After breakfast, he'd go back and harness the horses and go to the fields by seven o'clock. He was always out in the fields by seven. At noon, he came in for dinner—that was our big meal of the day was dinner. Probably had potatoes and meat, carrots—things that were grown on the farm. We raised our own chickens.

What kind of a farm was this? What was the main crop?

They raised potatoes to sell and they had cattle. Just general farming. The only cash crop we had was what cream we sold. We had seven or eight cows at that time. We milked the cows and then ran the milk through the separator and fed the milk back to the calves. The cream was sold. There was a truck from Traverse City came along every week and picked it up. Years ago, you could make a living, but not now. Can't raise enough—they don't get enough out of it.

You were quite a young girl when you came here in 1919. How did you meet Leo and come to the farm?

My brother worked for a man that lived next door. He was a lawyer and he owned that eighty. My brother worked that eighty for him.

Describe a day on the farm.

My part of the work was cook the meals and do the housework and bake the bread and churn the butter. Wash clothes on a washboard [Laughs]. We didn't have refrigeration. We just had the wood stove I've got now. We didn't have lights; we didn't have telephone. No television [Laughs].

You had six children here on the farm? Who decided what work was done around the farm?

Well, when the children were young, Leo and his father did the chores. The children had to go to the barn and help when they were big enough, help milk and clean the barn. That was the boys. I never asked the girls to go out in the fields—there was Marie and Evelyn.

The workday, especially in summer, must have been a rather long day.

Yeah, sometimes when they were hayin', it was pretty hot weather. At threshing time they had a threshing machine go through the country and we never knew

Haying time. Evelyn O'Dell (left), Mae Fitzpatrick with son Leo on the wagon, July 1, 1943.

134

exactly when it was gonna hit here. Sometimes they'd be at the neighbors and they'd quit at eleven o'clock and they'd come into your place expecting dinner at noon. I have cooked for about twelve men and didn't have any help.

Other times, they'd be threshing somewhere, we'd get word that they'd be at our place at a certain time. That'd give us a little time to prepare a meal. Threshing day was a big event because it was all the men in the countryside. They all came together to help each one thresh. So, there's about twelve to fifteen men. I can't remember their names—I think they're all gone. I did all the cooking. I had this table stretched out. Just an average meal, but more of it.

You were farming here in the '20s and when the Depression hit. Let's talk about hard times on the farm. Were there any hard discouraging times?

Leo had died in 1930. It was hard to make a go of it 'cause I was alone. During the Depression, I had the six children and they weren't very big. It was a hard time. We went without a lot of things they think they gotta have today. Grandpa was with me for three years after my husband died and he hired some young boy to help him.

When children got sick in those days, how did you take care of them?

Well, I was blessed. My children didn't get sick, not anything serious. Not any more than the measles or something like that. Only one time, one of 'em had underneath his jaw, swelled up. And the other one had a cut on his eye, he held up a cutter or knife and it dropped and cut him. I took him to the doctor in Rapid City—ol' Doc Miller. That's about the only time I had a doctor for them. He was a good doctor. He seemed to know what he was doing and he always came when you needed him. Lotsa people still owe 'im [Laughs].

How often did you go to town?

On Saturday night. Everyone went to town on Saturday night. You knew everybody and that's where you visited. Elk Rapids was pretty much the same as it is now. They used to have places to tie your horses up. In summer time, we went in a horse and wagon. In the wintertime, it was sleighs. No car. We got a Model T Ford in the '20s.

If we had to go to Traverse City, it was an all day trip, but not unless it was necessary. We went in horse and buggy. The roads weren't very good, they were mostly sand, the hills were quite sandy. There was no pavement. They had a livery barn in Elk Rapids where you could rent horses.

What changes do you think were the most important or significant in farming?

I think this big machinery—where horses would take a week to do, they can do the farming in one day. In a way it's a good change. In another way, people are gettin'

135

Mae Fitzpatrick making maple syrup, April, 1944.

lazy. They don't want to work any more. I think if more boys were raised on the farm, we wouldn't have so much crime.

It's been said that farmers are the last geniuses because they're so self-reliant. Is that a fairly accurate description?

I think they liked it because they were self-employed. They didn't have anyone behind them; they could do what they pleased and they knew what they were doing. They helped one another back then much more than they do nowadays.

You used to have the land cleared here and the land down to the lake was pasture land for the cows?

Yes. That's wet. That's what the DNR calls wetland. We're not gonna sell it anyway. That's part of the farm.

How do you feel about the farm being sold off piece by piece?

People have gotta do it because they're raisin' the taxes so you can't keep your places anymore. That's why the farmers are selling out. They can get more money out of the property than they can raising crops.

You've lived here on Torch Lake for a big portion of your life. What effect has the water had on your life?

Well, I think the water was good. I think that lake is an awful lot of company to you. To me, it's always been company. It's better than having close neighbors. You got something to look at. That I've always appreciated. The water changes and when the sun comes up over the water, it's just beautiful.

Helen Larsen

Helen was born Helen Bachi in 1913. Her father, Adolph Bachi, was born in 1879, the son of Swiss immigrants. Her mother, Lena, was a Bussa, a long-established and highly-respected name in Antrim County's farm community. She describes here her simple but happy childhood, the sudden death of her father, the unrelenting struggle to farm the land, the surprisingly numerous good times, and the strong sense of community exhibited by the south Milton farmers that made life more bearable. This 1993 interview is sprinkled with Helen's infectious laughter, illustrating further the enduring spirit of this pioneer family. Helen lives today with her husband, Frank, on the north end of Elk Lake in Elk Rapids Township. Her story begins:

My parents were Adolph Bachi and he married Lena Bussa. He took her to a new home that he had built for her, which is still standing and beautifully renewed. That's about a mile south of Kewadin on Cherry Avenue.

My grandparents came over from Zurich, Switzerland. They got here in April [1879]; my dad was born in June. They had gone to Kansas first. There was a dust storm out there and my grandmother said, "I won't stay here." So they came back to Elk Rapids—there were a lot of Swiss people around here. He bought the farm that my dad built the house on. He bought it from the Indians. There was a log cabin on it; they lived in it until they built a new home. The farm was fifty acres and my dad bought thirty of it and then they bought another twenty that faced on Bussa Road.

So you're from a real pioneer family?

We are, we really are. There's still a lot of pioneer families living around here.

My dad was a farmer. In the winter, they always let their teams out for logging. He had a few cherry trees on the place. They never sprayed with anything but Paris green, and only twice a season. They never had wormy cherries.

137

There was an enormous flu epidemic and he was one of the victims. He'd had the flu in the spring of 1918; he died in June of 1918. He was thirty-nine when he died. Mother was twelve years younger; she was born in 1890.

Even though your dad died when you were five years old, can you recall him for me?

I don't know if I remember so much about him as hearing people tell about him. He was a wonderful person. He smoked one cigar a day; he'd sit in a chair by the kitchen table while mother was doing dishes. He was a tall, very soft-spoken gentle person and, apparently, well-liked in the neighborhood.

He died when you were five leaving your mother with . . .

. . . she had me and my brother, Lloyd, and my sister, Josephine, was born in November after he died.

What did a young widow do with a large farm and three little babies?

My uncle, George Bussa, came to live with us and stayed with us until mother remarried three years later. He moved in the day my dad died—the cows had to be milked that night. This uncle farmed it for her and that's what we had coming in, was what we had—a few cows, a couple of cash crops, lotsa garden. He was just like a second father to me; he was awfully good to us kids.

John, Adolph (Helen's dad), and Emma Bachi on the family farm, c.1900.

138

In the winter the snow was up over the fence tops. Believe it or not, we haven't had snow like that since I was a kid. Uncle George would try to take us to school; the horse couldn't get through. He'd take us as far as he could and we'd have to walk the rest of the way. There were no plowed roads then.

I walked to [the Roberts] school—about a mile and three-quarters. I remember so well; we had art; we had music, agriculture, English, reading, spelling, penmanship––things you don't even hear of today. Eight grades in the school; one teacher taught them all. My seventh and eighth grade teacher was Raymond Sexton from Bellaire. Ellen DuFresne was a teacher; my aunt Erma Bussa taught there for awhile and Frances Drake taught there.

Frances Phillips was another teacher at the Roberts School at that time. [Laughs] She had an awful crush on my Uncle George. She thought she could get to him through me and she let me take two grades in one year and then skip the next one which was not very smart 'cause I got into high school when I was twelve years old.

You're surrounded by water, sandwiched in between two large bodies of water—Elk and Torch. Did the water have an effect on farming or the way you lived?

That's why this is such a great place for cherry growing—the effect from the lakes. The ground is very fertile in this general area. One year dad grew radishes; we grew beans; we grew potatoes, we had a fantastic garden; we raised an awful lot of stuff in it. Hay crops, corn—general farming. Radishes and beans were the only cash crops we had. We used to have a co-op in Elk Rapids and he'd take 'em there.

After my mother remarried, we had seven or eight cows. We had all the cream, all the whole milk unpasteurized [Laughs] that we wanted. Butter which we used lavishly. My step-dad would take a can of cream to the co-op in town; he'd come home, maybe they'd have $5.00 out of it. That kept us in groceries for a week.

Tell me about your mom. Here was a woman who was widowed with three little children. Describe her disposition and her personality.

She was pretty matter-of-fact. She liked to laugh; she liked to tell jokes; she liked parties. She was a good person, very talented as a seamstress and a marvelous, marvelous cook. She could just make something out of nothing. She was a good mother. One dish that I dearly love today is spatzels—it's fried bread crumbs.

Mother used to can, oh my goodness, the canned stuff she put up. We didn't have a lot of meat on the farm because you had to have every cream check to make do. But once in a while we'd have a beef or pig. They'd cut the meat in steaks and she would fry down pork and get lard out of it and store it in a big crock and brown those steaks and put those steaks in that lard—and another layer of lard and another layer of steaks. She put up pork chops like that too. They were so good. Then she'd can: we canned chicken; we canned pork; we canned beef. Dad hunted quite a bit, we had rabbits. We had a big boiler. I think she could do twelve or fourteen quarts

Helen's mother, Lena Bussa Bachi Hockridge, at age 19, 1909.

of meat. You boiled three hours. She canned suckers when they got them; it was just like salmon.

Lotsa jams, jellies, juice, lotsa fruit—what we grew on the farm or what you picked wild. She put up over five hundred jars of stuff a year. We ate good. We bought lard—cottosuet was the shortening of the day. We bought chocolate because she made an awful lot of chocolate cake, but we had our own eggs. A farmer then didn't need an awful lot of cash. When the taxes were due, I remember hearin' 'im scream how high they were, but dad would sell a cow to pay the taxes.

She baked a cake every day of the week. My dad [Glenn Hockridge] was a dessert eater, just loved dessert. I say "dad" because he came into our lives when we were still very young and he was dad to us. He loved life. He was a sailor. He had been in World War I, after the war he sailed all over the world. He came home and he dated mother. They went together three weeks and they married and he became a farmer. He was a good guy; he was really a good guy. Strict, made us kids toe the mark. He was a good father.

Being a farmer, there's a lot of work. Who made the decisions as to who did what?

We kids had to haul the water and the wood. Most times we had to feed the chickens. As Lloyd and I grew older, we learned to clean the stables, pump the water for the cattle, but dad did the milking. Once in a great while, if he couldn't be home, mother would milk. She told me one time, " Don't ever learn to milk, then you won't have to do it," [Laughs] and I never learned to milk. We put hay down for the cattle, go back in the pasture in the summertime and bring 'em in for milking—just all the things that goes with farming.

Our three barns had burned—the one on my uncle's place and Goodman's barn. The three barns went up in one afternoon—spontaneous combustion and the wind was just right and it took the other two barns. My mother had hers rebuilt. Fella from Elk Rapids came out and put up the stone basement. Then they had a barnraising. There must've been one hundred people there; the barn was up that

140

The Goodman family of south Milton, neighbors of the Bachis, enjoy a family gathering, c. 1910.

night. You just don't see that done any more—'course barns aren't being built anymore. Big dinner—the women all came and helped mother cook and brought stuff. Put up some tables outside with boards.

Why do you suppose that community spirit is gone; why has that changed?

People are selfish today, I think. I can't help but feel it's a different attitude about everything. You might pitch in and help if a neighbor needs something, but you don't go out of your way for it. We're all guilty of it.

What was a day like in the summertime, when you weren't in school?

We would be up about six o'clock. We'd have breakfast and dad would say, "You hoe the beans," or, "You hoe the radishes," or, "You hoe the corn today—and don't pull anything up that isn't a weed." We hauled wood. From the time I was eleven years old, we helped dad with haying. We put in enough hay for seven to ten cows and horses.

Dad would mow with a horse-drawn mower. Then he'd rake it and it would go in windrows and we'd put it in what we called haycocks. Then we'd bring it in. We always tried to finish haying. We had a wagon—dad would pitch it up on the wagon, and Lloyd and I would make the load. We didn't do any baling until the last few years that dad farmed before the war [World War II]. I don't remember that dad ever had a tractor, always used the team. I remember one team we had; one horse was the balkiest thing—Bob—I never saw a horse so ornery. If you wanted him to pull, he wasn't gonna pull. If you wanted him to stand, he was gonna run [Laughs].

Describe your kitchen; what conveniences did you or didn't you have?

None of 'em. We had a wood stove, big kitchen. We had to keep the kitchen range going and the one in the dining room. We washed dishes in dishpans. There was a kitchen cabinet—it had two bins, one we had flour in, and one we kept our bread in––two of 'em on top, one of 'em had sugar. Our milk was kept in the basement, but we had fresh milk twice a day, so we didn't ever have sour milk. We had a cream separator. Linoleum on the floor. We had a kitchen table; that's where we ate. There were seven of us 'cause there were five kids when we finally ended up. Mom and Glenn had two children: Beth and Richard Hockridge.

I remember Christmas. Dad would get a Christmas tree and we would decorate it, string popcorn. Mother had a few candles and holders she would fasten on the branches and, because we kids wanted those candles lit, Mother would do it. She would light them, but just for a second. We were satisfied with that. Christmases were very, very slim. I don't remember any toy but a teddy bear.

Was that typical or was your family exceptional?

No, no. Everybody was alike. When we went through the Depression of '29, it didn't mean anything to those of us that lived in rural areas because we'd never had anything anyway. I can't relate to that like so many people can.

Were there any other holidays that the family celebrated?

We celebrated the Fourth of July. We finished our haying and Lloyd and Josephine and I would go across the road over on the Hassett's place and pick wild strawber-ries—and, oh gosh, they were good. Mother would make homemade ice cream. That was our Fourth of July celebration; we did that every year. We had Thanks-giving dinner; Christmas was always a good dinner—we always managed that.

There used to be a lot of parties in the neighborhood at somebody's house—the older people. Everyone's kids went; it was a community party and you went. We had more fun; they danced; they played cards, sing. Didn't cost anybody a nickel.

Tell me about going to school in Elk Rapids.

We used to ride with different people that had cars and we paid fifty cents a week. One time my ride didn't wait for me; I said, "Well, there's a track across the lake, if I want to go to school, that's the way to go. So I'd go down to the end of Bussa Road and get on it [Elk Lake] and follow the sleigh tracks across. Everybody drove across the lake in those days with teams and sleighs. I'd come out by Dr. Ferris Smith's and walk the rest of the way to school and I was always on time. It was about four miles.

Since your childhood days, what do you think is the greatest change?

The population explosion. I don't think I like it as well. There're no neighbors anymore. You don't neighbor anymore. I haven't seen my next-door neighbor for at least three months. I'll see 'er tomorrow 'cause I'm gonna take her some Christmas cookies. You just don't do things as neighbors.

You've lived around the water of the Chain all your life; what's your favorite spot?

Elk River—with the stumps, especially when they're snow-covered. You can't beat that for beauty. I think that's my favorite spot in the area. I like to see the water and there are some gorgeous spots around here. I'm so glad they have preserved some of those spots because they're building condos and condos—it's just shutting out everybody. I realize it's money in their pockets, but you hate to see everything spoiled like that. The views—because when you can't see the water, you can't see it. You don't appreciate it, but there are some gorgeous spots here.

So the water has affected your life?

Oh, yes. I love it here. I think it's beautiful and I'm proud of living in a place like this. It doesn't mean I have to agree with everything [Laughs].

Helen ends our interview with laughter.

Dorothy Pearl

Dorothy Pearl was born Dorothy Waite in Kalamazoo in 1896. While a Detroit school teacher, she met Norton Pearl and they married in 1919. They honeymooned that year at Eastport on Torch Lake. During the ensuing years, she led a remarkable life, raising babies and leading women's organizations at a national and international level. She had been National Director of the Womens' Civilian Defense Program and, in 1946-47, President of the American Legion Auxiliary. In 1946 she founded Girls' Nation and Girls' State, to help high school girls throughout the country learn how their state and federal governments work. Dorothy was National Parliamentarian to the American Legion, and authored a book on parliamentary procedure.

She was active in the Republican Party all her life and into her 90s she served as a delegate to the Republican Party. She worked in the administrations of Presidents Truman, Eisenhower, Kennedy, and Johnson. Most surprisingly, this dedicated, frail ninety year old lady was the recipient of the French Legion of Honor in 1947 for her efforts in aiding French war orphans after World War II. The focus of this 1986 interview, however, is on Dorothy's life in northern Michigan.

Summer meant Torch Lake and Eastport. Six generations of Pearls have resided there. In 1949 she and Norton made major changes on the Eastport home preparing it for year round use. This interview was made in that same house on M-88 where she had honeymooned nearly seventy years earlier. It was five years before her death in 1991.

Describe your husband Norton and how you met him.

This was his birthplace. He was born on this site. There was a two-story building there; Norton was born upstairs in that house. His father, John Wesley Pearl, was the grocery man, the supervisor, the postmaster—they moved from Norwood down here. My husband's father, John Wesley Pearl, owned the whole end of Torch Lake at one time. He had a grist mill and a sawmill right on the beach.

Norton's father, his second wife, and his sister, and the daughter of the second wife were here living. He actually took care of that family. He hadn't gone to college until he was twenty-one. He had come to Detroit from Butte, Montana where he went as a teacher and then he became a ranger in Glacier National Park—he travelled the length of the Rockies as a ranger.

I was teaching at Northwestern High School and he was supervising the program then because there were fifty physical education teachers. He supervised all the activities. I got to know him pretty well. Norton was quite prominent in the field of education.

More interestingly to me was the fact that the Ford Motor Company had built the Ford Hospital—it was in the process of being built [during the war]. They took in the wounded—the Michigan and Wisconsin wounded [of World War I]. He served with the Red Arrow Division, went overseas as a unit [in 1917]. As an extra-curricular activity my husband was to see that those men got comfort from organized groups and entertainment. So I used to go to Ford Hospital and sing for 'em, and dance for 'em, and dance with 'em. That's how I got to know him pretty well. We were married the Fall of 1919—the eighteenth of December—and I came up here with him on my honeymoon.

When we came here for the honeymoon, we had to hire a team and sleigh to get from Central Lake over here through the snow. We took the train to Central Lake—it went from Detroit to Petoskey.

This house had a wood stove in the kitchen. This is where we spent ten days on our honeymoon. I went hunting rabbits with the fellas everyday and I think I saw more game than they did. I walked on snowshoes which I had never done. It was quite an experience for a city-bred girl.

That next summer he was hired by a man who owned a very famous boys' camp in Maine—Kinnewatha was the name. We bought a new Ford—$500 worth of car— that was something else. We drove to Maine. We must have had one hundred and fifty boys there—all from well-to-do families from "Down East" who used to, I can only say, dump their kids there for the summer. But the man who owned the camp,

Dorothy in her high school graduation dress, c. 1914.

he didn't like women much and he wasn't very happy on Norton insisting on me coming down there. But I went anyway. As it turned out, he got hard-up for a swimming teacher, so I began teaching swimming to the boys.

Anne was born in April of the next year. We came up that summer. There was a little boat house down on the lake. There was a tent down there—the kids and everybody used to be down there; I was up here cooking for 'em. So I put my foot down, I said, "I'm never going to Eastport again till you get me something to live in right on the beach." So the next spring, father and Norton pulled a boathouse out of the lake, turned it around, put a porch on it and a lean-to on it and I lived there all the years those kids were growing up.

I was down there on the beach, no electricity, no running water, wash for four little kids. Took the water outta' the lake and you put it on the old wood stove we had outdoors to heat it.

We finally built some log cabins down there; we built extra rooms. We lived on the beach, I'll tell ya, right close.

After Norton retired in 1949, we sold our house in Detroit and we remodeled this place. The winter I came up here as a bride, there was no electricity—the only heat was the wood stove—kerosene lamps. Had to wash and clean the chimneys. I'd never done that before. The "john" was down in that barn there where you had to go.

There wasn't an inch of paint on the inside of this house. Sand plaster—if you touch it, it falls off. It hadn't been painted, the woodwork hadn't been painted. I came into this situation.

Out in the woodshed was the pump. Downstairs you got your wood to the fire going in the kitchen. I really didn't know for a couple of years about cooking on a wood stove. I thought you put the wood in and let the stuff cook. Instead you had to keep wood in. I had things that I thought should be done that weren't done at all 'cause I didn't know how to tend fire. It was an experience; it was hard work for me, it really was. That summer almost finished me.

So you spent thirty years as a summer resident before you retired up here?

I spent a lot of years here with the kids, but, I'll tell you, they grew to love this place, so that they stayed here. I had four under four. Ann was two when the twins were born. They were fourteen months when Dorothy, the youngest, was born.

When you first came up, was tourism a lot different?

Oh, there was no tourism. I don't know what I'd call tourism until we'd been here quite awhile. There was the Park Place Hotel in Traverse City. Norton's father used to drive a team down to Traverse City every weekend to buy groceries. Fifty cents for a dinner at the Park Place Hotel.

In the days when his father had the sawmill, there was some boating on Torch, there was a steamer—but that was before my time.

Do you recall those days kindly or are they rough memories?

They weren't easy. They were pretty hard on me. Frankly, it was kind of hand-to-mouth. As I told you, I wasn't used to livin' this way. In Kalamazoo, we had a very nice home. We had chandeliers with gas lights, very nicely furnished. Norton—he was here and away. First summer he brought me up here, he wanted me to see where he lived on Torch Lake—the most beautiful spot in the world.

Tell us about the first electricity and how you got that?

That's quite a story. My husband was teaching summer school, so he was not here. He used to drive up weekends in the old Ford.

I was down there alone, no lights. I got wind that the electrical company was gonna run lines through Eastport and I got to thinking, I'm gonna see if they're gonna stop. There was a very nice crew of young men working, setting poles and running lines. Every Saturday night we had a square dance down here in the Grange hall. So I got these young men interested in the recreation on Saturday night to come up here and square dance. They didn't know how to square dance, so I taught 'em. They got to be real good friends.

I kept sayin' to them, "Look at me. Here I am without a light of any kind except an old kerosene lamp. Why can't you guys put some poles down to my cabin—just run two or three poles and give me a couple of lights?"

Well, they'd think about it. So, as it turned out, they did put poles down, just right down this little lane. They promised they'd put the line in so I could have some light. Well, one weekend, later in the summer, they came along and said, "We're gonna have to leave." "You haven't hooked me up with any electricity yet." "Well, we got orders, we gotta go." I said, "Look you guys told me you'd run me a line down here." On Sunday afternoon they came in their Sunday clothes and climbed those poles and ran a line down to my cottage. I was the only one in this community that had electric lights. (Laughs)

Where was your main shopping center?

Central Lake. Charlevoix was nothing but a resort town. I remember the big boat came in from Chicago to Charlevoix—people came just for the summer.

Aside from shopping, what were your sources of food?

I canned tomatoes till they came out of my ears. We had a great big garden all across the back here. This property runs behind the postoffice and down to the lake. We grew vegetables enough to feed anybody in Eastport that needed them. We tried everything—peas, corn, and potatoes. I even tried to grow broccoli.

Aside from dances, what other forms of entertainment were there?

Norton and others used to go to the Bay several nights a week and camp out. The kids sang songs, they had a bonfire. They ate their meals and stayed all night. Almost every night we had a fire down on the beach. We still do.

I liked the theater. When I was a girl in high school, I used to do lots of plays. My mother told me if I was in another show she'd disown me. But I liked it and, of course, that's carrying over right now. If I were younger I'd be in one of these plays they're gonna have up at the corner. I'm not about to learn a part anymore.

When did Eastport start to seem like home?

Not till I retired. You see, when Norton retired the pension was very meager. They had never been under Social Security in Detroit. He'd worked there over forty years. Actually I didn't feel at home until the Fall of 1964 when I moved and settled this house the way I wanted it. My husband died in 1960. I don't know, I guess it is home. This is the house where we had lived. But my kids were all grown when we came here to live. But I didn't raise the kids here—we lived in that old cabin on the beach.

I recall coming here in the summertime. I took myself down to the beach and I stayed there. I didn't get out and get to know too many people.

Torch is very deep. The first cabin we built on the beach—I talk about the beach. Norton's father owned the whole north end, he let it go—cut the lumber off—except for seven and a half acres right here.

There was seven hundred and forty feet of Torch Lake frontage. One of Norton's big things was that the families stay together and come to Eastport. When he died, I gave each one one hundred and three feet of frontage—four of 'em—on Torch Lake. So that everybody on the beach is a Pearl.

Who was the most memorable character you ever met?

My husband, Norton Pearl. He's a man that has a great story behind him. He was working in the sawmill at fourteen, taking care of his family here. His step-mother was quite ill with cancer. At twenty-one, he went to college. I would call him a pioneer.

If you could go back to those early days, would you?

Probably not. I like the experience of doing new things. But they're not so new to me anymore, but I'm not letting go of some of the things I think are important.

The Pearl "sumer cottage" at Eastport, 1920-21.

On the Pearl dock on Torch Lake (l to r) Dorothy Pearl Malasky, Jane Pearl Martin, Bill French, Joe Diamond, Otto Ohland, Adrienne Wright, Ann Pearl Bretz, Fran Bingham Foy, Betty Pearl Beeby, c. 1933.

Four Pearls: Dorothy, Betty, Jane, and Ann Pearl on the beach, c. 1925.

As President of the American Legion Auxiliary, Dorothy Pearl greets future President Dwight Eisenhower, 1947.

150

Amy Smith

Amy Smith was born on December 23, 1893 on a small farm near Clam Lake. Her mother, Marie Wildasen, had emigrated from Switzerland and married Abraham Steiner. Amy was the second oldest of eleven children. At sixteen, she married George Smith and raised three children: Gladys, Doris, and Kenny. Amy lived to be almost 102, passing away on December 4, 1995. In this 1987 interview, at the age of ninety-three, she talks to me about the primitive existence, the simple pleasures of a rural childhood, the hard work, and the joy of always living near the water. The lilt in her voice and her laughter throughout the interview belie her hard, pioneer existence. She begins by describing the American Indians who camped near their farm; it is still the Nineteenth century.

Clam Lake must have been a little different than it is today. Describe the family farm.

Oh, it was a lot different. There were quite a lot of Indians living there in the summer. They had canoes—they never had anything else to travel in. In the winter they would leave, but they always came back in the Spring. They put up little tents along the shore close to us. We were only a quarter mile from Clam Lake. They did their cooking, they caught a lot of fish—they kept us in fish. They were very good neighbors. Sometimes my mother would bake them a little pie.

One of 'em was Johnny Wabsquaw. Another was named Solomon. One was named P.M [Peter Mark]. Johnny Wabsquaw would come up to our house and he would play a big jew's harp—that was great. We'd go outside—we had a big pan, we'd put

The Clam Lake School, 1907. Amy Smith (center row) standing in front of her teacher, Mrs. Vance.

"I worked at the Pere Marquette Hotel . . . did you know you didn't even have electric lights." -- Amy Smith

chips in it, start a fire and cover it with leaves and make a big smudge [smoke]—and we'd all sit outside. That's the way we'd scare the mosquitoes away [Laughs].

The Indians used to have arrowheads to hunt with. We'd find a lot of them up around Clam Lake. When my uncles would plow, they would find skulls and jaws full of teeth and all kinds of bones, not too far down below the ground.

There were hills up above our house. There were blueberries and blackberries, strawberries. People would come from the other side of the lake to pick berries by the pail.

Peter Mark, known as "Old P.M.," 90 years old in 1908. Noted Indian hunter, fisherman, and guide.

I was a busy girl. We picked up arrowheads, we picked blackberries and sold 'em for ten cents a quart. In the boat, we'd go down the lake—there were resorters all over. We had a good life.

They used to call Lake Bellaire Grass Lake when I was a girl. There were no cars, but there were lots of motorboats. On Sundays, the lake was full of 'em, scared all the fish [Laughs].

And, did you know, the logs would come down the Grass River—we lived right there where we could see those logs. These men that were taking care of the logs, they had big spikes in their shoe soles and they would run all over those logs and they would keep 'em in order. They would drift 'em clear down to Torch Lake, down the lakes, clear to Elk Rapids.

I love the water. We rode around on the lake a whole lot. We'd row clear from our home to Clam Lake and that would be about three miles by water. We did grocery shopping—took us all day to row down and back; we were fooling around and didn't hurry. We also rowed up the river to Troutman's Landing—from there we could go to the store at Comfort.

At Comfort, there was the store; all the other buildings were shanties. There was a potato warehouse. The section men and their wives lived at Comfort. There were little shanties all the way down the railroad tracks where my husband's brothers lived and different men who worked on the railroad tracks. There was George's brother, Chris, his brother, Gay, and my brother-in-law, Jay Breece. They took sections of the railroad tracks and put in new tracks and kept the railroad in shape. They worked from Bellaire to Alden.

And down at Clam River there was Anderson's store. Bellaire was nine miles. If Dad wanted to get dry goods or clothes or shoes, he walked.

I did get my hand cut in two when I was about six. It was a nine mile walk one way to get a doctor, so Dad started out about 3:30 in the afternoon. He walked nine miles—there were no cars—and then he walked nine miles back. The doctor got there about eight o'clock and took care of my hand by lamplight.

With a family so large, who decided who did the chores?

Dad decided. We only had a cow. We did a lot around the home. I helped with the little children, little sisters and brothers. I got them ready for school. We had to walk three miles, summer and winter. It was the Clam Lake School.

Describe your dad; what kind of a man was he?

He was medium height, slender and good natured—good, clean man. My mother was a very nice woman, no swearing, no bad talk and not too much quarreling. My dad had a mustache and when we got too noisy, he would stick his tongue out to the edge of his mouth and draw in his moustache. Then the kids knew what was comin'. If they didn't, there was a little willow patch down by the crik that ran right by our yard—he'd go get a willow and when he came back everyone was real quiet [Laughs].

Mother could crochet, she could knit, she could sew, she could sing tenor. Of course, when she came over she talked Swiss—she had to learn English and she did a pretty good job, even learned to write English.

Little by little, we left home. I worked for different people. I worked for the neighbors. We had a nice neighbor by the name of Hasting—I stayed there, worked for my board and room and went to school. I was about eleven. I stayed with her because her husband went to a lumber camp, so she was alone and elderly. I did the chores around there, carrying water from the lake for wash water.

But I did work at the Pere Marquette Hotel. I worked there, and did you know at that time you didn't even have electric lights? A candle, you could light that until you got dressed for bed and then "Out!" There were no bathtubs, no water, bedrooms all upstairs. We had to carry water in big white pitchers up the steps—every room had that. People from Chicago and all over would come there and stay all during the summer. It was just north of Anderson's store on Torch Lake—about a quarter mile north of Clam Lake. It was about four miles from our home. You had to work very hard. You had to wait table, you had to clean upstairs, you had to iron. There were four girls. My table had eleven people. We had a colored man for a cook and he was very funny. His name was Jim.

Off and on, I would go home and stay a little while. We would go to country dances, my brother and I. I love music. As I grew older, I started to date. I was quite young, but I loved to dance and hear the music. Oh, I would walk three miles to get to a dance. Then I got acquainted with the man [George Smith] I got married to. We got married and I was sixteen.

My husband was working on the railroad track. We bought a little farm and I had my little girl there, named Gladys. My husband farmed and worked out; he also worked at the little Comfort store. There was a post office in one room.

We moved to Alden so my girl could go to school. We planned to go back to the farm, but she had to go quite a ways to school and she was just about six years old. Then we bought this house and I had Kenny and Doris here. They were born here at home. People didn't go to hospitals then; there was no way to get there in the winter.

Then the mail carrier retired while we were here. My husband said, "I'm going to Bellaire and take an exam." It was the year after World War I. George got this mail route and he worked on there for forty years. He went around with horses in the winter. Later on, he made himself a snowmobile—he got tractors and wheels and fixed the big ol' thing. He retired, he lived about six or seven years and then he passed away. So this is the way my life went.

I have always lived where I could see water, but once for a short time when we were on the farm. I can see Torch Lake here; I could see Clam Lake there. I could see Torch Lake from the other place we lived. I've always been happy to have lived near the water. I think Torch Lake is the most beautiful.

Play that over and I think that is it. If something sounds foolish, leave it out.

Amy with her daughter, Gladys, c. 1912.

155

Natural disasters were few on the Chain, but when tiny Spencer Creek overflowed, the force of water was felt by the citizens of Alden, 1910.

In the days before dime stores, Kmarts, and Wal-Marts, every small village had a general store. From the 1870's to 1920, Coy's store in Alden provided many of the necessities of life.

The SCIENTIST

1. Richmond Brown
2. LaVerne Curry
3. Bill Weiss

"Conservation is getting nowhere
because it is incompatible
with our Abrahamic concept of land.
We abuse land because we regard it
as a commodity belonging to us."

——Aldo Leopold

Whether it is the thrill of a fifteen-year old's catch of a thirty-one pound muskie (upper left), or Dell Turk's modest 1912 catch of perch (upper right), fishing was a pastime and challenge that attracted many. Frank Lyon's twenty pound muskie in 1907 (lower left) and the fine catch of northern pike (lower right) caught by Walt Lynn (left) and Jim Mariage (1940) is further proof that the Chain of Lakes offered some of the finest fishing in the Midwest.

Richmond Brown

Richmond Brown began his first summer on Intermediate Lake when he was three months old in 1925. His parents had bought a cottage there a few years earlier, at the end of World War I. With a degree in geology from the University of Missouri, Richmond made his career with the U.S. Geological Survey as a hydro-geologist. Today he spends his retirement with his wife Lee on Intermediate Lake, just two miles from the original family cottage. He is an active and outspoken advocate for water quality on the Chain of Lakes. In this 1988 interview, updated in 1997, Richmond speaks of his concerns for the water and his fond memories of a happy childhood.

When do you first recall coming to Antrim County and the Chain of Lakes?

We came up on the Pere Marquette Railroad. We didn't have an automobile at that time. We came from Columbia, Missouri by train; the principal train to come up on at that time was the Resort Special which used to come in to Central Lake early in the morning and go out, going south, late at night. We had a Pullman from Chicago to Central Lake. When we got here, the station agent I recall was a Mr. Gabrey—George Austin was agent before him.

We got picked up with a horse and wagon by George Hanna, a farmer on Intermediate Lake a mile and a half south of town. He took us down to our cottage. Later on we shipped all our clothes and books by leased freight. We had steamer trunks and the steamer trunks usually came a week or two after we got here.

You mentioned that your mother had all her children in the spring for a particular reason.

[Laughs] She wanted to be up here summers. She was very careful in child planning so that her children were born in the Spring so she could come up here and feel good and enjoy the summer. I was born in April. I was here the first summer when I was three months old [Chuckles]. The only time I missed was a couple of summers during the Second World War and three years when I worked in Colorado.

My father was Harry Gunnison Brown, my mother was Fleda Phillips Brown. My father was professor of economics at the University of Missouri. My sister, Cleone, the oldest of the children, was born before they came up here.

A friend, Herbie Reese, had gone into the wilderness areas of northern Michigan. He found Intermediate Lake an outstanding place to fish and he had camped at Birch Point on Intermediate Lake for several summers. A tuberculosis sanitarium had been built on Birch Point; that was in the days when they thought if they put people out in the sun, they'd get over tuberculosis. In part, because the treatment wasn't successful, the place went under and it was put up for sale. Dr. Reese told his neighbor, Dr. Herman Almstedt. The Almstedts rented the sanitarium the next summer.

When they bought the place, they invited my family to come up. My parents heard that there was a cottage for sale down the lake. It was for sale by Mr. Stevens who was president of the Central Lake Bank. The sale price was $800.00 and they decided it was something they wanted to do, so they bought it. This was 1918. My parents came up every year after that. My father came up the last time in '72 or '73.

Birch Point is about half a mile south of the bridge at Central Lake on the east side. It became a place for Missourians to settle in the summer. Of course, when we came up there weren't that many places on Intermediate Lake. When my folks got here, ours and Professor Green's, a professor at Notre Dame, were just about the only [families] vacationing on the lake in their own summer cottages.

The Maples, down at the south end of the lake on the west side, was a famed fishing resort and advertised in *Field & Stream*. The people who came up there, came to

Birch Tree Point on Intermediate Lake

Bellaire or Central Lake and then were picked up by the people at the Maples in wagons or cars.

What was so significant about the fishing on Intermediate Lake?

Well, it was outstanding [Laughs]. I'm sure that all fishing was outstanding years ago. Intermediate Lake is famed among those who know about it for having yielded the world's largest muskie—something over one hundred and fifteen pounds.

When we fished, the old limits were five fish of each species. Bass season opened the 25th of June; walleye and northern seasons opened somewhat before that. On opening day we would row from our house to the upper lakes. In fact, usually my brother would row to Six Mile Lake and we would camp overnight and we would row back down to Ellsworth or Wilson. We'd camp there for a night.

We'd get up at three o'clock in the morning or there abouts. We'd usually get into Wilson just about the time the sun was coming up over the woods. I'm sure I was not more than five or six when we first did this. It was the 25th of June 'cause that was the day the season opened. We went religiously every year. I remember getting up and putting on sweaters and more sweaters and a jacket so I wouldn't freeze to death because my brother did almost all the rowing. My brother thought, and rightly so, that he was much better at keeping the boat positioned for fishing than I was [Laughs]. He was seven years older than I was. I sat in the back of the boat trying to keep warm. In the early '30s, when I was a little kid, I would just row once in awhile.

The boat was a Mullins steel rowboat. It was shaped very much like a Whitehall or Ranger boat. It was particularly good to row because it was heavy and, not only was it all metal, but it had a skeg [a timber or series of timbers attached to the stern of a small boat, serving as a keel to keep the boat on course] which was about four feet long and six or eight inches deep at the stern. This was filled with lead which gave it additional weight and stability. The freeboard was only five or six inches, so it was almost undisturbed by wind—a beautiful boat to fish from because you just put it somewhere and it would stay.

I remember going through the rivers in the pitch blackness. We had a flashlight with us; we took sandwiches; we took canned stuff. We always made a fire and heated beans. We almost always ate fish for our main meal and usually for breakfast.

If we were a little late, we'd take a few casts in Ben-Way. This was a particularly good place to fish. Then we'd row up to Wilson. Usually, it was in the lower part of Wilson that we'd start to fish till we got as many fish as we wanted or till it was nine or ten o'clock and the sun was up and the fish weren't biting that much. Then we'd row on up through Ellsworth and St. Clair and Six Mile lakes.

We'd stay a day, sometimes for a couple of days on Six Mile. Then we'd turn around and row back down. If we hadn't caught as many northerns as we wanted, why we would usually fish for northerns in the north end of Ben-Way—in the afternoon you could almost always get all the northerns you wanted out of the north end of Ben-Way. There were big weed beds in Ben-Way. Northerns tend to strike more in the afternoon. Bass strike in the early morning and walleyes strike, I guess, when you get 'em.

We always got large-mouth bass and northerns. We always thought the fishing was better in those upper lakes—more fish in less time. Those are shallower lakes and they have lots of weeds, so they were a more suitable habitat for large-mouth bass or northern pike and for muskie, though we never caught a muskie.
It was true then though that if we went out in the evening, after dinner, almost always we'd get two or three or four fish in Intermediate Lake.

Richmond Brown (right) and Phillips Brown sailing above St. Clair Lake, c.1930.

Wasn't your mother worried about two little guys taking off on such lengthy trips?

When we were very small, we were told we could not go anywhere in a boat without adults until we could swim across the lake. Dad learned to swim from a book and he taught everyone up here how to swim. He taught all the people at Birch Point and he taught us, of course. He must've taught one hundred kids how to swim.

I was four years old when I swam across the lake and back—that was a half-mile. After we swam across the lake and back, we were able to go anywhere we wanted in the boat, anytime we wanted to. We had freedom of the lake and freedom of time. We were in the water for hours and hours. And, of course, we wanted to learn to swim because we couldn't go anywhere until we learned to swim.

There weren't mobs of people here. I remember occasionally seeing people fish and once in awhile we'd see somebody fish during the day when we were fishing. I'm sure there must have been half a dozen boats on the lake many evenings, but you just didn't see many people. The most people I remember was in the evening; there were quite a lot of these—maybe a dozen—inboard launches that went up and down the lake. The Longley's had one called the Alabess. It was probably twenty feet long; they had wicker chairs in the boat. You'd hear these one-lung engines putt-putt-putt up and down the lake.

There was nobody on the west side at all; there wasn't a single cottage all the way down to Snowflake. Snowflake was a spiritualist camp. My sister went to a seance there one time when she was in college and thought that was a fascinating experience. They had a school there; it was a village at one time.

Is the lake becoming saturated with people now?

Well, it certainly is relative to what it used to be. I've been active with the Upper Chain of Lakes Association and the last few years we've counted boats on the lake and several years ago we counted approximately 1500 boats—870 on Intermediate Lake and another 700 on the other lakes. So your talking about 1500 boats on the lakes compared to, probably, 50. So it's certainly more crowded.

Going back to your childhood, how many times a summer would you and your brother take these overnight fishing trips?

We always did it on opening day and a few other times. Usually my mother and dad would go once or twice each summer—we'd go up to Wilson and camp—we'd spend two or three days at Wilson, then sometimes we'd paddle up to Six Mile and back to Wilson. We'd take a canoe and the rowboat. My mother loved to camp in the upper lakes.

I get the picture of a rather primitive existence. Describe the roads and going into town for groceries. How much different was it then than today?

Mom, Dad, Rich at Wilson Lake

The road was a two lane sand road. The trees arched over the road most of the distance. It was completely shaded during the day. Milk and fresh produce was delivered once or twice a week by horse and wagon. We got groceries by taking our boat to town. My dad had fixed it up with sails. It was a fourteen foot boat; he had two masts and two sails and a jib—three sails on a fourteen foot boat. Usually, there were six of us in the boat; everybody would go to town. We'd load this with groceries for a week.

We went to Smallegan-Smith; it was the only grocery store in Central Lake at the time. They'd load the groceries in a wagon and take the wagon down to the dock, put 'em in [the boat] and we'd take 'em home. I was frightened to death. I thought sure we were gonna sink. My dad put up every bit of sail in any kind of wind there was and we'd just go flying home [Laughs].

We cooked on a wood stove. The cottage was unfinished—two-by-fours. There was a brick fireplace in it. We had an outdoor toilet, no running water. I didn't think having an outdoor toilet or no running water was a problem. There was no electricity. We had kerosene and gasoline mantle lamps.

REA [Rural Electrification Administration] came in the '40s and my folks were reluctant to get electricity at first. They thought it was too expensive and didn't think they had any need for it. Sometime right after the Second World War, they had electricity put in.

Is there anything unique about the Chain of Lakes or is water water?

The climate here is unique. It's a climate tempered by the Great Lakes. It's hard to find a place that has the through flow of water that you get here, protects you a little bit against pollution problems. Though the population density is increasing, it is still one of the less-densely populated lake systems that you find in the upper Midwest. Of course, Torch and Elk are big lakes and population pollution doesn't seem as great on those simply because the lake surface and volume is so huge in comparison to the number of people that are on the shore.

From what you said about water flowing through, do you see pollution as a big problem?

I see pollution as a problem and I see it as a big problem, but less a problem here than on a lot of lakes. I've spent a lot of time and created all sorts of antagonisms in this area by worrying about pollution problems. When we did this, we did it as the Upper Chain of Lakes Association—with unanimous approval of the members. When they built this new dam in '68, they set the water level higher than it had been and so it eroded shorelines significantly and the lake had a significantly higher silt level than it had had before. Trees were falling in.

We went to court to get the lake level lowered. After we got the court order, we didn't know how they were regulating the lake. The gauge in Central Lake, used for forty years, had been removed. So I testified on this.

164

They asked, "Where do you want this set?"

I said, "Let's set the dam [at Bellaire] at the lowest level that the lake had been on the presumption that, with the regulation we'll have, that will approximate the level it had had before. It won't go down to this level except in a period of sustained drought."

Well, it turned out, they were able to lower it much more rapidly that I had anticipated. So the average level was a little lower than it had been in many years. This got people upset.

The dam at Bellaire is considered by the Corp of Engineers to be an unsafe dam. The Corp of Engineers rated it as inadequate for one-half of a maximum probable flood. A maximum probable flood is one-half of the flood you would get from the maximum possible rainfall—the dam and the spillway are completely inadequate for that much precipitation. It's a hazardous dam.

There's contamination that takes place from farms in the Beal and Scott Lake area. There's contamination from run-off from fertilizing lawns. There's contamination simply because you cut down the trees that are using a lot of these nutrients and you let everything move through to the lake. There's some contamination from septic drain fields although that's probably the least of the problems.

With all these forms of contamination collectively, is there a point where the lakes become endangered?

Lakes all die anyway. It's how long it takes that you're concerned with. I suppose that what one can argue, as some people have here, that if it doesn't take place during my lifetime, it isn't significant. I don't know how many generations you've got to preserve it for.

The upper lakes are close to being eutrophic as they have low oxygen levels in the deeper holes and they have very significant weed growth. The water is warm because it is fairly shallow—sediment loads coming into them contain a lot of nutrients. The so-called eutrophic index for these lakes is in and out of the eutrophic range. If they reach that point, they deteriorate at a fairly rapid rate.

When you get eutrophication because of low levels of oxygen, it doesn't support the kind of fish most people like. It doesn't support the so-called sport fisheries of northerns and walleyes. You tend to get suckers and carp species that are less desirable. The lake tends to have thick growth of algae which, in some cases, will extend over much of the surface.

Intermediate Lake isn't really close to that. You have good transparency to the water. In terms of the lake actually becoming eutrophic and having extensive algae and large areas where there's no oxygen, Intermediate Lake isn't really in danger, certainly not in my lifetime.

You've spent the greater part of your life here on the water. How has the water influenced you?

Very greatly. I love to swim. I suppose it influenced me in what I did for a living because I went into geology in part because it was an outdoor field. I like to be outside. A lifetime goal for me was to retire here.

What is your favorite view?

My favorite view over the years has always been to go down on the dock early in the morning in the summer and see the fog rising out of the lake with the sun rising into it. You get the beautiful blues and pinks, just mirror-like water. I'm sure that's my favorite view.

I enjoy too much reminiscing about my youth here. To my point of view, at least, it couldn't possibly have been better.

LaVerne Curry

LaVerne Curry holds a Ph.D. in Freshwater Biology from Michigan State University. He has conducted forty years of water quality studies on Torch Lake and is a recognized expert on the subject. He has presented papers on his Torch Lake research in Czechoslovakia, Canada and, Sweden. Born in 1914, Dr. Curry taught at Central Michigan University and became Chairman of the Biology Department before his retirement in 1975. Today he lives with his wife, Kay, on the northwest shore of Torch Lake a few miles south of Eastport. He accepts the premise that Antrim County's Chain of Lakes is believed to be one of the largest spring-fed freshwater bodies in the world. I first interviewed Dr. Curry in 1986 and followed with two visits in 1997.

How did you first get associated with the Torch Lake area?

It was in 1944 and I brought a group of students from Corunna High School. We were going to spend a week at Camp Hayo-Went-Ha. The second time I visited was during the time we had made an extensive survey in the Upper Peninsula. I had a student with me [named] Gale Gleason. His father was Dr. Gale Gleason who was a dentist in Traverse City. On the way back on US 131 at Mancelona we cut off and came over to Bellaire and, if you remember as you come out of Bellaire to get to Alden Road, you get a beautiful shot of Torch Lake. That was the second time and I figured that, with luck, my third time I'd have my own place here and that's the way it worked out. So about 1960, we bought our property.

Mary Kay McDuffie gave me your name. Why do you suppose she recommended that I contact you concerning the water of Torch Lake?

Well, we've spent quite a good deal of time—students and Ed McDuffie—he was associated with us. His students at Bellaire High School helped to operate some of the equipment through classes we conducted up here for several years. The students were the muscle. I was just like the bone in an arm, they moved it back and forth.

Can you describe the equipment.

Oh, yes. Chemical testing involving water tests for oxygen, carbon dioxide, phosphates, nitrates, hardness, pH—getting into the physical characteristics. The temperature series that we ran—that, with the use of Kemmerer water samplers and various chemical reagents and devices in the laboratory. We used the lab at Bellaire. Ed was very instrumental in helping us set up a lab through the village government. Biological tests, using Ekman dredges and screen series—that sort of thing.

What we tried to do was to teach some the very basics of water quality determinations to the high school students. If they were going to stay around in this part of the country, they'd have some idea about what it means to have a good quality water around you—and Torch Lake, as far as I can tell, it is an excellent quality of water. It's one of the best in the United States.

When you say water quality, do you simply mean clean water?

I mean water that's biologically clean, chemically clean, bacteriologically clean and it's aesthetically a high quality.

What happened to the studies? Are they intended to be used in a political way—that is, for future planning of the lakes or development of the area?

Not that I know of. I have weather data that goes back to about 1955. It's sporadic because at that time most of our weather data was taken in conjunction with some sampling. For instance, if we had to take a water series down to, say, 300 feet, we'd take that along with the weather of that day.

It wasn't until 1959 or 60 that we were able to pick up recording instruments—a hydrometer for humidity, a thermograph for temperature and barograph to measure atmospheric pressure. We also picked up a pyrheliograph that would measure sunshine. That way we were able to put this whole thing together. The long range project was to find some information in insect emergence.

One of the things that was of interest was the sporadic feeding of the trout. A three-inch fingerling was eating something different than say a four or five-inch trout and finally a six-inch, then an eight or nine-inch. Each one had their own unique nutritional requirements and I wanted to know when these insects would emerge. It has a lot to do with day degrees, temperature of the water and that has a lot to do with the sunlight that warms it up. We're right back to some very pristine water here and the water is clear and it warms up and gets the temperature circulated a little bit. This incites the insects, and they grow and eventually they emerge and go through the larvae stage to the pupae and on up to the adult. Well, during this time these fish are feeding.

One of the things I find in a program like this is that it has its limitations. When you give it to the associations, they want it written in layman's language. They do not want something that is highly scientific because they maintain they do not have the vocabulary for it.

They wanted it simple. I kept telling them, "Look, if you want to sell a program to the DNR, you're gonna have to have these data as basic information so that they can start somewhere and go on with their own program." I think this has worked out well with the lake associations because you can see they're doing something in regard to this.

What do you see as the biggest problem?

I would say trace elements, residual heavy metals—stability of just insecticides. We used to measure it with our clams—put clams in a little case and take the clam meat and analyze it in a gas chromatograph or a photospectrometer. We could tell about insecticides—how they were leaching down from the orchards or how they were leaching down from the fields that the farmer was using to get a good crop.

You have some real problems—high water getting into septic tanks. What we have are some of the very basic problems that are indicative of our society.

You mentioned the insecticides from the orchards. Are there any particular insecticides that bother you?

We didn't have any here that we found that were coming into the lakes or the streams. Our testing wasn't that intensive. Most of them were biologically degradable.

So, the Torch Lake area doesn't suffer from some of the problems you found elsewhere?

No, I don't think so. The only thing we're going to suffer for is a slow nutrification, that's the nutrient material that's added to the water through nutrient conversion and more and more conversion around the lake—layering it up, right on back. Eutrophication, but we haven't reached that yet. They're taking steps on it, they're not allowing any of the people to build a tremendous number of condominiums. I was asked as an expert witness on the Sundown Condos down near Clam River. The only reason I was against that was the fact that the number of the people they wanted to have in the condo—that concentration of population would be almost the number per square mile you have in Bellaire. They did not have the septic or sewage disposal units in the condominiums that would be available in Bellaire. It's just a question of, "well, who will make the most money?" That's the problem.

I really believe that if we watch it, if we're careful of what we do as human beings— God created us so that there's room for everybody. Now we're gonna reach a point where there ain't no more room. If we're careful—we're not going to get everything we want, I know that. But we can get a part of what we want. I'm talking about myself as just a good old human being, living here, paying taxes. But you have to have a certain amount of open area, you have to have a certain amount of closed area too. They have to be distributed around. You can't have a mass of septic tanks put together here where there's one right after another for umpteen square miles because you can't handle that many.

Dr. Curry, 1986

How wide should a piece of property be on Torch Lake? How many human beings per how many square feet should there be?

That would depend on two or three things. It would depend on, number one, the soil. That would include sand or gravel, clay. The way the water is treated as it goes through the soil. Two, it depends on the slope. I would say a seven per cent grade—you shouldn't start to concentrate people in there because if you have people on the top of this seven per cent grade—if you have your lots lengthwise and a guy flushed his toilet here and if flows down to this one, to this one, down to the bottom. Obviously, this is the way you'd want to have it. You'd want to have your lots go across that, kinda like a belt that would go over it. So you're protecting the guy that's within a short distance of you. The third would be in the number of people that will be in your home. Septics today are no different than when they were constructed back in the '20s or '30s. Septic tank design is just about the way it was when it was born. The more you have, the worse the problem gets. The average life expectancy for a septic tank and tile field is twenty-five years.

Wouldn't the water from a septic field eventually purify itself going through the soil?

Oh, yes. That soil that you have around Torch Lake is a very, very thin—to me, it's a magnificent... I just can't explain what a fantastic life-giving thing this is. It's a living band that's no more than an eighth or quarter of an inch. I'm talking of this soil that converts these raw waste materials that originate from our home, our industries. They go into the soil, the soil has that capacity to break that stuff up and get that stuff changed around.

But, here's the point—it takes it so long—time, and man doesn't have the time to do that. That's the way we're gonna break up this good environment that we have. We just don't take enough time to let nature take care of it.

You use the word "magnificent.' Is it unique just to the Torch Lake area?

Oh, no. By no means. This an integral part of all soil formation. The only difference between the Torch Lake area is that we're in a northern temperate region and we have seasons. Again, we come back to the magnificent beauty that Torch Lake has.

What can we do—build better septic tanks? Not too many people along the shore of the lake?

I think if you were to put your septic tanks back. Along one lake, I found where they would use a fifty-five gallon drum—they run their waste into the drum and

Dr. Curry in his "jungle" 1997.

expect that to work as a septic tank. It was to save money, but in the long run, it doesn't save money. What's best is not to concentrate them. It's been scientifically proven that they work best if you have them spread out. Even where you have two, three farms close together, a dairy or beef cattle farms. Everyone of those critters that defecate on the land, the scientific estimates are that [that is equivalent to] seventy-five to one hundred and fifty people a day that would equal one cow. If you start to concentrate those, you don't have enough place for you nutrients to go.

This kind of soil is so thin that if you mow it very much, it soon turns to a desert. It means that nutrients rush right into the water. I had a friend come in here the other day, he said, "Curry, I look down here on the slope of your place and it's a jungle. When you look on the other side, it's all nicely trimmed."

 Well, all of the plants that are down in that jungle require nutrients and any nutrients we get rid of—the trees are constantly pumping this up during their growing season and the grass is growing it and that's why it looks like a jungle 'cause they're using that stuff up ... and it's not getting into the lake.

Are a lot of our problems just because people are ignorant? They're not doing things deliberately.

I think this is true. We have zoning ordinances—I was on the Board of Appeals for Torch Lake Township—I'd have a person come to me and say, "What about green belting, should we do it?" I would encourage it—wherever, whenever, however it could be done, do it!

Get that green belt in between you and that lake and it'll be a lot better. But the answer always comes back, "I can't see the lake. I'm in a beautiful spot. I wanna see it" Then I say to them, "Simply get up off your duff and go down and look at the lake. That will help you in two ways—number one, aesthetically, you'll see it. Number two, physically, you'll get exercise."

You have more than a passing interest.

I enjoy it. I understand it. I can tell you honestly—everyday I go out, I learn something new. I look forward to that newness, that new thing, whatever it may be. We have a fantastic environment today. It is absolutely glorious.

What's your favorite view?

Oh, a beautiful one. Sitting at that table out there and looking across for a sunset we get reflected. We have the sunrise and the sunset—both. If the lake is calm, along the east shore, the houses all turn a beautiful orange. It's fantastic. If you have a storm in the late afternoon, you're bound to have a beautiful rainbow.

If you could do anything different with your life, what would you do?

I think that's a very important question. I don't think I would do anything different. I would try to learn to be as healthful as possible to live longer in as good a health as I possibly could to enjoy as much as I could.

Bill Weiss

Bill Weiss lives on the shore of Torch River. He has spent most of his life on the Chain of Lakes, particularly Torch Lake. He holds a Bachelor's degree in physics, a Masters degree in oceanography, and a Doctorate in environmental engineering. He is the current Executive Director of the Three Lakes Association and is continually involved in monitoring the water quality of the Chain. In this 1994 interview, revised with him in 1997, Bill speaks here, not only with outstanding credibility and authority, but with a life-long love of the water he helps to protect:

My grandfather was the first to come to Antrim County. His name was Walter Jamieson. He came up in the '30s, bought about a quarter mile on Torch Lake. Through the years, he constructed a couple small cottages and a larger house. People would look forward all year to coming to Torch Lake to spend their summers. After World War II, my grandfather retired and spent as much time up here as he could.

In the 1950s, as you recall, Torch River still had a primitive unsettled look about it, certainly the Torch River shoreline did. I remember fishing expeditions when we would come down Torch Lake to fish in Torch River—it was an all day affair. You would station someone in the front of the fishing boat to watch for logs and stumps. I don't think we ever went as far as Elk Rapids in one day.

As a child, I can remember getting on the Jedge Jr at Clam River, doing down through Torch River, which was really a wild place. Most people had small fishing boats because recreational boating as we know it today did not exist. The Jedge Jr, being almost fifty feet, looked like it wouldn't fit through the river.

Most fishing spots seem to be sacred. What are your favorite fishing spots?

My father was the fisherman of the family although he always played second fiddle to Earl Pillman, the train master in Alden. Earl would always come in with these stories of huge fish, lake trout from Torch Lake. My dad would spend endless hours wandering up and down the lake. I don't think he ever caught much of anything. But his favorite fishing spot was Clam River. He'd go up at five o'clock in the evening, sit in the middle and cast—all artificial lures. I can remember going up there as a kid and never being disturbed. Rarely would you see another boat. Sometimes you'd see another fisherman or two.

We often had relatives that would come from Indianapolis or Chicago. Car travel was still kinda "iffy" even in the early '50s. It was a full day's trip from Indianapolis, so many would come on the train. That's usually when my dad would get his first round of fishing stories from Mr. Pillman—[Laughs]—get the bug to go catch some lake trout.

What do you see as the greatest changes in water quality from the time you were a young boy until the 1990s?

It's hard to separate myself as a child from being involved in the water quality business because I've tempered everything I've seen in what I remember from those days with what I know now. It's hard to have grown up here and not remember that special color in Torch Lake.

I can still remember some of the things we see today that are naturally occurring that disturb many people. They think they're unnatural things, but really they are natural. Such things as the pollen of poplar trees—gives you that little yellow sheen on the water. If the wind blows just right, it'll whip some of that organic material into foam. I'll get calls that somebody dumped their porta-potty—and all this soap, it's really natural material—just like you'd see in the Upper Peninsula at Tahquamenon Falls. The foam is the same there. Same derivative here as it is there—tannic material from rotting leaves or pollens, they cause foam.

The Alden Train Depot had been abandoned by the mid-1980's. It is resotred today as the Helena Township Historical Museum.

174

The classic story is the great Torch Lake "oil spill." A guy on shore overhears fishermen on Torch talking on their CBs about a black trail of oil on the lake. Phones start ringing, including mine, pretty soon everybody's on their way—sheriff, Coast Guard. When somebody finally tried to take a sample, they discovered it wasn't oil at all but discreet black particles. At last, a jar was dispatched to Doc Curry who immediately recognized it—the shiny black carapace of some "bug" which had just molted. The leftover body parts floated into a perfect windrow with a black sheen. Perfectly natural, but it caused quite a stir.

The lakes are slowly changing, in my opinion. It's simply due to the people that have settled around the lakes.

You mentioned that special color. Can you describe that?

Well, it's just a blue tint to Torch Lake that seems to be different. There are western lakes that have this fine glacial till in them that have a distinctive aqua-blue color—it's not the same color, but I think it is true that Torch has a distinctive color that no other lake has. I can't give you a scientific reason for that, it just seems to.

Is the change that's taking place because of all the people pose a threat to water quality?

I think to really understand our lake system, you have to look at a little bit of geology. In geologic terms, our lakes here are just like a flash of time in the billions of years of geologic history. All our lakes were formed after the last glacial period which was ten to fifteen thousand years ago. They're really like little puddles after a rainstorm in the span of geologic time.

We know from some newer work in paleo-limnology [the scientific study of ancient lakes, ponds and streams] where they're taking cores and analyzing these cores to try to determine what has happened. Since the glaciers, a number of the lakes along

The Jedge Jr. loading passengers at Clam River Bridge, c.1950. "As a child I can remember getting on the Jedge Jr. at Clam River, going down Torch River, which was really a wild place." —Bill Weiss

175

the northern temperate zone may have actually seen quite a few changes in temperature. This is research that's going on as a result of the fears over global warming.

The most significant event that occurred in our area was , of course, logging. That made a dramatic change in the watershed and the lakes. It was a massive removal of tree biomass. In most cases they were logged in a manner that all the slopes were left bare and huge amounts of soil eroded into the lakes. Now we have no way of going back to the 1600s, and I can't show you a piece of paper where the water quality parameters existed prior to logging. So, the best we can do is piece together the paleo-limnological data to try and understand what happened.

From the results of the EPA [Environmental Protection Agency] work that was done through the DNR [Department of Natural Resources] on our lakes where they took cores, show a pattern that huge amounts of nutrients eroded into the lakes after the woods were logged. After logging, the lakes, whatever condition they were in, were actually starting to clean themselves of the nutrients that washed in—and lakes have a way of binding up materials that go in to them. They settle out to the bottom, are buried and so most of those nutrients are not allowed to recirculate in the water.

As people started coming here in the 1920s and '30s, these were actually recovering lakes to an extent. They were still flushing out the excess nutrients. If you go just north of Alden and dig down, you can still find the sawdust that was underneath some of the more recent sediment that was left from the sawmills.

What we're seeing now, in real general terms, is that the effects of the logging have basically been overcome by the natural system. We have our second growth of trees, soil erosion has been vastly curtailed from those days, particularly in our area because we seem to have more nutrients in the soil to promote reforestation, while parts of Kalkaska County and the Upper Peninsula are still bare sand.

What we're seeing now is people have come and they've built right around the lake and they've installed their septic facilities. In general, septic facilities in sandy soils are excellent. They're particularly good from the bacteriological standpoint which is the public health concern. Sand is an excellent remover of the bacteria, so it works great. Our sandy soils are also a pretty good remover for nutrients. The ones I worry about are nitrogen, but particularly in our lakes, phosphorous. Phosphorous is the element of most concern because our lakes are what is called phosphorous limiting. If you were a little plankton in Torch Lake and you wanted to grow, you'd find that you had all the nitrogen, all the hydrogen, all the carbon and all the other nutrients that you needed. The one thing you would be limited on for growth would be phosphorous. That's common around the Great Lakes. That's why we've had phosphorous bans in detergents.

It's critical for us around our lakes because, even though we've taken it out of our washing products, it's still a natural byproduct of human waste. What happens is that the tile fields do their job—a lot of the nutrients will be caught in the septic tank and they'll be pumped up by the septic tank pumper and be removed to a field somewhere and be disposed of. So those nutrients usually end up back in some biomass—grass or corn or whatever it might be. But a significant amount of the nitrogen and the phosphorous that goes into the tile field seeps down into the ground. Our sands are excellent at absorbing those phosphorous nutrients as they go into the sand. The problem is that if your septic tank is fifty to one hundred feet away from the lake, there is a life span where this system begins to resemble a sponge.

My analogy goes like this: when that septic tank was first put there, the sponge had no phosphorous, because it had no water in it. Fifty years have gone by and those little drips of phosphorous have gone through. Our sponges in front of each little cottage are now completely saturated with phosphorous. So just like the sponge, if you put a drop of water in one end of the sponge, at the lower end of the sponge you're gonna get one drop of water or phosphorous out.

Since a lot of our homes were built around the early '50s, we're forty or fifty years out, not even counting the stuff that was here from the '20s and '30s. My personal feeling: we're about to run into the era when the sponges are going to start releasing more and more phosphorous into our lakes. We're just beginning to see, possibly, a lot more growth along the shorelines—various types of algae, grasses and weeds where, particularly in Torch Lake, we've never seen those before. As you release those nutrients, especially if they seep in out under the lake and they come up, say, through the rocks along the edge of the shore, this is nature's first remedy—it sends a plant out there—"plant, you're now able to grow." So the phosphorous will start to spur submerged vegetation; plants will start to grow. But it's very difficult to go out and quantitatively say "Yes, this is worse than it was ten years ago."

Bill Weiss monitoring the water of Torch Lake.

177

The upper Chain of Lakes, they're already at that point, they warm up quickly, they have lily pads and weeds, coontail—abundantly. We've always needed some of those materials—it's very healthy, very natural; they provide good fish habitat. In fact, Torch River is an interesting example. When I was a kid, we had lotsa green stuff growing on the bottom of Torch River—you couldn't hardly swim because it was there. When the swan population boomed about ten or fifteen years ago, they cleaned all that material out—all the way down to Lake Skegemog. Now, I'm beginning to get calls, now that the swan population has gone down. "Well, geez, there're all these green weeds growing out in front of my place. The river must be polluted." I've had a horrible time trying to convince people. "Well, no, the swans cleaned this stuff out fifteen years ago and this is just naturally regenerating. This was here thirty years ago—it was here when I was a kid. It's perfectly fine."

There are blue-green algae which love phosphorous and are not good for water quality. As was the case in 1976 when they had the spill at the Bellaire wastewater treatment plant. We did get a bloom of red-colored algae in that case. That's what we want to avoid. The green algae are primarily ones that beneficially use chlorophyll to replace oxygen.

The biggest thing about the other algae as a nuisance species is that they tend to upset the system when they get excess nutrients. They build populations very quickly, overgrow their food, starve themselves to death, and the degradation of their little plant bodies uses lots of valuable oxygen. In severe blooms, people see the color of their lake change.

What's going to happen with the upper Chain? You mentioned that it's in pretty bad shape.

Each lake is unique to itself and the smaller the watershed is, the smaller the amount of water that goes into the lake each year. How often the amount of water in the lake exchanges itself is a factor of what type of lake you will have and how many nutrients will be stored in the lake. Up here in our lakes, the amount of nutrients is pretty much the key. It all boils down, particularly, to the amount of phosphorous that's in the system.

The very small lakes in the upper Chain, their part in the watershed is pretty small, a lot of them are heavily agricultural, so there was some agricultural run-off. Now most of the lakes have been built around. They have the same people pressure that the larger lakes have. Because of the smaller amount of water, they simply don't have the resiliency to absorb large amounts of nutrients and dilute them as in the case of Torch Lake or Elk Lake. So when there are more nutrients, the system responds in very natural ways in growing more biomass in the lake either through plankton or aquatic vegetation.

The upper Chain is basically what would be called mesotrophic lakes now—not quite eutrophic which would be the most productive, but kind of in the middle range.

178

Banking ground on Torch Lake near Alden, c. 1900. Note people in foreground. "The most significant event…was logging. … It was a massive removal of tree biomass. …They were logged in a manner that all the slopes were left bare and a huge amount of soil eroded into the lakes." —Bill Weiss

Does eutrophic imply a dead lake?

Not necessarily. A eutrophic lake could be a highly productive lake with a large amount of nutrients in it. But it could mean that at times during the year there wouldn't be enough oxygen to go around, say in late winter under ice cover or even in the summer on hot days, there might not be enough oxygen to feed everybody that wants a piece of the pie. So when you start to discuss lake quality in those respects, a highly eutrophic lake may grow tons of bluegills and catfish and carp, but there wouldn't be enough oxygen for whitefish or lake trout to survive or breed, particularly.

So many lakes in Florida that are highly eutrophic, they're wonderful fishing lakes. They put out tons and tons of fish a year, but you wouldn't necessarily want to put your foot into them if you're familiar with Torch Lake. The upper Chain is nowhere near that bad, but it does have a higher level of nutrients in it. So the flow to the lower Chain has higher levels of phosphorus than the overall levels in the lower lakes. It's all part of the recycling system which incorporates a certain portion of the phosphorus from the plants and phytoplankton each year into the sediment.

But more and more of the phosphorus is released into the water and comes down and enters the lower Chain of Lakes through the Intermediate River. That's one of the stations where we've taken phosphorous readings and it [the Intermediate River] continues to be the highest level we monitor in the lower Chain of Lakes. That's not surprising anyone; that's what you should get and it's what we do get.

Unfortunately, the factors up there are no different than they are down here. To make those lakes any better, you'd have to restrict any agricultural run-off, try to get the septic tanks back away from the lake as far as possible, try to let as much water percolation into the soil rather than having it run off roofs and impervious surfaces, streets and roads to get into the lakes. Best thing, of course, is get those nutrients used up in someone's yard, or in a wetland before they get in a lake.

The same problem exists on the lower Chain of Lakes except that we have a much larger body of water. So we have a couple of things working for us. Number one, we have the ability for any small amounts to be diluted. And we have the fact that, every year, we have the drop-out as phosphorous is taken up in plankton bodies and they die at the end of the season and go down. There's the possibility that we'll keep adding to the phosphorous in the sediments, but we won't necessarily re-release it all next spring to be available for plant uptake.

Is the lower Chain big enough to wash out everything?

Yes and no. It's a flowing system and X number gallons of water that land in the watershed, if it's not evaporated, if it flows in, will go out and it will take with it whatever nutrients it can.

You mentioned restrictions on residents on the upper Chain. That'd be quite difficult to make people stop doing what they've always done, wouldn't it?

It's not just the upper Chain, it's all the lakefront property owners in the watershed, and as well as people who don't live on the lakefront. It's really everybody in the watershed that contributes to what we get.

Watersheds are the buzz words of the '90s, I guess you'd say. The soil conservation service has been working on this for fifty years. They knew that if somebody's on top of the hill and they fertilized their corn and they get a big storm, it's gonna run in the ditch, and in the gully, and into the creek, and into the lake—and they'd rather see the nutrients on the farmers field than in the lake anyway.

In layman's terms, how would you describe a watershed?

A watershed is just like a measuring cup with a spout. All the water that goes into that measuring cup is either going to stay in the cup, run out the little spout or be evaporated out the top. So whatever water we get through the air is not nearly as clean maybe as it used to be—we don't know—that comes into our cup. Now when it lands on the surface of the ground, there are lots of things that can happen to it. It can either just percolate into the groundwater, or it can be evaporated. But how it percolates in and what happens to it before it would run out a spring or run with groundwater into our lake is very important. If it percolates down through a dusty, dirty, oily parking lot, that's different than having it fall in a pristine wetland and maybe pick-up some natural organics but maybe actually leave some more of the airborne organic contaminants in the wetland before it moves into the river. So man's activities become very important.

Sawmill near Alden, c.1900.

Bodies are part of our problem. The more bodies we have, the more sewage we have, the more activity you'll see in the watershed. It's all so insidious. It's not just the sewage waste from people. It's just related to people. Somehow, once they get here, their activities seem to change things—building houses, building roads, paving, walking around golf courses. Sewage aside, we still experience a deteriorating water quality. In very subtle ways, compacting the soil, making the water run-off more quickly.

You see pavement as a problem. The more we pave and put in curbs and parking lots, the more damage we're doing?

It's a small insidious effect. Probably, the biggest thing is, how do you affect the flow of water when it arrives on our little square inch of area? In the old days, before we were here, it would fall on a forest canopy and dribble down. It might have taken weeks or days to reach the groundwater on someone's nice fancy lawn around Torch Lake, that rainwater is gonna go directly through the grass and into the lake—probably pick-up some fertilizer and go directly into the lakewater very quickly. The more disruption of the leaf cover and pine needles around our lakes, each little change that's made affects the movement of water.

This can be related to the big Mississippi floods of a couple of years ago. We know the upper Mississippi watershed states have lost 70-75% of their wetlands — mostly drained for farms. I read an engineer's estimate that those wetlands, filled with only six inches of water, would have prevented the entire flood—despite the heavy rains. Without storage area, the rainfall drained quickly to the rivers which couldn't hold it and the result was a flood.

All these little things change the system. Probably the biggest one is the fact that our lakes here are not natural anyway. They've all been dammed. So we're dealing with an ecosystem that was radically changed about one hundred and fifty years ago.

The lake levels would have been somewhat lower than they are now and the river levels would have been somewhat lower. There would have been a more pronounced narrows between Elk and Skegemog. That, to some extent, has changed the entire flow regime in the upper and lower systems.

Obviously, when they put the first dam in, there was erosion activity around the lakes because the water was higher and it was beginning to break new ground. I've heard people say there was forty or fifty feet more shoreline back in the 1890s in front of their property.

What is your greatest fear? Are we going to see these lakes destroyed?

I don't think "destroyed" in terms most people would think as unusable. I think over a significant period of years, we will see the nutrient level go up some. The changes that I'm seeing—taking chemical numbers—if there are changes, they're so small they'd be difficult to statistically validate. But the numbers that people generate often are the last things to change. The natural reactions of the systems to grow a couple more lily pads or grow a few more weeds here and there, those are very difficult to qualitatively go out and describe from year to year. That's pretty difficult science to do and draw conclusions from.

Of course, the size of our lakes is the great factor. That huge pool of water out there is going to assist us; it's going to take many, many—maybe decades—for some of the sponge effects to kick in. There's always the possibility that we'll come up with some better technical solutions to relieve the pressure.

The geologic perspective is that the systems operate in balance. Often times, a very small percentage to us might be enough to kick that out of balance. It's not always very much.

What can the average property owner do?

The solutions are about the same that we've had for about the last thirty years; they really haven't changed. Number one is maintaining your septic tank. A number of the older ones are being, periodically, moved further back. And that helps because it gives the area that is now a sponge a chance to slowly release phosphorous at a decreased rate. It gives a new area a chance to start filling up as a sponge. Of

The Cedar River, a vital tributary of the Chain.

course, if people just use less water, they tend to stress their septic tank less.

It looks like lawn fertilization is still one of the biggest prime culprits around the lakes. People do like their lawns right up to the edge; they like to fertilize 'em; they like 'em nice and green. It's been pretty well proven that they can have just as verdant a lawn without any fertilizer at all just by watering more often with water from the lake.

We've always thought the land and the water are ours to use. That's a difficult mentality to get over. People often think that their use of something gives them the right to abuse it.

I'm not sure we will get out of that rationale and, quite frankly, it's very difficult for me as well because I have my property and I want to do with it what I want to do, too. I've acquired a lot of my property to make sure nothing happens to it. It's an educational process that goes on from generation to generation. Breaking the mold. When my grandfather came here, the last thing they worried about was hurting the lake. We used to bathe in it, never thought anything about it. As times changed, the rules have changed.

The latest controversy is whether allowing Shanty Creek [golf course] to withdraw large amounts of water from the Cedar River to irrigate and make snow will damage the river. Now everyone should be able to picture that removing water from the river—and probably allowing more to evaporate—then putting it back into the watershed at a different location is a change.

The natural system will react to that change. Is that abuse? Depends on whether you golf or downhill ski, I suppose. If you want to see a great example of subtle changes that can occur, visit a wetland that's being used to treat sewage effluent. You don't have to go farther than Bellaire. Wetlands normally are extremely diverse in plant life. But when the water table is raised, it eventually will kill the trees and shrubs. As more nutrients are added, nature will grow what can utilize them best— cattails. If you visit the Houghton Lake site, you see huge cattails for miles. Still a wetland, yes. Is it the same, no. Give Bellaire another fifty years, it may look the same.

Lots of lakes in southern Michigan could probably be called "abused." Unfortunately, more and more people are voting with their feet to leave those lakes and come to ours. Keeping nature from reacting the same to our increased human presence is the challenge we face.

The Jedge Jr. cruises the Chain, c.1950.

1. Terry Wooten

*"Poetry affords us a respite
in which we may gather renewed strength
for the old struggle
to adapt ourselves to reality."*

——*Robert Haven Schauffler*

Terry Wooten

*Terry Wooten is host, poet, and storyteller at the Stone Circle ten miles north of Kewadin near the west shore of Torch Lake. The Stone Circle, built by Terry, is a triple ring of large boulders forming a natural amphitheater. It is the center where poets and storytellers and visitors gather each Friday and Saturday through the summer to exchange stories of everyday life and lore. After twenty years, Terry has settled in; he is part of the community. It is a surprise to many that Terry was selected to the first team of the 1966 All-State High School Football team. Today he is a noted and respected oral poet in schools and other forums throughout the Midwest. Terry is listed in the **Dictionary of Midwestern Literature** and is the recipient of the 1997 **Michigan Creative Artist Award.** We are sitting near Terry's circle of stones as he tells his story in a 1987 interview, which was updated in 1997.*

Terry, let's go back to the time you were nine or ten and talk about your childhood.

I grew up two miles north and two miles east of Marion [in Osceola County] out in the country. I had a habit when I was six or seven of roaming from the early hours of the day till nighttime. Sometimes I wouldn't show up till dinner time. My mother always said I had a very big imagination. I think I had a poet's mind back then and didn't know it.

186

I had my own set of traps from the time I was six—trapped muskrat, beaver, mink. I can remember coming over a hill zeroing in on the house lights in November.

When you were on the farm and you began drifting into writing, what did your dad think of that?

Surprisingly, when I showed him a couple of my first writings, he was really in to it. He really pushed it.

Earlier you mentioned the abuse in your family. Tell me about your dad's drinking.

I think it was there from the time I was real little; I was just too naive to know about it. I have a memory of him coming home and sitting in the yard sick and vomiting out the side of his truck. It got progressively worse until he was beating my mother up quite a bit. I have real terrible memories of standing upstairs in my sister's room—my sister and I standing in the middle of the room just terrified because we could hear my dad whacking my mom around downstairs.

There was one time when I was twelve years old, I went downstairs and stopped him one night. He was gonna fight me. I could handle my dad physically from the time I was twelve or thirteen years old—it affected me more than I realized.

I think that gives me some insights to kids when I [perform] at schools because there's a lot of domestic violence that still goes on, especially when things are so economically depressed. It's one of my gifts that I can touch kids who maybe aren't considered gifted because they've got some emotional problems behind it.

I've always considered myself a positive—an optimist. I refuse to let the negative side take over. So I used that latent anger and sadness I have inside me as a fuel for my art. It's like a booster rocket. You don't see very much anger show up in my writing. That's the reason why I stress family so much and the stability of family. Even at the Stone Circle, it's a family thing.

Life slips by, day by day, like a field mouse, as Ezra Pound said. The days are just never full enough and you try to appreciate each moment as if you're not going to be there the next day.

Who was the most dominant influence in your life?

I think an awful lot like my Grandpa Helmboldt—I can see mannerisms that I do. My Grandpa Helmboldt was a bootlegger; he was a carouser. The Helmboldts were a rough bunch. He was always telling me about Indian burial grounds out north of Park Lake. He probably affected the poet side of me more than anybody; he really fed my poet's imagination although I didn't realize I was a poet at the time. He was a storyteller—we call 'em bullshitters, I guess.

My Grandpa Wooten didn't drink—he was real conservative. I'd have to say my mother and my two grandpas were probably the dominant influence. My mother would talk to me from the time I was young. She took a real interest. My mother had a mystic side to her. I would talk to her—I was curious about everything from reincarnation to sex—from the time I was four or five years old. I would sit at the kitchen table and talk to my mother for hours.

Let's talk about Park Lake. Tell me why it's such a part of your life?

Park Lake's a little ghost town situated in between Marion and McBain. It was about five or six miles as the crow flies from where I grew up. My mother had grown-up there, my grandparents, my great-grandparents had first moved there. I spent a lot of time there. When I was little, we'd visit my grandparents. I was always running around the countryside out in Park Lake.

I have memories of the train, it was just a great thrilling experience—you'd be out in the yard and you'd hear this train whistle blowing which was real eerie. It just didn't fit in with the surrounding countryside—the sound of the birds, the tractor sounds, all of a sudden you hear this wailing siren-like sound. It just thundered through. The ground would start to shake. I'd run down there. It was scary as could be to watch—the train coming around the bend. I'd get up on the skeleton building with the whistle blowing, it was terrifying. I loved that. I was always a thrill-seeker.

I read Thoreau when I was in the sixth grade. From there I got into Pound, Shelley, Keats, Byron—and I was on my way.

There was a woman in high school who really got me going—Sonya Titus. She insisted we keep journals and write things original and think things out. Don't regurgitate the same old things you've been hearing. I started delving into my deeper self and found out I really liked it. She got me started, plus I remember her voice—she had beautiful articulation. I fell in love with her voice.

She was way too progressive for Marion. They kicked her out after three years. She was too good of a teacher. They got rid of her.

When I got to college, in my freshman year there was a woman who reminded me a lot of Sonya Titus. We had this conference half-way through the semester. She said, "You're real good. Have you ever thought of becoming a writer?" Yeah, I had—I thought a lot about it. That was kind of the push.

You've mentioned writing, but I know you as an oral poet. Let's talk about the oral tradition. How accurate is the oral tradition?

It's quite accurate especially when you're taking it from voice to voice. I'm a voice stealer, so you better be careful around me because if you say something that will fit into a poem, you'll hear yourself at the Stone Circle or wherever I happen to be speaking.

There was a storm six, seven years ago that raged through here. Everybody was all excited, they'd run out of their houses and look at the destruction. My father-in-law said they saw a cloud with four little tails like tits on a cow coming through the area. Great! So I said, "A herd of small tornadoes hanging from a big black cloud like tits on a cow." I took the first four lines from him.

There's the area of oral hearsay where we've been told about something that happened—we haven't actually experienced it. We're passing on someone else's experiences. Do you encounter much of that?

It's kind of a magnification process. We all want things to be a little bigger and a little grander than what they really are. That's the way we remember things; that's the magic when you're sitting around Thanksgiving or a family reunion talking about that night you got a flat tire in a blizzard and you almost froze to death. Ha-ha-ha, wasn't that fun? You don't remember the practical significance of it. I think we all live with myth.

It's part of the dangers with the written tradition rather than the oral tradition. All history was myth. That's how gods were created. There's an old warrior three, four generations back, before long he was five hundred years old. So there's a danger of inaccuracies there, but at the same time, it's maybe closer to what we want to believe the way things are. So it's maybe closer to the spirit of things.

Maybe oral history is, if not more, at least as accurate as the written word. If you can manage to capture it. The problem is if you don't capture it, it goes off into thin air. That's the disadvantage of it. There aren't as many trained in it anymore. The history tradition was an oral tradition.

Anybody is capable of saying something creative, we do all the time. It's the poet's job to steal those things. I steal everybody's voice and make it my own. I live my life in rural Michigan, so I can fit in with those people, and I'll speak for them and they can understand it. It's real different from academic poetry that most people don't think they like. I see poems as songs that you say.

I'm real pleased that the oral tradition has given me more strength in my writing; it's like another booster rocket going off.

For some reason you wound up in northern Michigan. You married Wendi and you're living on Torch Lake.

No better place to live really. I met Wendi who was one of the most sincere people I've ever met. There was no doubt from then on. Twenty-two years later, here we are. I imagine northern Michigan around this area will be our home base for the rest of our lives 'cause we both really like water. If I have to be around water, there's such a freedom and open space up here.

Why do you have to be around water?

It's something your spirit gets addicted to. You grow up in that environment—you need it. Why do people have to build houses on water? Why is the most prized piece of land along water? It's something that's real deep in all of us. We came from water originally. I think even though most people don't think about that, there's something real deep in people that's attracted to the lakes.

The Grand Traverse region has attracted a tremendous number of artists of all media: poetry, pottery, watercolors—maybe more than in other regions. Can you speak to that, why that is?

The openness. Twenty years ago there was a back to the land movement; they came out of the hippie generation. They wanted to get away from the city, the hustle and bustle. So they brought the hustle and bustle up north with them. You can't conceive of moving back to the city once you're up here. For me, it was a little easier because I grew up in northern Michigan. I know how to survive on not very much.

It's such a tourist area. There's a market for art, especially pottery, water color. I don't know if that breeds the best art, but it's there. I see Elk Rapids and Traverse City as almost like the San Francisco area. It just attracts a real creative group of people.

Friends gather with Terry Wooten for an evening of storytelling.

190

As the sun sets, the fire is lit and the myths and legends pour forth.

How does the land affect or help your art?

I'm a very earthy person. I gotta have soil under my feet to feel, to gravitate.

Couldn't you do that anywhere else? Couldn't you be in Iowa and write poetry?

No. I'd be too far away from the water. I went through a stage of writing about animals and the earth. I think artists are in the forefront. They have invisible antennas, they see into the future, they're quite a few years ahead of most people. They see problems developing; they sense things. They look a little closer at things than the average person.

Up here you're closer to the land. Maybe it's a form of escaping what's happening downstate. At the same time, if we don't get a grip on it, it's gonna happen up here.

I feel at home with northern Michigan people—the rural people.

Is the land and the water one and the same? Torch Lake, for instance, are you influenced by it?

The old Torch Lake, the archaic Torch Lake with the pine trees, the old forests all around it. I'm always attracted to a simpler time. I go back when there weren't as many people. The Indian people were here. I'm attracted to its water because it's a powerful lake; I'm attracted to the spiritual power of it.

It's rather depressing what's happening to it, all the houses around it. I suppose it's inevitable. It used to bother me a lot—the new Torch Lake.

191

Where we're at is a very special place. On this hill overlooking Torch Lake one day I had an awareness attack. I was too angry about what was going on around here and it was affecting my health. Every time they saw a view of water, they wanted to build a condo. A voice inside me said: "Don't worry about it. This is just another phase. We've dealt with glaciers, we've dealt with so many different phases. We can deal with this too. It's just a temporary phase. Ten thousand years and all this development will be gone" So I stopped fighting so much. I don't agree with it, but I realize I've got to survive.

Inevitable? You mean you can't influence or change it?

To a point, that's just beginning to happen. The farming techniques have got to be changed. The way people build their houses; they can't crowd them right up to the lake. The drain fields. Just too many people.

In the old days, there just weren't as many people. They were still littering and polluting, but there just weren't as many of them. We've got to get more responsible about how we live on the land and realize we're just one link in a chain of events.

Terry ponders the future of the land and water.

DRUM

I've got an imaginary shaman's drum
made of a warrior's skin and bones,
and I worship the polluted lakes and rivers.

Surfing the semis,
riding the oil-stained
asphalt and cement wave
of the late 20th Century
bumping down a worn out freeway.

Looking across the water
at a shoreline that used to be solid trees,
all I can see are new houses,
strip malls, golf courses and casinos.

So I don't get too depressed
I keep reminding myself
we're living between the glaciers.
Then all this development
for quick money
is just a blip in eternity.

It puts life back into focus
like Bob Marley sang,
"Cuz none of them can stop the time."

Terry Wooten
1997

The Chain of Lakes offers many quiet spots for reflection and meditation. For many, it is the chief attraction of the water and it is a major factor in the struggle to preserve the quality of life on the Chain. Whether it is the simplicity of two young boys waiting for a strike at the Alden dock, the rugged shoreline near Skegemog Point where a small girl relaxes peacefully, or a primitive dock where a young man enjoys the refuge of the upper Chain, these late nineteenth and early twentieth century photos attest to the need for secret spots, quiet places, and a touch of wilderness that offer the possibility of escape.

The BUSINESSMAN

1. Guy Dean
2. Lyle Paradise
3. Harold Wilke
4. Joe Yuchasz

"Handshake was ample.
. . . all those people were not makin' money every year,
but they had no trouble gettin' money
because if they said they were gonna pay it back,
they were gonna pay it back."

——Guy Dean

The Jennie Silkman, a sixty-foot tug, was owned by the Cameron Brothers Lumber Company at Torch Lake village. The boat often performed double duty by carrying passengers as well as towing booms of logs and wood scows. Built in Milwaukee in 1874, the Jennie Silkman spent her entire thirty-four years on the Chain of Lakes. She is shown above with a group of passengers at the Eastport dock, c. 1908. Below, the Jennie Silkman just off the dock at Torch Lake village with the Grass Lake tug at her stern.

Guy Dean

In the waning days of the Great Depression, Guy Dean came to work for the Farmers & Merchants Bank in Alden on the east shore of Torch Lake. His boss was Fred Aemisegger whose reputation for high ethics, honesty, and dependability made the bank a landmark institution. Fred was proof that a man's word should be sacred and that a handshake was a binding contract. During World War II, Guy served four years in the Army Air Force, flying thirty-seven bomber missions out of New Guinea. In 1945 he returned to Alden. Guy Dean eventually became president of the bank, now known as the Alden State Bank, and continued the Aemisegger tradition of compassion, accommodation and understanding until his retirement in 1987. Married to Leone Kinnison in 1942, they resided in Alden, raising five children: Guy Jr., Bob, Doug, Jeff, and Lori. I interviewed Guy, my good friend and former boss, in 1986. Two more visits added to the interview, the last in 1997. Guy continued to serve as senior member of the bank's Board of Directors until his death on December 17, 1997.

Guy, we're going to talk about your life in Alden.

You're not gonna talk about all of it [Laughs].

Tell us when and why you came to Alden.

I came here in 1938; my grandmother knew people here. I was a Traverse City boy and I finally got a driver's license; my grandmother didn't have anybody to bring her out here. Ol' Violet Aemisegger was some kinda shirt-tail relation to her.

I got acquainted with a few people. I don't exactly know how it came about, but one time I was out here and old Fred Aemisegger, he was the banker then, he said, "How'd you like to go into the banking business?" I said, "Well, I'm getting outta school, it sounds good to me." I came out here and started working. He was a real swell guy.

197

Fred Aemisegger

Got out here and started huntin' and fishin'—couldn't leave. Starvin' to death, but couldn't leave.

Why couldn't you leave?

Well, the beautiful lake, wonderful people, all the things that you really wanted to do. But you couldn't make a dime in the bankin' business [Laughs].

Did you ever think of leaving?

Not really. Only time I got close to leaving was when I came back outta the service. I'd been working for Uncle Sam, ya know; I was really rolling in the money. I purt near stayed in the service. That was the only time I thought of doing anything different. I'd been used to starvin' to death so long on that forty dollars a month I'd started with [Chuckle]. He'd raised it up to about a hundred when I got back out of the service. That wasn't much, but then it started gettin' better.

Let's talk about Fred. There aren't too many people now who knew Fred Aemisegger.

He was just a plain fine person. He was a man of his word. That's the way banks were run in those days. Whatever he told you, you could believe and whatever you told him, you better be telling him the truth, 'cause if you didn't you weren't welcome around him.

Can you think of an example?

Well, I've seen it. I wouldn't give any names—the families are still around here. When they let him down, that was the end—[Chuckle]—and that's the way the business was run. Accounts were run by rules and regulations. It's terrible now; it's just a dog-eat-dog business, but we still run a community bank—there's still room for it and we're locally owned. But it's a hard job.

Three was the top employment. We had an extra one in the summer when the resorters were here. Usually Fred and I ran the whole thing all winter—just sit there and look out the window most of the time. Everything was done by hand—had a couple of antiquated adding machines, the rest you posted by hand—all your book-keeping, savings and things.

Summer you got busy—had to work to beat the band—put in fifty, sixty, seventy hours a week sometimes. Couldn't hire steady employees 'cause you couldn't afford 'em as soon as September popped up. In the winter months you just didn't do hardly anything.

How were the chores—what was the division of labor between you and Fred?

Well, he did all the important work and I did all the unimportant work like sweeping the floors and filling the ink wells [Laughs], shovelling the snow in the winter, keepin' the furnace—throwin' the ol' coal to her. That was the way it started—janitor.

You were more than a janitor.

Well, I did all the janitor work, but I also had my little postings to do. You were jack-of-all-trades right from the word go [Laughs].

You started toward the end of the Depression. There must have been some awful bad times.

In '38 when I started working here, it was picking up then. It was a farming community; everybody was farming. There was nothing else here. You had Antrim Iron Company in Mancelona still going. The rest of the boys, if they didn't go down state and work for General Motors or Ford, they lived on the farm, fiddled around.

Of course, the resort area picked up and kept a few of the kids from going to the cities—and Lamina Tool came in to Bellaire and a little factory in Elk Rapids. That took a few off the farm but kept them in the area. The whole history of it kept going like that. Your resorts—now this is going to be one of the biggest in the United States. You can't stop it now. Got the Arnold Palmer golf course—there's Jack Nicklaus involved. They're just going crazy. Now, you get another little injection of skiing in the last fifteen years—that throws millions of dollars in this area.

Does that affect the bank?

Sure, it affects everything—gasoline, all your motels, restaurants—it indirectly affects the bank. You get a little lull in the spring and a little lull in the fall till the snow gets here. If you have a good snow here that means another ten million dollars.

The bank was one of the few to stay open during the Depression. Do you recall the stories of how that happened?

Well, I wasn't in the business during the Depression, but they had ample funds—assets and liabilities were offsetting each other. They had no reason to close. The money was available for the people. The bank had a reputation for being pretty sound and solid. They didn't panic.

The Alden ball team, c.1940. Bottom (l to r): Joe Day, Guy Dean, Ed Chapman, Guy Barber, "Tunk" Smith, Nelson "Gus" Shishler, Fred Day. Back row (l to r): L.V. Smith, Lester Smith, Albert Burfiend, Melvin Harriman, Gust Schuler, Robert Blissett, Ganzel Finch.

In those days, it was so small. The bank had a total footing of two or three hundred thousand dollars. What they did was they got cash together. A bank of that size had eight to ten thousand dollars around in the vault. That's what we were supposed to have. Fred blew that up to one hundred thousand dollars by getting it in from the Federal Reserve and other places. So he had this cash money laying there. Anybody come in and wanted their money, he says, "She's right here, you can have it" [Laughs]. That was his method of operating. There was no run on the bank. They had confidence in him. It was a private bank in those days—McPhail, Bloomer and Aemisegger—and all of 'em had good reputations.

You mentioned Fred's code of ethics. Was he so different or unique from most bankers?

Oh, I think so. He was a little more stubborn and believed that's the way things are supposed to be. You said something, do it! If you didn't do it, you were mud. I think he was more set in his ways than most bankers. Handshake was ample. Gust Schuler, "Dutch" Merillat [local farmers]—all those people were not makin' money every year, but they had no trouble gettin' money because if they said they were gonna pay it back, they were gonna pay it back.

I've heard similar things about Guy Dean.

That's where I got all my training—from Fred Aemisegger. Of course, a lot of it rubbed off with what I had in my own mind. So it stuck around for quite a few years. Now there's no such a thing—you gotta have everything documented, written or you just don't get involved.

Nobody's word is any good any more—[Laughs]—as far as the state and federal government's concerned.

200

Describe your attitude toward money. What is money to you?

Well, money's something that rattles in your pocket. When there's none rattling there, I get a little nervous, but other than that, money doesn't mean anything to me.

Let's talk about the lake. You've lived here overlooking Torch Lake for sixty years. What's your favorite view?

What do ya mean? This is it right here—just lookin at that lake—knowing it's there, that anytime you wanna to go down and stick your feet in it, or take a jug of Scotch and go out in a boat. You don't need to take your water with you, it's right there, its' clean and pure. That's hard to come by.

But that's why this country will always be good, right here in this local area, within fifty miles of here. Torch Lake, Elk Lake, they're private lakes. There're no big industrial developments around them. You can hardly find a motel on any of 'em. There'll never be this expansion like Houghton Lake and those places. Our Three Lakes Association isn't gonna allow it. In fact, they're gettin' tougher, which is good.

Guy Dean (2nd from right) with the crew of "The Eager Beaver," a B-25 Mitchell bomber. New Guinea, July 25, 1943.

201

Guy Dean's favorite fishing spot, Clam River and Clam Lake, c.1940.

They're gettin' meaner. They're gonna control these people. They're not gonna let 'em do these funnel projects where they buy one hundred feet of lake frontage and eighty acres of condominiums in back of it. They're gonna stop those, and that's what has to be done to preserve your water purity. In other words, you don't want too many people.

Describe the Three Lakes Association.

It's comprised of anybody on Torch, Clam, and Lake Bellaire. They're a bunch of hard fighters. They believe in preserving the water purity; they believe in preserving the Elk River Watershed. They were instrumental in the Grass River project and they're gonna keep this lake [Torch] in the shape it's in right now.

What do you think of the term "gold coast" that's often used to describe the region?

'Course everything is the gold coast. Where there's a lake, everybody's got a gold coast in their area. Torch Lake you could call a gold coast. The million dollar mile going into Traverse City's a gold coast.

If people who have property for sale will stop these developers from over-developing, there'll be no need using the word "gold coast" any more. They'll slow 'em down till it's done right.

You go into Traverse City now, every place that's on the Bay, they're stickin' up a two-story motel. You can hardly see the Bay anymore. But there's nothing you can do to stop that. People are getting a terrific price for those pieces of property. If they've got 'em for sale, somebody'll buy 'em. No, we don't want 'em here. That's why they're holding Shanty Creek and Schuss Mountain back—let's not overdo it.

Guy Dean in 1997.

Make 'em do things right, it holds 'em back. Of course, in many cases, no one knows what right is. So you have the DNR, you have everybody coming in tryin' to figure out what's right. When they develop these hills, don't let the sand all run out in the lakes. They don't know how to do this—they build holding ponds. They spent half a million dollars just tryin' to hold a hill there.

Besides all this, what's your biggest concern?

Right now, I have no concern. The only thing we have, maybe, is the influx of people—some people pollution, which is not the biggest pollution factor. People are very helpful. If one man moves his septic tank from the front to the back of his house on this lake, the next ten neighbors will do it. These people [Three Lakes Association] are doing their job. The water quality has dropped some, a little, not much. You can still drink the water. The water quality hasn't been bad at all.

It's people problems. You've got to have proper sewage. Bellaire's got a sewer problem. The bloom in Lake Bellaire—they're havin' some problems there. You'll see a slow, steady growth, but no big developments. It's organization—the Three Lakes Association is what changed attitudes. Showing them that you have this lake, keep it clean, you're the only one that's got that clean a lake, be proud of it. Torch, Elk, the whole Chain is very clean.

Where's the best fishing spot on the Chain—your personal opinion?

[Laughter] Well, Clam Lake probably. It's a little of everything there. Good fast-moving water. You get bass, pike, perch, all that type of fish. Lake Skegemog, it's a little too short—you gotta go back in those stumps. So, I think Clam Lake is probably the best fishing in the area. Elk Lake—you're gonna catch a few rainbow and a few trout out there, same in Torch Lake. As soon as the boats are off of Clam in September, you can go out there—people don't tell you what they're catchin'; they got their own fishin' holes; they don't even tell their neighbor [Laughs].

If you had it to do all over again, would you do anything different?

I'd do the same thing—maybe a little bit faster and a little bit harder, but I'd do the same story. Can't think of another place to raise five kids and live. I've just been very fortunate to be able to do it. I think that's the whole story.

I think I'm lucky. I went through some of the horse and buggy age, farming community. This was an agricultural state, now it's a big industrial state. I've covered a little territory. I'd like to see what the next fifty'd be.

One that didn't get away, c. 1909.

Lyle Paradise

Lyle Paradise was born on May 25, 1903 to Jack and Leafie Paradise on a forty acre farm in Milton Township, south of Kewadin. He is known as a tough, feisty, and unique character whose life was shaped by adversity and hardship as a farm boy in south Milton. Though Lyle was a businessman most of his life, his memories focus on his early childhood. He has owned Paradise Pines resort in Elk Rapids for more than forty years. This 1987 interview was made with Lyle at his cabin resort; I visited with him again in 1997. Today, at 94, he resides with his wife, Wilma, in Elk Rapids, a quarter mile north of the resort. His story begins:

There was six of us in the family. My parents were Leafy Moore Paradise and Henry Jack Paradise. In my younger days I went to the South Milton School, stayed with my mother and father on a small farm in the South Milton District. My dad was crippled up—he had a stroke when he was younger. He had a rough time; my grandfather helped out.

So my older sister, Rhea, and myself, we stayed with my grandfather and grandmother near Kewadin. I was in about the sixth grade, then I went to the Roberts School. I worked on my grandfather's farm. That was the next big farm after the Hoopfer farm. Farmers get up pretty early—back in them days, six o'clock. Milked the cows. I knew how to plow and drag and harness the horses. One time, we had

205

kind of an ugly one, just puttin' the harness on, picked me right off my feet and threw me up agin the cement wall [Chuckles].

After eighth grade we went down to Kewadin for examination. I passed my exam. My sister and I started to school in Elk Rapids.

Do you recall any of your friends or playmates?

Bussas, they were farmers; they had a better farm. Maurice Hoopfer, the Foxes. All of these people were, more or less, pretty well-to-do farmers. The Hallers. I went to school with Donald Haller. Went to school with the Bussa kids.

Some of the teachers I remember. One is Gerda Peterson. She married Charlie Anderson. 'Course there was Professor Fleming. He had a nice little cottage right at the Rapid River bridge. Truthfully, I learned one thing, it'll always stick with me. This one teacher taught us how to write. When I write a check right today, I follow that line. It sure done me a lotta good, I'll tell ya that.

I'll tell ya, one thing that pays off is to come up the hard way. I never had a nickel laid in my lap and I don't think there's another man around here that's done as much work in their life as I have. I've done more work than two men. Walkin' around right today and I'm still gettin' around.

Lyle as a high school student.

Do you think coming up the hard way helped to shape your outlook?

It sure did. To learn the value of doin' somethin' for yourself and learn the value of money. What it's like when your mother had to go down to the grocery store with eggs and bring back a little bag of candy to go around six of us kids. I had a mother that had to carry water from a spring to do washing for us. My mother used to take in washings, wash by hand.

Very poor farm. It was only a forty acre farm and the soil wasn't good. The same old house is still there, that green tarpapered house down the old clay hill. We grew corn, potatoes, raised just enough to get by, that's all. Had milk, just a small barn.

Before my dad died, he had to have that leg amputated; he dragged it along the ground. Young kids, they made fun of my father—I thought about that a lot of times. I was kind of ashamed, ya know. You look back and ya see where you coulda done a little better.

206

Describe your brothers and sisters.

My older sister, Rhea, she graduated from the twelfth grade. The youngest one was Alice—she passed away quite young. Then Joe, then Evelyn, then Raymond.

When we got a little older, I always liked to mess with cars on my grandfather's farm. He bought me a 1912 Model T, the first car I drove in my life. I was only twelve years old. I had to use cushions in back of me. Anyhow, we drove that back and forth from the farm to high school here.

Living on a farm, what did you do in your spare time; did you have much leisure time?

Oh, yes. I was always tinkering around with the Model T Ford, that's for sure. I guess I was born to be a mechanic. When I had any spare time, I'd tear it apart whether it needed it or not. My grandfather, Joe Parady, was real darn good to me. I'd take the car, come down and take a few of the girls out. There wasn't too many of the young ones that had a grandfather that was as good to 'em as my grandfather was, I'll say that.

When you came in town, do you recall the blast furnace in Elk Rapids?

Oh, yeah. Back on the farm, we used to always watch after dark—then they fire it up, the old flames would shoot up. I remember when we'd come to town back in the horse and buggy days—we come by the old furnace. The road was real close to the river then for the simple reason the big ol' sandhill was workin' it's way all the time. The furnace was right near the waterfront, had the ol' railroad bridge. I remember the white kilns they had. They had the Bee Hive where the men stayed.

I remember the logs. They used to float the logs down through the river. Right where that power plant is now was a sawmill. I used to get on a log, go up to that sawmill. 'Course the flour mill was right over there. The town was a pretty busy

The Elk Rapids Iron Company blast furnace, c. 1910. "I remember when we'd come to town back in the horse and buggy days; we come by the old furnace." —Lyle Paradise

old town in the daytime. I forget how many saloons, about four. I was real young, I can just recall.

You lived in between Elk Lake and Torch in south Milton. Did you get on the water much?

Oh, yeah. Purt near got drowned on Elk Lake. That's about as close a call—in fact, years back, there was several of 'em; one of the Haller boys and another man got drowned in Elk Lake.

My cousin, Floyd Hassett, and I, we used to like to get out just as it freezes over and we could chase fish down through the ice. Of course, we tested the ice before we got out. We went out quite a ways—way out. It just happened that we was comin' back

Iceboating at 40 mph on Torch Lake.

in towards an opening near the Hoopfer farm, where the grapevines are. Come up a wind that night, and the ice looked just as good as ever. I'm tellin' ya, I went down, standin' on my tip-toes with skates on. I was ahead a him—and broke through the ice. Zero weather. Anybody thinks they can swim with skates on, they're nuts. It can't be done. Anyhow, he scooted out to one side soon's I went down. I broke ice from there to shore. When we got up to the house, my clothes were frozen stiff. I've had so many narrow escapes—if anybody knew all the things that's happened to me. I've outlived a cat's life more'n a dozen times. I really have.

We did a lot of fishin'. We used to catch—darn good fishin'. I had a fish shanty and caught a lotta perch right near Kewadin, good perch grounds. We had these leaded spears. They'd hang with a hook. You'd have this hole about two foot square. I'll never forget one time when the fish wasn't bitin' good, we'd go out 'n do a little skatin' and come back in. I left my decoy down in the water. I'm not kiddin' you, I saw the biggest muskie—it just startled me. Boy, did I start workin' that decoy. Anyhow, he never showed up again.

We used to spear a lotta pike and muskies and suckers. 'Course, they's always suckers; when you couldn't get nothin' else, you see a bunch of suckers come along.

We used to be so foolish. We get to goin' around to beat the devil and jump over open cracks. That's no kiddin'. We used to make ice sails out of canvas— shaped like a kite, ya know? It had a big long wooden arm on it, dragged on the ice. Two of us on a good strong day—boy—that'd take us across Elk Lake in nothing flat. Probably going forty, fifty mile an hour. I'll never forget one time, I had a brand new pair of shoes on and we's comin' so fast on the way to the shore, we both set down on our shoes and, boy, it just tore our shoes to smithereens. Give us kind of a sore bottom [Laughs].

I worked on the farm for a number of years. I quit school in the tenth grade. During World War I, I went to Detroit. I was so young I couldn't get a job in a factory. I had a cousin, one of the Hassett boys, he was working in a restaurant— Walker Brothers Catering Company. He was tellin' me how much money he was makin'. Back in them days, bucks was bucks. I was washing dishes, "pearl divin'" as they call it. We worked twelve hours a night, seven days a week. During that seven days, we had a half a day off. In fact, back in them days, it wasn't too bad comin' from a poor farm, you had all the ice cream you could eat, and bananas. Right to this day, I ain't too fond of bananas [Chuckles].

Getting back to the north country, which lake is the best fishing lake of all the Chain?

Back in them days, really, Elk Lake seemed to be more populated. I know all about Torch though. I had a Chris-Craft boat. Years back before they was any cottages, I could go down through Torch River wide open.

Did you find your way through the stumps of Skegemog all right?

Oh, sure—and I got propellers out there now [Laughs]—I didn't find 'em. There's two of 'em still layin' around. When I'd hit a stump, it'd bend the drive underneath. But, you'd usually get back in.

You've seen a lot of changes in all the years that you've been here. Now the shoreline is almost all populated. What do you think is the biggest danger or problem to the water?

I think it's caused from pollution, of course. There's gettin' to be an awful lot of swan, now you've got Canada geese and all of the seagulls. I think that's a problem.

209

Truthfully, I've had septic tanks here—we're hooked to sewers now. I wouldn't be surprised but what they could do a lot of checking on septic tanks around Torch River. You can't tell me that some of that isn't gettin' into the water system. Lot of these old places weren't built properly.

You grew up in poverty in south Milton and you quit school, went to Detroit. Why did you move back here?

I came back after the war [World War II]—1949. These cabins—they were just shells. I started this from scratch. I've got this place now; what do ya want me to do—give it away? Nobody can take this away from me; I'm gonna take care of my little woman. I think some of these real estate people think I'll kick off anytime and they'll buy it for peanuts—that's about the way to look at it. But I'm gonna fool 'em; I'll stick around as long as I can. Nothin' scares me. You had to struggle and fight for everything you got.

Is there something that attracts people to this area, something that makes them return?

Oh, sure. The nice water—these lakes here are really something. It's a rat race in the cities. It's a good place to come up and relax—even if you have to struggle to get through life.

Anybody that's been around the salt water, around Florida—people that come from Florida, they can't get over the clear water. Friend from New Jersey came here, he can't get over the clear water. The water is so filthy around Jersey.

The Ruth and other lake steamers cruised the Chain when Lyle Paradise was a boy. Stopping at Rex Terrace on Elk Lake and other resorts was a daily occurrence.

210

Harold Wilke

Harold Wilke was born in Springfield, Ohio in 1902. He left his home town when he was sixteen and briefly attended Ohio State. He moved north to Detroit. Harold was always interested in electronics and has been a licensed ham radio operator since 1924. He was a radio operator on the Great Lakes when only Morse code was used. He drifted further north and by 1950 he was owner and operator of the boat shop at Torch River Bridge. Harold Wilke died in 1996. In this 1995 interview, in his home just a mile north of Torch River Bridge, he recalls his early life, his experiences at the boat shop, and, with modesty, the many lives he saved on Torch Lake:

During the Depression, I had a radio service shop in Flint. It was a nice hobby, but it didn't pay very well. I eventually got into the hardware business. But I always maintained the contact with radio work. At one time, I had two hardware stores: one in Flint and one in the little town of Goodrich. In both of 'em, I had a workshop in the back to repair radios.

When did you serve on the Great Lakes freighters?

That was 1924. They were from five hundred to six hundred foot bulk carriers: ore, coal, and grain. They were just starting to put radio transmitters on lake boats at that time. They travelled from ports on Lake Erie, Lake Huron, Lake Michigan, and Lake Superior. The longest trips were from Buffalo to Duluth.

The old time captains resented the radio operators because when the radio was on, the owners had their finger on the captain. Before that, he was boss of everything. He had to answer to no one—made his own decisions.

211

I was on the Angeline. The one I was on the longest was the Michigan—it was a six hundred foot freighter owned by Cleveland Cliffs.

We were in Marquette one time. These two captains had sort of a rivalry. Lake Superior was rolling pretty bad. This one ship went on out. The other captain said, "He can't beat me." So he followed him. We got in that storm out there and it took us twenty-four hours to go from Marquette to Sault Ste. Marie. I was at that radio trying to get location reports which were very crude at that time. We finally got to the Soo without any problem. That was about the worst storm I was ever in. I was new to the water. I'd never been on big water before.

Let's jump up to Torch Lake. In 1950 you came up to Torch River Bridge. Tell us how that happened.

I was very interested in buying a hardware store in Suttons Bay. That summer Doc Crow came to my place, he says if you want that place at Torch River Bridge, I think it's for sale and you can buy it. So I came up and bought it. Bill McCaslin was the real estate man.

I wanted to get up in the north country. I love the north country. I ran the boat shop here and the hardware store in Goodrich for two years. I bought this house about 1961. But I've lived right in the area since 1950. 'Course now I'm only here about five months a year.

Compare prices at the boat shop in the 1950s to prices today.

An eighteen to twenty foot boat for storage—I would take the boat in the fall, I would winterize it, put it up on supports out of the water for the winter. In the spring, I'd put it back in the water, have it all tuned up for the owner when he came to take it out—the price was forty-five dollars. Today, I think it's something like four hundred dollars for anywhere near that same thing.

Harold Wilke's boat shop at Torch River Bridge, c.1955.

We rented rowboats without a motor for a dollar, two dollars with a five horsepower motor for all day. I made a living, but I never made any big money—no.

Let's discuss the merchants at Torch River Bridge during the '50s.

Dan Way had a grocery store there—I don't think anybody knew how many poor people that he helped with groceries for nothing; he never made his charities public. Harley Rice had a grocery store; he was in competition with Dan Way. There was a barber shop—Bob Savage, the barber. He and I went fishin' in the wintertime. There was Nichols' Hardware.

Do you recall any accidents on the water?

One time, friends of mine were here in October—kind of a rainy, blowy day. I looked out the window here; I saw a sailboat out there. The mast was up and the sail was part way up. I couldn't figure that out. I figured it got blown out from somebody's dock. So I went down to the boat shop—we always called it the boat shop, not marina—and we got in a boat, came up here to get the sailboat. There were two boys hanging on that sailboat and they couldn't get in the boat. Everytime they'd go to get in the boat, it'd upset again. See, it was waterlogged. It was very cold and they'd given up. They'd already said good-bye to each other—they figured it was their last. I got there and got them in the boat and took them back down to the bridge. Their father was Doctor Brown over on Crystal Beach Road. Incidentally, I saw him about three days ago down at the bridge. He reminded me of that incident.

You saved their lives.

Yeah. Then another time, they called me and said there's somebody out over toward Alden in trouble in a boat. It was a nice sunshiny day, but it was windy and there were white caps on the lake. So I walked out toward the end of the sandbar—I couldn't see anything. I went back and got a boat and went out. I got part way over and I saw a hand come out of the water—it's all I could see because of the waves. Went over there, there was an aluminum boat, had two old people and their grandson with them. They'd upset and they were holding hands across the top of the boat—the old man and the old lady were. The boy was in pretty good shape; he was about sixteen, fairly husky. So I got him in first because I knew I'd have to have help getting the old people in. I got the old lady in the boat. She fainted right away. The old man was hanging on to the boat and he didn't want to let loose. I threw 'im a ring life buoy with a line on it, told 'im to grab ahold of that. We had to really talk rough to him to make him let loose of the boat. We finally got him in, and we took 'em down to the boat shop.

As we went past the gas pumps to turn around and come back, I hollered to one of the employees to get a bottle of whiskey in order to give 'em some stimulant. Got them back to their motel. They never even came around to thank me after that [Chuckles].

That's five lives you've saved on Torch Lake and you were no spring chicken then.

Yeah. It was quite exciting. I was forty-eight when I bought the marina down there. I don't know if you know it, but I'm ninety-three now.

Do you recall the marathon boat races that came through Torch River in the 1950s?

Each person had their own particular motor souped up to run these races. I never paid much attention to 'em, but I had a fellow working for me, a young kid, he was one of the best mechanics I ever had. His name was Heber Nothstine. He was active in the marathon races. His father was a dentist.

Let's talk about your customers.

I had one customer—I took care of all his boats—lived on Elk Lake. About two years after I retired, I was living up here. He made a special trip from Elk Lake, came up to the door. He said, "I just came up here to thank you for all the good things you did for me while you were in business down there." That made me feel pretty good.

'Nother thing that might interest you. That old bridge used to turn with a wooden key. I did that one year. There was a bunch of kids there to help ya—they just enjoyed helping. A lot of times a boat wanted to go through—there were no kids to help. I had to do it myself; I got tired of that. I got a horse and a half motor; I spent the winter figuring out how to electrify that bridge. I got it all figured out with reduction gears and everything. Morris Booth, owner of the Jedge Jr., said, "You can't turn that bridge with a horse and a half motor." I said, "Oh, yes, I can." He says, "I'll bet you a quart of whiskey that you can't turn that bridge with a horse and

Looking south on Torch River at the bridge, 1985.

a half motor." I said, "That's a bet."

So I got it all wired up with a reversing switch up on the bridge. I went up and threw the switch and it just went "uh!"—wouldn't move. I had to change from 110 to 220 volts, and that worked fine. The problem was that the resistance of the long wire coming from the electric service in the building out to the bridge was too great, but the 220 would overcome it. 'Course, like I told ya, I been working with this electrical stuff all my life. There wasn't any problem after that.

The first time Booth came up there in the spring, he blew for the bridge and I went out and threw the switch and it walked around nice as good be. He went on up to Clam River, he came back and tied up, came in and handed me a bottle of whiskey [Laughs].

How often did you turn that bridge?

I turned that bridge about three times a day. One Sunday, I turned it about thirty-five or forty times—that's when there was heavy traffic. When I came up here, there were only three boats you had to turn the bridge for. There was the Jedge Jr., another fella had a fishing tug, and a fella name of White had a fishing boat that wouldn't go underneath the bridge.

I can't see any reason for anyone having a thirty or forty-foot yacht on Torch Lake. It just doesn't make sense to me. If they had access to the Great Lakes, I could see it, but they're stopped at Elk River.

Were most of the people you served summer people?

Most of 'em were homeowners. There were a lot of people who would come up and rent cottages. It's hard to rent a cottage now.

The tourists are more demanding. I had a cottage down by the bridge, rented it for years. I don't have much good to say about renters. People would come in with great big Cadillac cars—you could see money there. When they left, the place was in a mess. You take ordinary people would come in here, maybe factory-working people. They'd leave the place perfect when they left. That was the difference in them.

Have you seen the quality of the water change since 1950?

Very much so. I wouldn't drink out of Torch Lake now. But at that time, if you wanted a drink of water and you were out there, you just dipped outta the lake and drank it. There wasn't anything to it. I think there's too much septic tank effluent going into it. Just too much pollution in there now.

When I came up here, there were three houses on Torch River. Today, it's all built up solid. Now you can go along Torch River and you can see a black oil smudge from the outboard motors.

215

There are a lot of myths and stories about Torch Lake such as it never giving up its dead. Have you ever heard any of these myths?

Well, I can tell you one true story. I don't remember what year it was. I had sold this fella a twenty-five horsepower Johnson, which was the biggest outboard motor you could get at that time. He was a schoolteacher from Cincinnati. He took that boat—they were doing some work on it, so he took the air tanks out of it. Then he and three other fellas—one was the purchasing agent for Chevrolet Motors, one was the mayor of Cincinnati—all four were summer residents. They went back across Torch in this metal boat toward Alden where their cottage was. The waves were pretty high and this one big wave hit 'em and slapped 'em sideways. The next one swamped 'em. Without any flotation, that boat went right down. The school teacher was a real strong man—he swam that long distance to shore. The mayor of Cincinnati, they found him clinging to some wreckage, but he was dead. Figured he had a heart attack. The fella who was the purchasing agent for Chevrolet is still there—they never did find his body. He's still in Torch Lake. [Roy McDuffie Sr and Joe Lambert survived. Al Cash, mayor of Cincinnati, and Jerry Haley of Detroit perished in this accident.]

I came up with an outboard motor looking for these fellas. I couldn't see anything. Then the Coast Guard came over, they dropped a string of flares, and that's how they found that one fella clinging to the wreckage. That's one of the true incidents of Torch Lake not giving up its dead.

See, what happens is that it's so cold that stomach contents don't ferment and form a gas that bloats 'em and brings 'em up to the surface.

Looking south as Torch Lake, eighteen miles long, fades into the horizon, 1985.

His widow had to wait seven years before she could collect any insurance because the body wasn't located.

You've been all over—Florida, boating on the Great Lakes—looking at Torch Lake, is there anything special or unique about Torch?

Clarity of water I'd say, much as anything, yes. The clarity and coolness of the water. I live on San Carlos Bay in Florida and the water there is—I don't say it's polluted, but it's not clear. The multitude of mangrove islands give off something that stains the water. It's kind of a brownish color.

You were born in 1902 in the horse and buggy era. If you had to list one major change or invention, Mr. Wilke, what do you think it would be?

I'd say the popularization of the automobile. I don't think there's any question about it. When I was a kid, maybe ten years old, I lived on this farm away from everything. It was two miles to the station depot. When the trains from the city would come out with relatives to visit, we'd hitch up the old horse to the buggy and go meet 'em. As far as we ever got from home was maybe five miles—that was a long way, five miles.

Television has had a detrimental effect on our lives, if anything. It's cut out sociability altogether where people used to have card games, neighborhood gatherings—that's all out anymore. For instance, we used to have a group up here in later years that every Saturday night we'd meet and play cards. It disappeared.

Looking back on these past forty-five years that you've been up here, any regrets in making the move?

None at all, no. I think the best move I ever made was to get away from that southern part of Michigan. I can't think of doing anything different. I've often thought if I'd gone all the way through college, I would have taken electrical engineering and I woulda spent my whole life tied down to a desk probably. I would have hated that.

The sixty-five foot Ruth stops at Skegemog Point Hotel before heading up Torch River to Alden, c.1910.

The Oddfellow, later the Ruth, cruises through Torch River Bridge heading into Torch Lake, c.1900.

Joe Yuchasz

Joe Yuchasz left the Detroit Police Force in 1945, the same year his dad retired as a police-man. With his wife, Mary Frances, and three children, Joe settled in the Kewadin area after World War II. He stayed until his death in 1994. For more than forty years, Joe headed the Northwestern Specialty Company, a construction firm that performed any needed building chore. Known sometimes as a hard-nosed, practical businessman who knew how to make a buck, or as a soft-hearted, generous soul who would volunteer his entire workforce for chari-table works, he was a pioneer in the postwar boom as it began to change northern Michigan. I interviewed Joe at his home in Kewadin in 1986.

Joe, let's begin by telling me how you happened to settle in northern Michigan?

My dad retired from the Detroit Police Department in 1945 and he bought a resort on Birch Lake. In the process of remodeling some cottages, I came up to help; I was between jobs in Detroit. To make a long story short, we never left. When fall came, we just put the kids in school and stayed.

Did you start the business right away?

We got the assumed name [Northwestern Specialty Company] about a year later. We started working right away, naturally. We did a little work for the church. Pretty heavy in mill work, made all our windows and doors. I had been doing that in Detroit, had a little cabinet shop there. So we just drifted into this kinda work.

Basically, you got here at just the right time, before the big boom.

Exactly—postwar. We can get all the business we want right now. We don't want too much. Everybody's accusing me of wanting to go out of business. Well, I do and I don't. I gotta have something to do. I have to have someplace to come to every morning at eight o'clock.

How many men did you have working for you in those days?

There was Joe Bussa—Don Swindlehurst worked for us for awhile and Roy Hoopfer—three or four guys normally for the first four or five years. That's when we found out there were no plumbing supplies available around the area and we put in a line of plumbing supplies and it went hog-wild. I had to pay sixty dollars a piece for toilets—that's what got me excited. Soil pipe was practically unavailable.

Friend of mine in Detroit made a connection for me with Norwest Plumbing—a wholesale house. I was buying toilets from them for seventeen-fifty a piece. They were B grade toilets, good enough for cottages. I bought fifty of 'em, and sold 'em for twenty-two fifty. They went so fast that I bought another fifty, and then I bought twenty-five more—I sold them. It was gettin' pretty close to snow flying.

I bought fifteen ton of soil pipe, sold all of that. Things were flyin' outta here so fast and I bought so much stuff off the company that year—I bought $34,000 of stuff and they gave me an adding machine and it's setting here yet. In fact, they didn't believe I could sell so much stuff, and I didn't even half try.

How do you account for such a shortage of toilets up here?

I suspect that—it was after the war—and all the guys come home from the army—all the farmhouses needed toilets. Three-fourths of the folks installed them themselves—we put a lot of 'em in too. We did a lot of plumbing work. We'd do anything—we didn't care what it was. We tried to be in the home building business, but we got into everything—plumbing, wiring. In the early stages—1955 or so—cement was such a pain in the fanny, we ended up buying a little transit mixer—two yards. Well, you couldn't do nothing with one, so then I bought a three yard. Then, if you got to mix it, how the hell do you batch 'em? So I had to buy a little batching plant—a used one.

Explain a batching plant.

That's where you put the gravel in and you can measure it out and drop it into the trucks. Then I finally got a four yard truck. We started a transit mix plant before they had one in Traverse City. As time went on, people started building homes and cottages and the cement business got bigger and bigger. About ten years ago, we sold it.

What do you do if somebody doesn't pay you? Ever had that situation?

Not too often. In the early days, we had a little bit of that. I talk plain English pretty much. If you sit down and talk to me, I ask you right out, "You gonna pay me?" In fact, I write a contract—I request a down payment and progress payments. The only time I can get hurt is on the final payment. By that time, we're normally friends. One or two times in my life did we end up on a bad note. I've probably done five or six million dollars worth of business here and ninety-nine per cent of the people are

A-l. You get a few dunkies that try to work you over and you stop them before they start.

When I was on the police department, I learned to recognize bullshit when I see it, and if I see it, I let you know I'm seeing it. What the hell they come here for?—they come here to get a job done, to ask the price and when you give it to 'em, they either nod their head or shake it. Simple as that. If they want the job, it means they wanna pay for it.

So, really—truly, business has been good for me up here. I lived a helluva good life. I didn't have to take any shit from anyone for forty years. I worked at different places in my life and every morning you're a son of a bitch. Every morning, the world's coming to an end—you gotta do this or you're gonna get fired. No one can fire me. In fact, when I kid around, I say "I'm the last son of a bitch that's gonna get fired around here. The last one!"

What's the strangest or oddest job you ran into?

Moving a building. When they relocated M-72 at Bates, the railroad bought a couple of houses off people. They contacted us to relocate the house, so we took the job. We bought a couple of big I-beams—ten by ten—wide-flange beams, fifty foot long. Slid 'em under the house and went to pick it up—couldn't pick the house up. It was so damn heavy, we ended up pouring concrete pads and jacking the thing up and had two big earth movers to pull and we just strained like heck to get it there. We opened up one of the walls to see why it was so heavy and the thing was solid brick. They had bricked in between the studding to fire-proof it. The house shoulda weighed twenty ton, the damn thing weighed fifty ton. But we got it there. That was the goofiest one. Coulda lost money, but we didn't.

Let's talk about labor conditions in those early days of forty years ago. How did labor practices differ from today?

Joe's fleet at Northwestern Specialty in 1955.

221

I recall one situation. Buck an hour was what we were working for—standard wages. Never forget, one time I was in a saloon, ol' Rollo Western came up to me and gimmee hell because I was payin' guys a dollar an hour. "Hell," he says, "you can get all the guys you want for sixty cents an hour." "Yeah," I says, "I can get 'em for sixty, but if I can't get a buck's worth out of a guy, I don't even want him on the job." We pay what a guy's worth. I want a guy that can put out.

Did you have to deal with labor unions?

One time they came through makin' little noises. A guy came to me and wanted me to organize my men. "Why the hell should I? You're the one that wants 'em organized—go out and organize 'em!" That was many years ago. We never had any trouble.

You seem to know how to handle these guys? Where did you learn your negotiating techniques?

Again, I learned on the Detroit Police Department. I was on the Department for four years. I was working right down in the good neighborhood—First Precinct, downtown Detroit—and if I didn't learn anything else, I learned to spot bullshit when I could see it, and I was hearing some, and I wasn't buying. As you get older, you can tell what a guy's feedin' you, whether he's pullin' your tail. Lotta people think I'm kinda hardnosed. I'm not really. I'm the easiest guy in the world if you're smilin'. You can con me out of anything.

We all worked together—like a big family. Nobody fought anybody—a plumber didn't screw around with the electrician—in fact, it might be the same guy half the time. The same guy that poured the footings was the same guy that put in the light sockets. No sub-contractors. You monkey around with sub-contractors, you had to wait until they get damn good and ready. This way I had perfect control.

One big happy family—you must've had a lot of loyalty. Is twenty-five years the longest anyone worked for you?

No, "Buck" Bussa worked for me forty years. He came right outta the air force—he never did work for anyone else. He tried the farm for one year and he didn't like that too hot. Top man. I think of the top men like Charlie Cole—worked for us forever. He worked in the cabinet shop for fifteen, sixteen years. He could make those windows blindfolded. He was not a carpenter before—he was a farmer. He made all these cabinets around here. All the drawers are dove-tailed, all the little extra things you don't normally do—we done all that. We ran all our own trim, all our casing, shoe molds, we run it all.

Instead of sending a guy home—that's one thing I could never do—send a guy home with a half a day—a guy could drill holes, something—even **you** could do that. If you went to college, it'd take a little longer to teach you [Laughs].

We're slowin' down a little bit. We had twenty-eight men at one time. There were nine houses under construction at one time. All that work, all of that baloney, all that effort, I can't say it wasn't good, sure it's good—we made money, but we didn't make no ton of money. I'll be honest with you, I make just as much now and I only got five guys. You just don't have the grief, the screw-ups—and we probably charge a little more too.

Let's talk about the lakes area we live in. How is construction different in the north country than in the city?

Well, when we first come here, it was all cottages—hell, everything you done—we built a house for $3200 thirty-five years ago—that was a classy, top job for us. We were a little independent.

Aside from all the cottages that led to a lot of business for you, in what other ways has the water—the Chain of Lakes and the terrain around it—affected your life?

Well, it's sweet and simple—it brought the people up that wanted to have a cottage on the lake. That's the dollar and cents side of it. It happened to be a helluva good area. Look on a map of Michigan—where do you get so much waterfront in such a close area? Everybody keeps thinking of factories or industrial, which I'm not against, except you don't need no foundry up here. Nice little shops we got here—naturally the cherry industry. That's just right for small areas; you don't need no damned foundry up here.

What's your favorite lake up here?

Well, I think Elk—Birch Lake is a nice little small lake. Of the big lakes, I think its Elk. Torch is a long, skinny thing—but it's so damn cold, you can never swim in it. Sure it's beautiful if you're standing on a hill and looking at it. So's Elk. Don't you think so?

If you had to do it all over again, would you do anything differently?

I'da done more faster. I was always nervous; I was always thinking I didn't have the ability. That holds you back a little bit. When you get to be forty, you get a little braver, and when you get to be sixty, you're braver than shit because nothing can happen then, you know? If I knew what I know now that many years ago, I'da went in full blast. In fact, I'da bought half of Torch Lake [Laughs].

I was offered Elk Lake frontage. I bought ten or twelve lots here [Birch Lake] for $450. For ten dollars a foot I could have bought on Elk or Torch. I said, "Who in hell wants to be over there? All it is is woods and trees?"

My dad and I went up to Creswell Road on the Bay. There was three miles of frontage for sale—three dollars a foot. We looked it over and everybody agreed. We called the owners, we find out they're a couple a bullshit artists—I coulda bought the damn thing for a second-hand potato digger and four dollars down. Now, I'da done that. At the time it seemed so fantastic, outta reach—three bucks a foot, and I know they didn't need the money. At that age, though, you believe it's three dollars, they mean three dollars. I find out later, three dollars is what they ask, they'd probably taken a dollar and a half. Three miles! Now, that I'da done different.

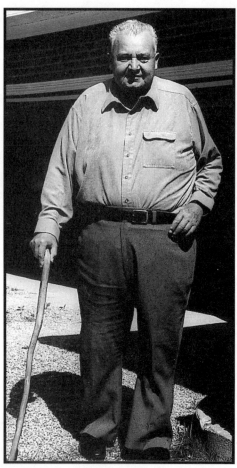

Joe Yuchasz in 1986.

The *SUMMER RESIDENT*

1. *Warren Daane*
2. *Ellen Moore Poulson*

*"The color—there are days up here
when the color is a color that you can't believe.
Perhaps you take a picture so you can remember that,
take it home and show it to friends.
They say, "That's not real. You've had it painted.
Nothing is that blue, no lake is that blue."*

——Ellen Moore Poulson

Warren Daane

Warren Daane was born in 1911 and first came to Elk Lake in 1925. His father, Gil Daane, a successful Grand Rapids banker, built a summer home on four hundred feet of lake frontage in that year. Warren became a prominent attorney in Cleveland, but he keeps returning. Except for a tour of duty during World War II, Warren has spent every summer here for seventy years. I interviewed him at his Elk Lake summer home in 1995.

Describe your first impressions of Elk Lake.

We knew nothing about it except that it was a beautiful lake, as was Torch. Torch was supposed to be a little better, more beautiful. It still is ... , but it certainly has changed.

In what way has it changed?

In those days we drank the water. We pumped it out—you can no longer do that. It isn't pure enough. It was pumped up into the garage, into a big tank there and then it came down to the house. It was used for everything.

We kept testing the water every year. Ten to fifteen years ago, the test wasn't so good. I'm no technician, but it just said it was not drinkable. So we put in a well—now we have well water and don't use the lake water for anything.

What do you think has been the greatest change up here in the last seventy years?

The increased population around the lake and the increased water traffic. There were so few years ago. Across the lake, the only one was Elkazoo Woods. That girls' camp up towards Skegemog—Chippewa Trail. It was run by Lena Morgan. My sister went there, as a matter of fact. I think Dad sent her there as punishment, but it developed that she had a better time there than she had here [Laughs].

Of course, these jet skis will drive you crazy. This is a quiet area in here, so the jet skiers like it. They're not cheap. I understand they cost five to seven thousand. It doesn't appeal to me. I'm not going to be riding them.

What are your first memories of the lake?

The first time I came up, we drove a boat up from Holland—probably eighteen feet long. It would go about fifteen miles an hour. I had an uncle and a guy named Joe Jessick from whom we'd bought the boat, and we had quite a trip coming up because the boat had two gas tanks. We started coming up the coast and we started running into heavy weather. We needed more gas—the pump from the back tank to the front tank wasn't working. So we came to a grinding halt. We threw the anchor overboard and the rope broke. I'm fourteen at the time; my uncle was nineteen. We went up on shore near Hart, Michigan and called the Coast Guard. This was in June of 1925 and it was awfully cold. It took 'em four hours to get us back to Whitehall. We came up from Manistee on about the fourth day. We sure were pleased to see the power plant where we were landing here in Elk Rapids. We finally made it.

They had regattas in those days and we put [the boat] in the regatta and I got the cup here now—showing G.L. Daane as the winner. It was a handicap affair and we won it in 1925. The big thing in the regatta was always the speedboat test.

Dad was a golfer. One of the reasons he agreed to come up was because the Elk Rapids Golf Club had opened about two years previously. At that time, it was started by resorters and used mainly by resorters.

Do you know who the people were that started the golf course?

The new Elk Rapids Golf Club, c. 1925.

Ferris Smith didn't play golf, but he was one that was in on it. C.C. Carver, the local banker, he was in on it. There was Frank Standart, he was pretty active. He was a resident here. Dr. Oughton, who ran the Keeley Institute for alcoholism down in Dwight, Illinois, he came up in the summers too and lived right on Elk Lake.

Bev Cary was prominent in the golf club—he was an avid golfer. Ben Marsh was active in the golf club. He was a very sophisticated guy, probably as sophisticated as there was up here. He became president of the Michigan Bell Telephone Company.

Donnelly from Toledo built a couple doors up, then Mort Broughton came along from Kalamazoo. Mort really used to run the golf course. I used to play golf with him and my father every day. In the early days they had three caddies—Tony and Johnny Pink and Lee Bachi. We'd generally snag the caddies.

Of course, there wasn't as much play then. It was open to the public, I think, for seventy-five cents compared to the ten dollars today. There were no electric carts—it was all walking. There were no pull carts, as a matter of fact. This was back in the '30s.

The Point up [the lake] here was owned by a fellow named Alec Park. Smilin' Ed McConnell* owned it at one point. He was very heavy—probably 250-300 pounds—and when it came to playing golf, he had a big Packard and he would drive this Packard around the course [Laughs] between shots. That's the only way he got around. No carts, but one car.

I used to play tennis with Willard Wilcox [of Wandawood Resort] and we'd row to town to get to the tennis courts. About the only town person I remember playing

Crowds gather on the shore to enjoy the annual Regatta on Elk Lake, c. 1925.

Spectators gather at the Regatta on Elk Lake, August 14, 1925.

with was a fellow name Bob Banninger whose father was in the shoe business.

How would you compare the village then to the changes that have taken place today?

It seemed a little more of a village. A village does have its charms. One of the things I always enjoyed was the horseshoe court. We'd go down the main drag in those days and we'd watch these guys playing horseshoes and they were awfully good. It was right next to the bank. I didn't know them, I just admired their ability to throw horseshoes.

I recall Frank Sobbry. He was the mayor; he ran a garage where Dick Palmer is now. I remember Roy Winters—he lived up here. The one-armed sheriff Asa Maxwell—I didn't know who he was, but you could recognize him.

Let's go back to your childhood in the summer here. Give me a description of a typical day for a young boy on Elk Lake.

I generally played golf once a day. I generally tried to work in a tennis game. Of course, work in a few swims. I've never been much of a fisherman, but on occasion I would go over to Stevens Point there—Smilin' Ed's Point—and pull in a lot of perch and bass.

At night I used to have dates with a girl down in Traverse—then there was Dorothy Oughton here. The place I went to the most was the O-At-Ka Beach dance hall. It was ten cents a dance. And the Rainbow Gardens [in Elk Rapids] which was five cents a dance. 'Course those were prohibition days—there was no hard liquor sold anywhere. I don't think they made much money, but it was the only place you could go to dance around here. It was live music. It was good fun, I can assure you of that.

I went to college in '28, but I was still coming up here in the summers. So I saw more of Elk Rapids than I did of Grand Rapids in those college years. There were four years at Princeton, then three years at the University of Michigan law school.

Let's take one last look at Elk Lake.

It sure brought me a great deal of pleasure and relaxation. I wouldn't come back if I didn't enjoy it. It's very peaceful—a getaway from the city life. I've been most happy to have been able to spend as much time as I have. I think Elk Lake is a beautiful lake. It's a great place to come for the summers.

The view of Elk Rapids that fourteen year old Warren Daane saw for the first time as he boats into Elk River, 1925. "We sure were pleased to see the power plant where we were landing here in Elk Rapids." —Warren Daane

*[*Smilin' Ed McConnell was a popular radio and television star of the 1940s and '50s. Hosting the Smilin' Ed's Gang on radio and the Buster Brown TV Show, his children's puppet show was famous for Midnight the Cat, Squeaky the Mouse, and Froggy the Gremlin. Smilin' Ed died in 1955.]*

Ellen Moore Poulson

Dr. Carl R. Moore, Chairman of the Department of Zoology at the University of Chicago, met his future wife, Edith Abernethy, at the University. Edith was a primary school teacher at the Chicago Latin School. In the late 1920s, they discovered Elk Lake. A few years later, Ellen was born and they brought her north. She has been on Elk Lake for the past sixty-five summers. In 1986, I interviewed my longtime friend, Ellen Poulson, and updated the interview with her in 1997. Her affection for Elk Lake is strong and she speaks warmly of the "sparkling water, dancing water."

More than sixty years ago you found Elk Lake?

Yes, I was brought up here as a baby by my parents. They had dreamed of a place that was peaceful and quiet—where they could grow their own food. They came up in 1927 and built the cottage, very simple as they called it a shack. I was brought here as a baby in 1932. The summer years—we came up around June first—so we had June, July, August and September here. We had no electricity, kerosene lamps. We had a two-seater outhouse. It scared me to death to go out during a thunderstorm at night. That was really overpowering. During the Second World War, I had a feeling that maybe the Germans were coming to America—I was afraid I'd be in the outhouse when they came with their armored cars.

What do you remember most about your father?

He loved to fish, he loved to play a good game of baseball, he enjoyed gardening. He adored nature. As a child, you think he's just "Daddy." But the bigger picture was that he was doing studies on genetics, studies of sex differentiation.

Tell me about your mother. You speak of her in glowing terms.

She's a gift to the world, one of God's gifts. She's a woman with high energy, high intellect, with rousing good humor. She used to write for radio—Fred Allen, Edgar Bergen—and we used to listen to the radio in the utmost silence waiting for her ideas to come through.

The garden here was a big part of our lives, and the apple orchard. We planted the seeds, we picked them and canned them and all the winter long at dinner parties, she would say "Uh-huh. This is food from our garden in Michigan."

She made us take naps up here—it always used to irk us—we would have to spend one hour in our rooms. She would allow us to take books in with us; we developed wonderful reading habits during that hour. I went in disliking mother and the hour, coming out loving a new book. She had reasons for what she did.

In a general way, let's talk about the impact this place has had on your life. For sixty-five years you've sat about fifty feet from Elk Lake .

Rarely did it sitting—it's been a very active existence. Our life is centered on the water. Certainly the lake has touched every day of our life that we've spent here. When I'm away from here—all of us, we take it home with us and it's a refuge in our mind. When I'm caught in the traffic, sometimes I close my eyes for a moment and think of the water lapping at the shoreline and long for the peace that we find here.

Let's talk specifically about some of the ways the lake has touched your life.

I like to watch its moods. When I wake in the morning, the reflections of the trees, the approach of a storm—right before a storm hits—very often the waves turn deep turquoise as the dark clouds approach. There is a wildness in the waves as the northwest winds whip the water into a frenzy. That's a favorite!

I think of it as an always changing thing. When we come up early in June, it's almost too cold to swim in, except one can freeze bit by bit and get into the water, then when you're all frozen it doesn't matter [Laughter] because you don't feel it.

I love the way that it warms up especially on the hot days when the sun is out. On calm days, the upper levels will be very warm. There'll be five inches of almost hot water and then it swirls. But down on the bottom, it's always quite cold. In August, it's just delightful—we used to refer to it as being a large bathtub. Then in September come the equinoxal storms. There'll be a hard blow for about three days from the north and we refer to it as the lake turning upside down. Suddenly, there's that one day when the cold water is back. You know swimming is practically over for the year.

You spoke of the marshes, watching the grass and weeds in Torch River.

Ellen and Harris Moore on Elk Lake, 1933.

As you leave here on Elk Lake—clean and sandy bottom—you go through the narrows into Round Lake [Lake Skegemog] which is clay and dark, with a great deal of silt in the water and you can't see down through it. But there are many, many weeds, and then to go into the river—again the water becomes quite clear and the seaweed bends in the heavy current. As a child, I always used to think of it as being many mermaids swimming underneath there, waving and undulating back and forth.

Elk Lake is just another lake. All of these things could have occurred on any other lake. Is there something unique about it?

Oh, no, no. Yes, Elk Lake is unique, it's not just another lake. When people in Chicago ask us, "What is it like, tell us about Elk Lake." We sometimes figure two to three miles wide and about nine miles long. We used the words "glaciated" and "spring-fed"—and you sputter these words out as if I'm gonna take a trip. But when you stop to think about it: glaciated. Think of when the glaciers were here millions of years ago. Spring-fed—the springs come out of the sides of the hills . . . and it is clear. Lord, help us, I hope we can keep it clear.

Elk Lake is special in my mind because I love it and when you love something, that makes it special. I suppose the history you have with something is very special. I've spent every summer of my life more or less here. It becomes part of you.

The color—there are days up here when the color is a color that you can't believe. Perhaps you take a picture so you can remember that, take it home and show it to friends. They say, "That's not real. You've had it painted. Nothing is that blue, no lake is that blue." But it is. You've Torch Lake, Elk can get just like that—colors of turquoise, colors of blue.

233

Ellen Moore Poulson, 1997.

Sometimes you can stand on top of the sand dune across the lake and watch the color change. If it's one of those days with cumulus clouds and the sun's going down, those clouds can scoot across and you see the dark shadows. You can see sandbars, then there's a drop-off—see the concentric rings of levels of color.

The reflections of light on the lakes are intriguing. I looked at it as a child—I love the ways the waves refract the sunshine. You can see the water in two ways: if you soften your vision, you can see the bottom, you can see the sand and the ripples and pebbles. But then on the surface, you get the refraction of light and if you can see both of them at the same time, you have a painting in your mind like Escher used to do. Sparkling water, dancing water.

I love the shadows in the lake, underneath a boat hoist where a boat is hanging above or where there's an overhanging tree. I like to see the minnows that come—they're always in a pattern. It seems as if they get a message all at once; they all turn one direction or follow in a circle or scoot away. I always wonder how they communicate with each other.

Petoskey stones—I always like to find them in the water; they're so easy to find in the water. If you look on the beach, you can't see them because without the water to bring them to life, they just look like another gray stone. But on a calm day, about eight or nine in the morning, to go in that water barefoot and find a Petoskey stone or an occasional Indian arrow—personally, I feel more natural in the water than I do on land walking. When I go to the water, I feel as if I've gone home.

Could this have occurred somewhere else? We're talking about that uniqueness again.

I suppose uniqueness is a coming together of many, many levels of something. The people that bring something to it, and the people who came here are very special. But I'm sure the Indians before us were special. Miss Morgan and Miss Simpler at the girls' camp [Chippewa Trail] were magnificent people. It's anybody who's loved the lake, they bring themselves to it. I think nature speaks to us, we are one with nature. We must guard it, we must not let it go.

Are you a different person because you've spent so many years on Elk Lake?

All the things that we go through in life add a certain quality to it. It's like making a good hearty stew—salt, bay leaf, hambone—and if you left out that hambone you wouldn't have that element. I suppose we're nothing but a pot of stew [Laughs].

If I'd grown up in Chicago and gone to Lake Michigan, there would have been the Lake Michigan quality. It's a beautiful lake—and those people who live in the high rises near it and get to see it from a different perspective have another quality in their lives. But they love it too.

Do you think it's in danger—the lakes, the water?

Oh, I think so. I think all these qualities of our lives are. When I find a beer can in the water, it makes me feel sick.

What's the biggest problem on the Chain?

Taxing of the lake properties. I feel like our property will be taken away from us because of the taxes.

I don't see a mowed lawn out here.

You never will [Laughs]. There's no lawn here. We want it to be natural always. I understand there are some portions [of Elk Lake] that are getting polluted. People feel that they have to have a lawn and then they put some fertilizer on it . . . and that gets in the water. I passed by Birch Lake yesterday and there were two or three people out with their lawnmowers. I closed the car window—I thought, these are the noises of the city. When we came here, all of us enjoyed a place that was natural and we've kept it as natural as possible. There are no fences, we have pine needles, natural Michigan flowers.

235

The Italianate home in Elk Rapids, known today as the Widow's Walk (above), was built after the Civil War, probably 1868. Italianite homes often have a cupola on a roof that has a large overhang with a deep, highly-decorated cornice featuring massive brackets. Shown here in an 1890 photo, it was built originally as a rectory for the Episcopal church (note the cross in the chimney). It served, however, as a residence for the Fitch Williams family during the latter decades of the nineteenth century.

Built in 1895, the Richardi House in Bellaire (below) was built during the 1890s in the Queen Anne style. Queen Anne homes usually display a variety of shapes and textures. Gables, dormers, chimneys, and round turrets are used freely. Smooth boards mixed with clapboards and shingles add variety. Shown here in 1905, the home attests to fine craftsmanship of the German workers of Richardi-Bechtold factory.

Both homes stand today as representations of fine architecture and shining examples of historic preservation.

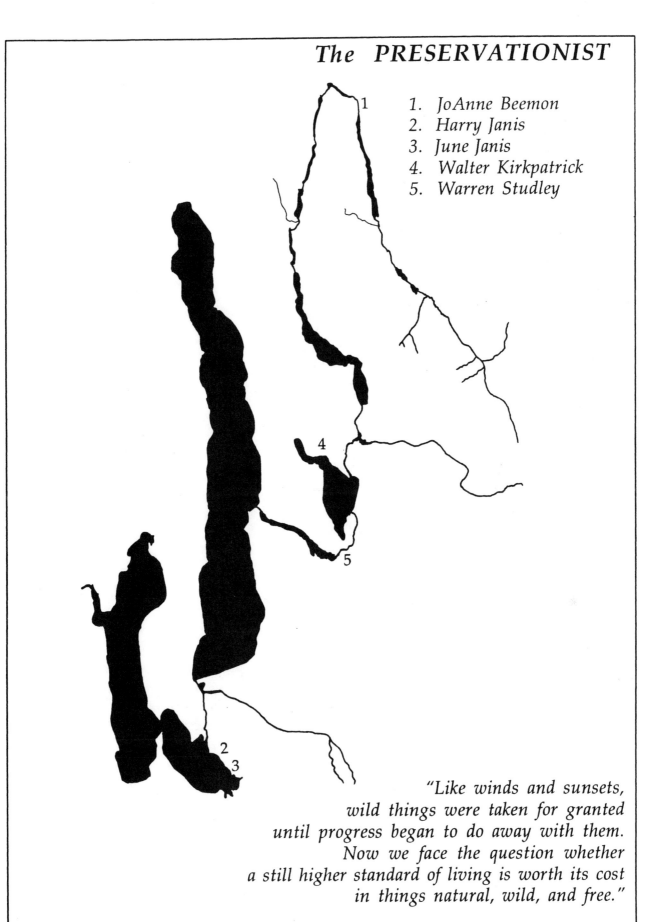

The PRESERVATIONIST

1. JoAnne Beemon
2. Harry Janis
3. June Janis
4. Walter Kirkpatrick
5. Warren Studley

"Like winds and sunsets,
wild things were taken for granted
until progress began to do away with them.
Now we face the question whether
a still higher standard of living is worth its cost
in things natural, wild, and free."

——Aldo Leopold

JoAnne Bier Beemon

JoAnne Beemon was born near Grand Rapids to Ray and H. Roselle Bier. One of eight children, she came to love the waters of the Grand River. Graduating from Forest Hills High School, she attended Grand Valley State University. Living today in Charlevoix with her husband, Richard, and five children, she is a teacher and Christian environmentalist. She is the driving force in protecting the St. Clair Lake/Six Mile Lake Natural Area. Near the northernmost point of the Chain of Lakes, the Sinclair River remains in its natural state, untouched, due mainly to JoAnne's passionate efforts. She was named Environmentalist of the Year by the Northern Michigan Environmental Action Council. We are sitting a short distance from the Chain in Ellsworth as I interview JoAnne in 1996.

You preserved this Natural Area with just a handful of people. The volunteers must be an amazing group.

We started off in 1993. When I saw this little area, I went to an established land conservancy, and they shook their heads and said, "There's not much money down there. If you're really serious, bring us $3,000 to obtain an option to purchase." We desperately needed them—they gave us credibility. We raised the money; we shook down our relatives and sold cookies and tee-shirts. We paid that first piece off—seventeen acres. We moved on to the next piece.

Describe the volunteers—who are they?

We have a retired Ford Motor Company man, Harold Shirey. We have an artist, Ron Tschudy. We have a writer and sales rep for a local newspaper, Cherie Hogan. We have a photographer–dreamer, Phil Ohmer, whom I absolutely love. I'm a housewife and a teacher and a Christian educator. We have another teacher, Michelle Nerone, and Mary Frey, editor at the Antrim County News. Then we have a retired school teacher, Betty Hoffman. Basically, we're people who care about a beautiful place on earth.

If you could single out one major issue that we need to focus on, what might that be?

More and more over the years, my focus has been on protecting the environment. For a lot of years, we've been called tree-huggers and crystal worshippers, but for me, I've never been able to separate who I am from my environment around me. Degradation of the environment was always personally painful. As I have learned on my own spiritual journey, I have become more aware. What I'm seeing is that we cannot spiritually disconnect ourselves from our world.

I'm kind of the person nobody wants around. The environmentalists don't want a bible-thumper around. They want to talk about species diversity and biological factors. Certainly, the church has been very relieved to be left alone by the field of science. The church has never really embraced science and still would like to think that the sun and the planets and the stars revolve around it—the Church.

The primal people have always known that we're all interrelated, that there is that God-spirit in us, that God is not somehow removed and we have to get in touch with that very inner-relatedness.

What I see as a society, we have a pathology of disconnectedness. We don't know who we are and we do not know where we're going. We had hoped for so many years that technology was going to give us the happiness in our families and the convenience of leisure time. All these promises—we put a lot of eggs in the technological basket. What we find is a society where we have become disconnected, where our time is filled with fillers like mall–walking and the drugs.

In our technological world, we went so fast, our God became technology. We worshipped at an altar of cost-effectiveness and profit incentive. We ceased to prioritize what was meaningful, what was moral, what was spiritual, what was becoming more God-like in us.

I think technology can be a wonderful thing. We have not prioritized the direction

The Sinclair River, 1997. "We have these fountains of life coming out of our ground that nourish us, that we can share." — JoAnne Beemon

of our technologies; we have not made them meet standards of morality or priority or spiritual wellness. We have worshipped pure knowledge. We're constructing super-colliding super-conductors while people starve. That doesn't make sense to me. The pursuit of pure knowledge is good if that knowledge is used for the betterment of creation, or the betterment of people or the betterment of our place in life.

We all seek to be effective, we all seek to be contributors and, in a way, we all seek to be creative artists. When we cannot be creative, when we cannot contribute in ways that feel good, we seek power in other ways. What we see is a generation of disconnected youth and it's not surprising. It's not because we are bad moms and dads, it's because we are disconnected from our earth and from our society and from our world. What we're talking about is: who are we? Who are we as people? What is my place on this earth? How do I live peacefully on this earth and how do I live with interconnectedness?

You mentioned primal people knew about this connectedness. Are you referring to Native Americans?

I'm referring to Native Americans, to Africans, to aboriginal people, peoples all over the world. You find these wonderful creation myths. What's so wonderful is that

The Sinclair River, 1997. "Every day changes, every day is a new day, every day is a new Monet." — JoAnne Beemon

they're so close to what science is telling us, that in the beginning there was created the heavens and the earth, and the earth was without form and void, and darkness fell upon the face of the deep.

Where did the dust come from? Where did the water come from? It's coming back to this understanding where the principle of uncertainty—that the more we know, the more we find out that we don't know. Somehow viewing things changes them. All things are interconnected; what we're seeking is that connectedness. Primal people knew that and felt that and ritualized that.

What's so amazing to me is that the great prophets have all had the recipe for full-ness on earth. That is: love one another, love the Lord thy God, and to live simply, to shun material things. That, basically, is your recipe for earth care.

One of the things that blows my mind about living is that when I think of this water right here—in places in Africa the whole day is spent going for water and coming back—we have these fountains of life coming out of our ground that nourish us, that we can share. The gift of life, that's what water's all about. They're coming right out of the ground and they're flowing, and they're full of life and they're miraculous, and they're good and they're pure and they're clean. It's a miracle. It's a sacrament to receive this. Life is a sacrament. When you start to live with that awareness of life as a sacrament, life is a gift.

The river that I love—when I think about it, I think of that place as a sanctuary, a sanctuary of God's creation. It's a place that feels to me fresh from God's hand. That

241

ever-renewing, that ever-changing, that ever-healing that water brings, that the Creator manifests that's revealed in those lush earth gardens—it blows my mind. These rivers are so unique in the world.

What is so unique about the Sinclair River? What was your reaction when you first saw the Sinclair River?

We lost a major battle to protect two thousand feet on Lake Charlevoix. I was heart sick, I was in mourning. My husband said, "Get in the boat, let's take a ride." Somehow it heals me to be outdoors. So we discovered that a river comes out to this lake we were on. We went into this river and it was like being pulled and embraced by all this wildness around us. As the sun went down with shades of pink and the sounds of the birds, it just seemed to me that all was pure and serene and good in that special place. We couldn't see anything, not one man-made structure. Everything was so fresh and pure, I didn't want to go home. I wanted that feeling to last forever. It was right there that I knew I had to do everything that I could so that my children and other people's children might be able to experience that someday.

You have compared it to the Garden of Eden and Walden Pond. Some people might think that's an exaggeration. Could you defend that statement?

Every day changes, every day is a new day, every day is a new Monet. One day, going into the river, a rain had just fallen. The wind before the rain had blown the pink petals of the wild roses down onto the green lily pads, and in between were white water lilies. It's just incredibly beautiful—how can anything be so perfect and so alive?

You call yourself a Bible thumper, but you seem to have reconciled your spiritual beliefs with

The wings of a blue heron lift it from the marshes of the Sinclair River, 1997.

242

your concern for the environment quite well; they seem to be very compatible. Why wouldn't the environmental movement buy into this Christian view?

I think it's starting to happen. What we need to understand is that what gives us happiness is not material things, but that we must love and embrace our physical and that also means that we can love and embrace this world around us and we have forgotten to do that. The time has come to come back to that. There's a saying: "If we continue on this path we've chosen, we will inevitably end up where we're going."

Now connect this to the Chain. To some people, this may seem a bit high-flown. They might say, "How do I implement this?"

I love to take children into the Natural Area. They come down and they're clamoring like little ducks and they'll be going, "Mrs. Beemon, why are we here? What's so special about this river?" They're throwing rocks at things—it takes children probably twenty minutes before they can see what's around them. They're so used to things being in a little box and all the words and pictures being right there for them. They have to stop and learn again to listen and see. Then all of a sudden, they start to be amazed. They start to see things move, and they start to see life.

We have to relearn how to see and relearn how to listen. What we want those children to experience is the miracle of God's creation and that God's creation is good. We were given a special responsibility to steward that creation, to till it and keep it.

I want my children to see the river and I want my children to experience the beauty of life and see a deer crash across the river in the fall. I want them to see the mink pull a fish out of the river and haul it back to shore, and to see the osprey and the eagle. Our children should have a birthright to see those things. Who are we to deprive them of those things for our convenience today?

I will know that we are starting to get well as a society when we invest as much in clean water for our children to drink, clean air for our children to breath in a sustainable environment as we invest now in things like savings accounts and second homes and college accounts. What we need to know is that this is the earth that must sustain us. We cannot love each other, we cannot love our children unless we create a sustainable environment—and we cannot do it the way we're living now. We have to make some choices here.

God did some things out of necessity, but the brilliance of the cardinals, the beauty of the waterfalls, those were given out of love. The world is so abundant with all those wonderful lovely things. Anytime we destroy a creature like a Piping Plover or a Spotted Owl, what we're destroying is the evidence and glory and the revelation of God's love. How could anyone choose to do that?

Some might think that this tiny strip—the mile and a half Sinclair River—in a chain of water which is seventy-five miles long—what is so important? Beauty aside—how can the quality of the Chain be affected by this tiny little strip? Take a look at that for me.

243

JoAnne Beemon stands at the kiosk near the shore of the preserve.

This is one of the longest untouched, undeveloped pieces of waterway on the entire Chain. It's a navigable river so you can go up and down the river. There are absolute worlds in that little river. There's the real dark shady spot where the cedars come over the water—they make little rooms. There are the open ponds, there's the lush ribbon of underwater garden. There are lily ponds. They change every week.

Everything is being developed. If it's on water, it's being developed. If we can save one little spot and one child can experience the awe and beauty of that natural community—I have known many people who have not been healed in churches, but have been healed spiritually in the outdoors. I want people to experience that awesome wonder of God and how they experience that is their business, but I want them to see that.

Part of loving God is caring for creation. How can you love God and destroy God's creation? Over and over in Genesis, God said, "This is good." In the story of the Ark, God didn't say, "Bring on the cattle for hamburger and chicken for drumsticks for your barbecues." He said two of every living thing. In those wonderful old stories, what we're being told, very gently, is care for all things.

What I'm trying to do is protect one little sanctuary. I think our world is going to change; I think we are in transition. We don't want to look at it because to look at it we might have to question capitalism, we might have to question how we live our lives in this country. Is technology always good? Do we need to seek knowledge constantly? We might have to say technology is not what's going to save us.

Describe capitalism in terms of saving the water here.

Who has a right to pollute and destroy our waterways, our wetlands, and our water for profit? Who has the right to put the poisons in the air that are changing species at the North and South poles?

We need to join together. I'm talking about a shift in consciousness to a point where we could no more destroy a beautiful wetland than the states would war against each other for water rights.

What do you say to people who say we can't stop progress?

We have to define what progress is. If progress is quality of life, do little packages of McDonald's and Burger King plastic toys around the house make us feel better? Does it make us feel better that we can now spend our money on a car that totally disintegrates in four or five years, or that we have throw-away clothing? The world is so full of stuff. We have all this stuff and yet we're empty inside.

If we got to know those wonderful ponds and rivers beside our homes—even the ones that have garbage in them—if we started to clean them up and we started to listen to them—I just see that we could be a whole new kind of society.

The Sinclair River, 1997. "This is one of the longest, untouched, undeveloped pieces of waterway on the entire Chain." — JoAnne Beemon

245

Harry and June Janis

Harry and June were both born and raised in the Chicago area. Both attended Northwestern University where they first met. Harry served three years in the Army Air Force and they were married in the last year of World War II. In 1957, they purchased a log cabin on Skegemog Point and reside in the area today. Both have been recognized for their work on the Lake Skegemog Natural Area Project; many awards have been presented to them, including the Keep Michigan Beautiful Distinguished Achievement Award, and the Chevron Conservation Award. Their greatest joy and pride, however, is their family: three sons and daughters-in-law and seven grandsons. Harry and June have been the driving force behind the Skegemog Natural Area. They tell here how it happened. This interview was conducted in 1995 with a follow-up visit in 1997.

To preserve seven and one-half miles of shoreline is an amazing accomplishment. How did the Skegemog Project get started?

June: It's not as easy a question to answer as it might seem. We both became involved in the Elk River Watershed after we moved up here in '66. The Elk River Watershed was formed through the efforts of the Three Lakes Association, the Elk-Skegemog Lakes Association, and Warren Studley of the Antrim Soil Conservation District. The effort was to inform people of the importance of the whole watershed and to include others than riparians in the effort to protect the waters.

One of the efforts we had was protection of the vulnerable areas. Grass River and Skegemog came up as two of the main wetlands in the area. Through Margaret Campbell and Warren and others, the Grass River project got started. Harry was the first chairman of the environmental group for the watershed; he, in fact, brought The Nature Conservancy into the picture for the Grass River project. We were going to wait for the Grass River project to be finished and then start work on Skegemog because the group couldn't do both at the same time. Obviously, it's a good thing we didn't wait because Grass River is still a work in progress.

246

How would you describe a watershed?

June: It's like a basin where all the liquid that comes down on to it goes to one spot and comes out. In the case of the Elk River Watershed, it all comes out at Elk Rapids into Grand Traverse Bay.

Harry: That's where the original concept back in the '60s came from—the first watershed council—from the fact that the water flowing by Elk Rapids can come from miles away because it's in the same watershed. The whole watershed determines what the rest of it is. Anything that starts upstream is going to wind up here.

June: Including Ellsworth and that pollution from the steel mill which is no longer in operation.

What was happening with Skegemog that prompted you to get involved? Was there a need that was felt?

Harry: In the early years when we were summer people here – from the mid-50s until we moved here permanently in 1966 – we lived on Skegemog Point on what was then Round Lake, now Lake Skegemog. We always looked at the swamp and we said how wonderful that all this is wild and will always stay that way. However, they were starting to fill from both sides into the wetlands, in some instances in a very poor way. Regulations were very lax at that time. What really got it going is when they put a road through with the permission of the DNR and put in a huge amount of fill for two homesites right in the middle of the swamp. Subsequently, a trailer went up on one of them and we knew that it was not going to stay wild forever. We had always hoped it would. That was the reason for starting something to try and save the swamp.

I started out by making a list of everybody who owned property in the swamp. Of the three thousand acres, about one half was state land, the rest of it was in twenty-two private holdings. I wrote a letter to each one stating what our goals were and asking for cooperation and comments. I got nothing back. June said, "That's not the way to do it; it has to be done by personal contact." She started out to do it. She was the one that had all the optimism that this really could be done—that you could bring twenty-two separate parcels together into one entity—three thousand acres! It's now almost entirely in a protected status and there are seven and a half miles of uninterrupted shoreline that is forever wild and protected.

June: It was the days before computers and instant communications. Earl Dunn, who was chairman of the Elk River Watershed at that time and became first chairman of our group, went to the Kalkaska County records and got detailed up-to-date records of who owned what. A great deal of effort was getting sponsorship and recognition and approval because if you just went to a private property owner and said we want to buy your land, they'd say, "What do you want it for and what's up?" So we were very lucky in getting involved with The Nature Conservancy in Michigan.

247

We also worked with the State Natural Resources, the Forestry and Wildlife, particularly the Wildlife Division, because part of the land was already in their ownership and the land that we would acquire would ultimately go to the State and it had to have their approval. Then we got the approval of the Soil Conservation District and the various counties. The final three sponsors were Elk-Skegemog Lakes Association, Kalkaska Soil Conservation District and Clearwater Township—they were our three primary sponsors and they have always been very helpful.

There must have been some huge obstacles aside from just getting responses from letters. The cost comes to mind as one obvious obstacle. What was the total cost of acquiring the land?

June: It was in the hundreds of thousands. Our first fund drive was in '76.

Harry: It was in excess of $300,000. This was a major obstacle. The Nature Conservancy was willing to lend us the money, but ultimately it would have to be paid back. The money came from two sources; over a period of time we developed a strong following for this project and a regular newsletter and occasional meetings brought together a large group of people, mainly riparians. Over a period of time, the number that contributed was somewhere between two to three hundred. About $90,000 was raised over a period of years from this source. The rest of it came from the Michigan Land Trust. June and I and a couple of others made a presentation to put before them. After that it was much easier to get grants. Throughout the history of the swamp project this has been the mainstay of our funds. It finally got to the point where the DNR, with the help of The Nature Conservancy, automatically filed when we had a need and it became a lot simpler. But that first one was a big task, putting together a presentation for them.

June: Also the $90,000 was used as matching funds. The Land Trust usually required matching funds and so when we acquired land through private contributions some parcels were turned over to the State as part of our matching funds. So we didn't retain any of the property or cash.

We were lucky in the timing. We should have started earlier when land was even cheaper—we could've gotten more as contributions from landowners. But we were lucky in that we got the project going before the prices went up the way they are now.

Were you paying the full assessed value of this property?

June: Usually it was the appraised value. There was never any condemnation, it was always through contact with people who had property for years and weren't going to do anything with it. Others wanted to see their land preserved. Society's attitudes were good and laws were just emerging in the '70s that supported environmental efforts. It could be very different now.

Did all of the twenty-two owners agree to come into the project?

June: It was piece by piece. Our first property that we acquired was Stella Copeland's. It was so very exciting to have actually acquired something. Acquiring the railroad right-of-way took years. Without The Nature Conservancy, so much of it would have been impossible. I just can't overemphasize the role that they played.

Would you identify them as the key organization?

Harry: Oh, yes. Tom Woiwode who's been the director of the Michigan Chapter for many years now has been just splendid. There were many people throughout the life of this project who were part of it and helped—they helped a lot. It wasn't something that could be done by any one or two individuals. It was a group effort of many people. June was certainly the catalyst, but it was an effort that was shared with many, many people.

June: The Audubon people were great. Elk-Skegemog members were just super. Warren Studley, Ford Kellum from Audubon, Bill Arvison, June Mason, Dr. Bill Scharf, the Frenchs. There were always people who were there and shared their knowledge and interest. A.V. and Emmie Williams from Audubon. From Elk-Skegemog there were Mark Sammon and Earl and Lorraine Dunn. There were Paul and Delphine Welch, Warren Goodell and Ed Krigbaum, also Esther Amidon of Clearwater Township was very helpful.

Harry: A Clearwater Township official who gave us a great deal of help was Bill Hecker. He used to be a junior high teacher in Traverse City. He lived on the edge of the swamp and he was one of the very few people who was intimate with it. He loved the swamp. He could go through it on firm ground that he knew. For most people to go into the heart of the swamp it could be quite dangerous. But he would go through there at any time of year. He was also very helpful with Clearwater Township contacts.

June: I miss so many of the people we've worked with. You just can't measure it. Some of the garden clubs contributed funds; Elk-Skegemog Lakes Association contributes to the annual maintenance, and they have six hundred members. When you think of the number of people who cared, it's endless and exciting.

Do you have an ongoing organization now?

June: The organization is still functioning, but since the land acquisitions, opportunities have diminished. The need for massive fundraising passed, so the urgency is gone. We meet now just twice a year. The State DNR people and the Forestry people are responsible for maintaining it with the direction of Wildlife. They've been super in keeping out the garbage and motorized vehicles.

When you mentioned Clearwater Township, it would seem in some cases the local government would fight the acquisition of such property for a preserve.

Harry: Clearwater Township and Kalkaska County were very cooperative. The thing that is key for the future is the master plan for the management of this area. It was drawn up with specifications; there would never be any motorized use; there would never be any roads into it. The only thing permitted would be perimeter parking areas. There would only be marginal cutting of the area, strictly for wildlife purposes. This was set in a plan approved and signed by the Natural Resources Commission. There will always be a need for a continuing committee because we want to be sure that the tenets of this plan are carried out. The DNR has certainly been very, very cooperative. Denny Vitton, the local forester, attends all of our meetings—he offers a lot of input and he's been helpful in getting some of the summer help programs for the boardwalks and trails that have to be maintained.

An interesting thing that was done a number of years ago by committee members, the DNR and Dr. Bill Scharf, then head of the Biology department at Northwestern Michigan College, were two signs at a lookout off of M-72 describing the swamp and its topographical features from the highlands to the lowlands.

What did you find in the way of wildlife and plant life when you went in there?

June: The present walkway, using the old railroad right-of-way, was done with Denny Vitton and Bill and Pat Huxtable who were just a tremendous help on this. The goal was to provide access and not damage the land. There are creeks that go through with marsh marigolds, fern, and moss. My expertise is in trying to find people who know what they're talking about. I make no pretense at identification as such. The walkway was done in a beautiful way. Denny Vitton designed the type of fiberglass matting and wood chips in areas where you didn't need boardwalks; boardwalks can be expensive to maintain. Also, the use of fiberglass matting and wood chips allows the flow of water without hindering the hydrology. The final platform at the end, which is really floating, is in an amazing area.

Harry: The other access point is off Torch River Road. That was the estate land of Rudolph Zabel who owned the mouth of the river and most of the north shore of Skegemog. The old boathouse was there. Paul and Delphine Welch—she was the granddaughter of Zabel—negotiated a special price with the estate to buy this land. The boathouse was torn down at their request and a platform was put there.

The third trail initiated a major celebration with several hundred people attending. We finally acquired the two filled-in sites of the lakeshore and the trailer was removed. There was a two-track road which is now a foot trail. These three are safe places where you can get into the swamp and appreciate it.

June Mason, a Traverse City naturalist, compiled the plant list and Dr. Bill Scharf, who is nationally known for his work in gulls, was the bird man—he identified a number of species. We have animals as large as black bear in the swamp, and otters and beavers. There are osprey and we've had an eagle family for a long time.

You've had a fair amount of success, June. What particular skill is required?

"The goal was to provide access and not damage the land." —June Janis

Visitors are encouraged to stay on the boardwalk.

Looking west to Lake Skegemog.

"If you step in the wrong place you're just going to sink." —Harry Janis

"Just looking out at the water; the waters in this Chain of Lakes are very unique . . . We need the swamp!" —Harry Janis

"There's more to life than just green lawns. There's so much of nature that's beautiful on its own." —June Janis

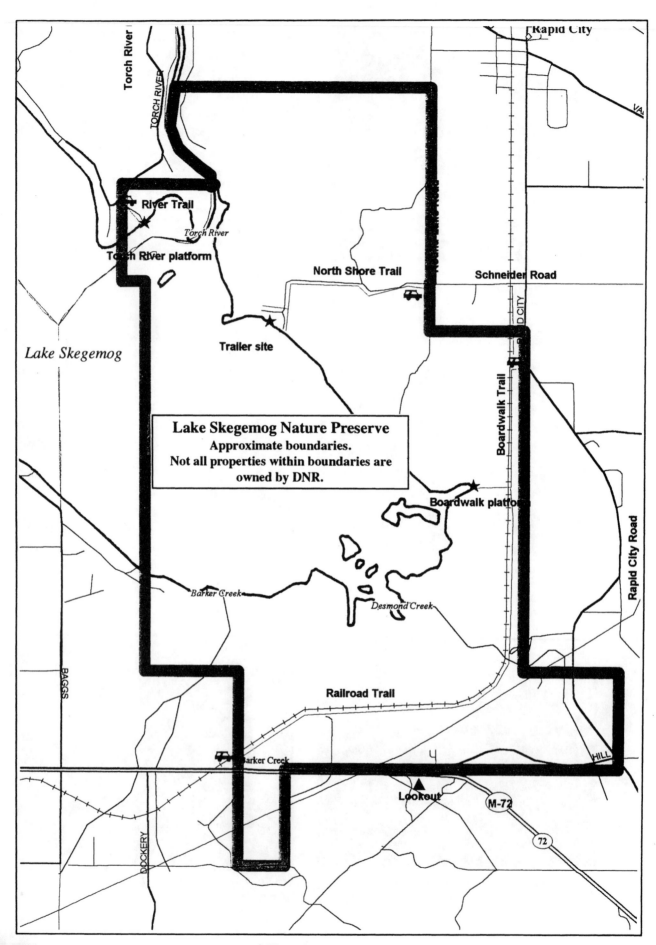

Lake Skegemog Nature Preserve
Approximate boundaries.
Not all properties within boundaries are owned by DNR.

June: The interest. The experience of working with individuals in government at all levels makes you realize that they are just people, limited by their own legal restrictions and interests. Having the back-up of individuals in the community and organizations, so they know you weren't just some nut out on your own. That it was a good cause. I found it was easier to work with people in Lansing because they had authority to act. Local officials, well-intended as they might be, can be very limited as to what they can do as individuals. They must wait for approval from those who are higher-up.

There have to be compromises; you can't have it all your way. But if you start out with high goals, you have something to compromise down to.

Harry: June was head of a five hundred member League of Women Voters in Illinois; she was also on the Michigan State Board. She had a wealth of experience in dealing with political people.

Let's go back to the beginning. When you first looked out across that swamp and realized that it was going to be developed, did you have a vision of what you were headed toward—the size, the purpose?

June: The main goal that the committee had was to protect the integrity of the whole area. As far as development, boardwalks, education—I don't think any of us had any grand plans for it. We had many discussions on the future and the final decision was to try to keep the area free of "people impact." If you start improving the area, you change it.

What are the consequences of all this, the unanticipated effect of what you were doing?

June: It's sort of amazing to me to be used as an example of what can be done because when we were doing it, we certainly didn't think of our efforts as an example for conservation. We were very concerned about something that involved us locally as well as the whole community and the whole state. We think it is a very special area. We don't think of ourselves as being trailblazers, but between the Elk River Watershed and the Grass River and Skegemog, I think we were there early. People often have a great desire to save their backyards.

Harry: Going back to when this first started, there were not many organizations set up that could do something like this. We had previous experience with The Nature Conservancy in Illinois, but it wasn't set up in Michigan yet. But we knew what they could do. Probably the most daunting part of it, when we first looked at this and realized that even with the comparatively low prices for swampland, it would take hundreds of thousands of dollars. June was always the optimist; I wasn't as optimistic. My lord, there's twenty-two private parcels here. Where on earth are we going to get those kind of funds? June said,"We will." We did and she did.

On the seven and a half miles of shoreline, there is no dwelling of any kind. It's all in a wild state.

"On seven and one half miles of shoreline, there is no dwelling of any kind. It's all in a wild state." —Harry Janis

Describe the danger of going in there.

Harry: There is quicksand in many places where, if you step in the wrong place, you're just going to sink. There never have been any tragedies, though over the years—during hunting season this a very popular place for deer—you hear about having to go in for a helicopter rescue because the hunters have gotten lost.

June: You can't keep people from going in on state land, but our committee is trying to avoid responsibility for encouraging people to go in. This is the beautiful part about the railroad right-of-way. It may not be the most exciting way, but it's the safe way of seeing the property.

We haven't mentioned the Massassaugas—the rattlesnakes. We've never seen one except when we were with George McDuffie, the local "snake man."

The word "swamp" has, to a lot of people, such a negative connotation. If I were to go there today, what do you want me to see and enjoy?

June: You can appreciate quiet. You can see the various pines, tamaracks. You can look at all the undergrowth, the spaghnum moss, the ferns, labrador tea. The cedar. The beauty of the shapes are just exquisite.

In the creeks, just to see what it was and what it should always be. There's more to life than just green lawns. There's so much of nature that's so beautiful on its own. Everybody who goes will see their own thing.

Harry: It's a great birding place. Starting in spring, you'll have a lot of wildflowers—the orchids, the lady slippers will be out. A multitude of other flowers later in the summer. There're fall colors particularly from the viewing platform at the end of the boardwalk. You get a wonderful look out over the bayous and Lake Skegemog and the narrows going into Elk Lake. Also, this is a planned and popular area for cross-country skiing in the winter.

Are you perfectly content with the success of the project? Is there anything today that bothers you; is there some fear or concern?

Harry: Not really. The DNR has been very cooperative in following the guidelines. They plan on a wildlife cutting every ten years. The one done seems to be reasonable and not very large. If there's any apprehension at all, it's that a citizens' committee always has to stay involved because you never can tell what happens with state politics in the long run and whether they will carefully follow the guidelines or whether they will try to change it.

June: Of course, there's always a chance that they'll decide to sell it to private people. The pendulum swings as far as environmental issues go. We've always taken for granted, the last few decades, that people would always care about the environment—that protection and various regulations would always exist and that people would honor them. Nowadays, there's always the threat, not necessarily government budgets, but from individuals. You don't know. All you can do is keep your fingers crossed and keep vigilant.

Harry: There's a new tendency in government to reverse some of the laws that have to do with wetlands. This could be a real hazard anywhere wetlands are involved.

Your work with the preserve here is more far-reaching than one might imagine. You've affected the water at the east end of Skegemog, and that all flows into the rest of the lower Chain and into Elk Rapids.

June: One of the important things for the riparians is the water quality; the swamp acts as a sponge to help prevent flooding. All the plants help purify contaminants coming down. So there're many selfish reasons for doing it. The easy, glamorous part, strange as it may seem, was the acquisition of land. You can touch it and see it and smell it. But maintaining an interest in protection and stewardship is a harder thing. Selfishly, I'm glad we don't have too many man-built structures to maintain.

Harry: There are so few wetlands left. It is so highly important that what is left be protected. They do so many good things in water purification, fish spawning habitat, animal refuge, nesting and fly-by areas. The old philosophy of years ago: "It's a wetland, let's fill it in"—that's what happened to most wetlands in the United States. The very tiny amount that's left is a valuable resource that we should do everything possible to protect.

Just looking out at the water—the waters in this Chain of Lakes are very unique. There are not many areas where you have such great clarity. In Torch and Elk, the wonderful colors, it changes all the time. We need the swamp!

June: Personally, I just think it's important for individuals to realize that they're not going to take their land with them to the grave. "This is my land. I can do what I want with it." It's not so! You can't take it with you. What you leave behind is what you're remembered for—or maybe even better, forgotten for. As we live on the land and water, we have to remember: We're just visiting.

We're on the west side of Skegemog Point; we're looking in the wrong direction, we're looking west. It points up the generosity of your efforts. You have no personal gain.

June: Oh, we do. This is our foot in the door of heaven [Laughter].

Harry: ... and it's where we live.

Lake Skegemog is the dark body of water at the lower left. The Nature Preserve is identified by the jagged shoreline at the bottom and running along the right (east) side of Lake Skegemog to Torch River. Notice Skegemog Point (left), a peninsula which creates the "narrows" connecting Lake Skegemog with Elk Lake (left center). Grand Traverse Bay is seen in the upper left and Torch Lake is seen in the upper right.

Walter Kirkpatrick

Walter Kirkpatrick was born in 1908 on the family farm one mile south of Rapid City. His parents, D. Reid and Estella Kirkpatrick, settled in Kalkaska County in 1901. Walter spent his entire adult life employed in northern Michigan. His first job was as a Dairy Herd Improvement tester in Leelanau County. After graduating from Michigan State College, he became Antrim County Agricultural Agent (as County Extension Agent) from 1938 until 1968. His life has been devoted to serving the people of Antrim County, especially the farmers. He has always lived close to nature and he has a personal and intimate knowledge of the land and water. Today he lives with his wife near the western edge of Bellaire. He begins his story in this 1997 interview by describing life on the family farm:

We had about 160 acres, had about fifteen dairy cows, had an orchard, some cherry trees—we used to ship cherries by train to the old Central Lake Canning Company. In those days, everybody grew a few acres of potatoes for a cash crop. The only trouble was in the fall when you had your potatoes harvested, you often didn't have any cash [Chuckles]. The price was maybe ten cents a bushel.

When I grew up we had "potato vacation." Every school in the county and northern Michigan had from one to four weeks of "potato vacation"—potato harvest. The children were needed for help. Potatoes were dug by hand, had to be picked up by hand. That was the source whereby many families in the towns earned enough money to buy winter clothes for their children. It was automatic, everybody raised potatoes. The pay for picking potatoes was normally two cents per bushel—you could pick one hundred bushels a day. The "potato vacation" was part of the curriculum, part of the life-blood of the community.

There were six of us children—three boys, three girls. We went to school in Rapid City. We walked a mile to school and a mile back every day. We had folks there that walked four miles. The Ruttan boys from northeast of town walked four miles in, four miles out every day. Every one of 'em graduated. We didn't need physical exercise provided by the schools in those days—we all got our exercise walking to and from school in the early 1900s.

This part of the state was opening up. Agriculture was the only occupation in those days. Land was cheap. We had a lot of native hemlock—twenty-five, thirty inches in diameter. Great beautiful logs today. Originally when the land was lumbered there was no value to the hemlock except the bark for tanning—it has a chemical called tannin. They barked 'em, sold the bark for tanning; they shipped it to Boyne City tanning factory. Hides were shipped from South America by the carload, they'd tan 'em. On one five acre piece, my father had twenty-six decks of logs high as you could put 'er with horses and just burn 'em up—clear the land off—get it ready to till.

As you talk about those days with a smile on your face, a thought comes to mind: Were those days the good old days?

They were good. You lived close to nature. Farming was largely subsistence farming—you grew practically all your food. Some people took their wheat to the flour mill. But you could buy the flour and the sugar and a few other things of life and you lived pretty good. Chickens, hogs. We didn't have any government bureaucracies around to tell us how poor we were, livin' below the poverty level. I imagine everybody lived below the poverty level. But actually, poverty isn't how much money you take in, it's how you spend what you have, and how you do with what you have.

Were the Kirkpatricks considered to be successful farmers?

I think so. He was looked to by people in the neighborhood as a successful farmer. My father was one of the early farmers to grow alfalfa and use purebred dairy sires; we had one of the better herds in the area. Up to that time, timothy was the big crop. Of course, timothy didn't have much protein for a dairy cow.

I've heard it said that farmers, because they're so self-reliant and solve so many of their problems, are the last geniuses on earth. Looking back to your life on the farm, does that make any sense to you?

Yeah, because if it was available, you didn't have the money to buy it. The old saying is "Necessity is the mother of invention." I have a hunch that I've seen more new things developed on the farm than anyone else, and then industry takes 'em over. Commercial outfits take the plan and kinda smooths 'em up a little bit and charge twenty times more, and you're in business. I've seen right here in this county—a stone picker. You picked stones by hand, but Orville Walker, Tom Coulter—they put together old potato diggers and put the tractor on 'em when the tractor became available in the early '30s and '40s, started pickin' stone mechanically. Jay Williams of Bellaire put together what was the very first "Trashy Corn Planter." Herb Reilly put together a very early mechanical tree planter.

Another genius: Bev Veliquette of Kewadin. Well, the old saying goes "If you want to have something done, if it isn't available now, don't hire someone that knows it can't be done. You hire someone that doesn't know it can't be done"—Bev was one of those fellas. There wasn't anything that he couldn't do. He built one of the first pole barns. Later he wanted to move it. The Ag engineers said pole barns can't be moved. Well, he went in and braced the poles, sawed 'em off at the ground, put the tractor on and hauled 'er over where he wanted it.

Farmers have gotta be self-reliant. I've known farmers that couldn't or wouldn't put a board on a barn, they'd hire someone to do it. But the people that get ahead are those that train themselves to do the job. That makes the difference between success and failure.

"Another genius: Bev Veliquette."
—Walter Kirkpatrick

When you think of other good farmers throughout Antrim County, who comes to mind?

There were many throughout the county. One of the good farmers was Bill Hoopfer in south Milton Township. Bill was very successful, he didn't overspend. He didn't have a lot of money and he did a lot of things himself.

Of course, Charlie Anderson. Charlie was a worker and a planner—wasn't afraid to get out and work. The old saying is that "A lot of people don't get any place because they don't plan to get any place." Of course, after you get the plan, you've got to carry it out. I think of folks who were great planners, but when you go to visit 'em, they're in the house playin' cards in the middle of the afternoon when they shoulda been out farming.

In the '20s, things were starting to go bad economically even though people didn't realize it. Farmers were usually the first to suffer. Were you feeling anything at this time, did you sense anything going wrong?

They were beginning to feel the pinch. I think it was '31, with something like fifteen dairy cows, three or four sows, hogs, chickens—the gross income for the farm that year was $625. A good year in those days was probably $1200 to $1500—cut in half. The taxes were high—couple a hundred dollars a year. That's when a lot of people throughout the whole state, especially northern Michigan, let their land revert back for tax title. They couldn't pay their taxes.

Let's talk about the Depression of the '30s. How bad did it get?

It was around '33, my brother sold off the dairy herd at the farm and took over the Kalkaska Dairy. I remember some real good cows going for $30 or $35 dollars at the sale. But who had $30 or $35 dollars? Not very many. It was tough going for farmers for many years.

Farm families taking a lunch break while picking huckleberries near Bellaire, August 6, 1919.

From 1938 to 1968, you were the Antrim County Agricultural Agent. Describe the duties of that job.

At that time we were probably the key person in the county—in a county like Antrim, we had no veterinarian. At the time I came in we had 1150 farms in Antrim County [approximately 175 in 1997]. To a great extent, in 1938, farming was still, to many, many of those folks, very important for growing their own food, surviving. There were only two farms in the county that didn't have dairy cows—probably a few more that didn't have pigs, but most everybody had their own chicken flock. Today you can't find a chicken flock. I might say too, we had 450 commercial potato growers—although they averaged about five acres per farm. That's only about 2200 hundred acres. Kitchen, over at Elmira, grows that many acres himself. At that time, the average production per acre of potatoes for the state was ninety bushels. Today, if you don't get 600 to 800 bushels per acre, you better be out of the business. I'm sure Kitchen averages 800 to 1000.

When I came here, you'd say something about conservation or saving the soil, they didn't know what you're talking about. So all the terminology for conservation, ecology—they've got a dozen different words that have been coined since that time— they never existed back then. So it's been a matter of education. That's our job as Extension Agents: education. Education of the rural people, and it's voluntary. We don't have a fixed audience. If farmers don't want to come to a meeting, they don't have to come. But if the people that come start adopting new practices, the neighbors see them and they adopt them. So indirectly, you'll affect them all. In those years, it was recognized that it took seven years before a new farming practice was adopted; today you adopt the practice at once or you may not stay in business.

Where was the turning point in this environmental awareness? Was there a particular event?

With the dust bowl in the West, people became very conscious of the fact that we'd better tie our soils down; there was a universal cry for that. Locally, people—at first—didn't see that plowing up and downhill was a bad practice—and it's harder on your horses to go uphill than it is down. It's far easier to go around a hill. So we had to educate them. They're going save fuel, they're going save the energy of the horses, also the tractors, and by saving water—catching it on the way down the hill, getting the water to soak into the ground, they're gonna grow better crops, even if they don't improve their fertilizer program.

Water itself is a controlling factor. We don't realize it but one pound of dry corn requires seven hundred pounds of water. One pound of dry alfalfa requires twelve hundred pounds of water; it's gotta transpire up through that plant to make one pound of dry matter. So we talk about nitrogen, phosphorous, potash—really, water is far more critical than people give it credit.

What's the most serious problem relating to pollution on the Chain of Lakes?

I don't think there's any visual threat that I can see at the time. Some of our septic tanks could be seeping into the lakes. Eventually we should go to a sewage collection system and treatment. But there're various thoughts about what is clean water after it goes through a collection plant. Not all sewage disposal plants produce the good water they are supposed to.

You hear an awful lot about nitrogen and about algae in the lakes. But you never hear the fact that from one good electrical storm, for every inch of rain per acre—that's 27,000 gallons of water—you get fifteen pounds of nitrogen, and I think a lot of algae comes from that. Electrical storms produce nitrogen which winds up in the water. There's a natural pollution.

Let's talk about the soil in Antrim County. How would you describe the soil: good, rich, thin?

We have all types of soil in this county. Generally speaking, the soil laying west of Torch Lake is pretty good quality. We come this way [eastward], Helena Township has some good soil, especially up on the hill, but as you go east, it becomes sandier. Forest Home, fairly good soil, but quite a lot of sandy loam. Central Lake has quite a lot of better type soil—it will have some clay in it, what you call loam. Banks Township is pretty good except it's pretty hilly, lot of moraines. The moraines will start south of Charlevoix and they'll be fifteen miles long. But they're very productive. Echo has some good soil and as you get down in the river bottom, some is sandy and some is better than others.

But as you go to the east side of the county, you've got—apparently centuries ago, there was an outwash from the lakes and it's pretty sandy. Fact is, Losey Wright, who was a farmer here in Forest Home Township, originally he was born and raised

Working the old grain binder. "Water is the controlling factor…one pound of dry alfafa requires twelve hundred pounds of water." —Walter Kirkpatrick

in Star Township. He said they put a well down a hundred and some feet and it was sand the whole way. No hard pan, nothing to catch the water and keep it from going. It's kinda like a sieve: you put 'er in the top and it keeps on going. You've gotta have humus in the soil to hold the water.

One of the first projects I had was grasshoppers. We had a lot of grasshoppers, so we put on a grasshopper program. Why do we have grasshoppers?—because we had thousands and thousands of acres of plains and open land, stripped of all its timber and the fires had kept the second growth from comin' up. It bein' dry, that's what grasshoppers liked. Of course, fires make for good blackberries and raspberries and blueberries.

In '34, '35, '36, we had tremendous dry weather. We actually had a lot of dust clouds comin' over here from the west—very distinctive. The old sayin' in the west was the supervisor would appraise the various farms by just standing in his front yard and countin' 'em as they went by [Laughs].

It affected us. As it gets dryer, the grasshopper has an affinity to grow longer wings and then we get a trade wind—a southwest wind—and that just blew millions and millions—billions of 'em—up here. The first year we mixed four hundred tons of bait. In those days we didn't have chemicals to spray; we didn't have the sprayers either. The government furnished our arsenic and banana oil or molasses mixed with sawdust for getting the right flavor for the grasshoppers, which they liked. Then we bagged it; we bought burlap bags by the bale. Every township in the county used bait. You could band the edge of your field or cover the whole field. It was very effective.

If you hadn't done that, what would have happened to the grasshoppers and what damage would they have done?

They eat all the hay, corn, everything. At that time, we were growing quite a lot of vegetable crops: carrots, string beans, red beets for the canning plants at Central Lake and Ellsworth. They'd clean them all up too. Pickles, cucumbers—we had a lot of cucumber acreage in those days.

What effect does the Chain of Lakes and the water of the Chain have on farming?

Very much, because it extends your growing season. In the spring, it doesn't freeze as late, maybe the last frost in the Alba, Mancelona, Elmira area would be Memorial Day. From here [Bellaire] west, especially Milton Township and Elk Rapids Township and the west side of Banks Township, Torch Lake Township, possibly the last frost will be May twelfth, May fifteenth, sometimes even as early as May first. That means you can get your corn in earlier, potatoes, and it's excellent for fruit, too; it makes fruit possible in those areas. Again, in the fall we'd have a killing frost over in the Pleasant Valley, Alba area, often two weeks before the west side of the county––maybe a month. Here we were thirty-five, thirty-six degrees. On the west side, maybe forty.

What actually is happening? Does Torch have an effect in changing the air?

Oh, yes, it warms things up. As the air cools, the water starts cooling. But, at the same time, the water's so much warmer than the air that it warms the air and that keeps it from frosting. So it gives us a longer growing season over in this area.

In the eastern half of the county, you pretty much have to go to corn, forage, potatoes, and livestock. You're pretty much limited to those things. Tree fruits are out. On this side, you can start throwing in fruit and vegetables which makes a lot of difference on a farmer's potential income.

'Course, Lake Michigan is the first big buffer and then as you come over Elk Lake and Round Lake [Lake Skegemog] and Torch Lake, it helps again. It has a lot more influence than what we might think. Of course, we need to remember that Torch Lake, as far as inland lakes in Michigan go, has the greatest volume of water of any lake in Michigan; that means there's a lot of latent energy there, heat or cold. In the fall, the lakes provide a vast reservoir of heat that moderates the area; in the spring this water is a vast reservoir of cold that holds temperatures back, making for ideal tree fruit production.

What's your personal feeling about the Chain of Lakes? Do you have any affection for any of them?

Oh, yes, it's a great asset to the whole area. We've only been able to develop them since REA [Rural Electrification Administration] came in. The first REA pole was set over at Elmira in May of 1939. The first meeting I conducted as an extension agent was to promote REA. We still didn't have a pole in the county. We didn't have a

263

foot of line built in northern Michigan. No electricity outside of Michigan Public Service area. REA was first started with the idea that utilities would run lines out through the rural areas.

The utilities missed the buck a lot by not being farsighted and seeing what could happen. They were used to serving towns and cities and if they didn't have 125 people per mile, they said they couldn't make any money. Well, REA showed 'em they could. REAs were organized and financed through government loans to bring electricity to rural areas, not make money. We have to realize that at that time, electric milking machines were just coming on the market and being perfected. Electric pump units had not yet been developed, electric refrigerators were brand new and unaffordable for many. Electric freezers had not yet been developed plus dozens of other electric gadgets that, today, we take as ordinary.

We've been talking about Antrim County's past and future; you might be interested in a situation I encountered about 1966: An eminent professor of one of our state universities, who was an authority in population growth trends, came out with a forecast indicating that Antrim and other northern Michigan counties would continue to lose population through the '70s and '80s as it has for the past forty years. To me, it seemed that this good man was basing his decisions entirely upon past census trends.

I dropped him a note and pointed out that to me there were other factors that should be considered besides census figures—such things as the new Social Security program that was just beginning to be used by retirees and company retirement programs. The improving roads north and south such as the new I-75 and improved US-131 was tending to eliminate distance. There was recreational attractiveness and being a good place to live which northern Michigan offered, availability of labor and giving a good day's work. Electricity is now available throughout all the northern Michigan areas with home heating units and home water units making for "city living in the country."

Needless to say, the reply I received was not very complimentary of my suggestions, but now thirty odd years later, I leave it to you as to who was closer to projecting the future growth trend of this area.

So REA and the paving of the roads around the Chain was the big impetus for development?

Yes, and the modernization of automobiles. Of course, as we become more of an affluent nation, that all added together. But the roads made it possible for people to come. Once people have running water and electricity, somehow or other they don't want to live where they don't have it.

Let's change the subject for a moment. As a final question, describe the conditions necessary for "skating down fish."

In the first place, you've got to have clear ice. You have to have real cold weather—down to twenty or thirty below zero. Quiet—it's got to be quiet for twenty-four to forty-eight hours and then the ice will freeze like a mirror. Then you can see through it. If it gets too thick you can't see through it, so it's got to be between three quarters to an inch and a half. The day we took the pictures, the boys were complaining because they were skating uphill all day. Of course, the ice was bending under them and actually they **were** skating uphill [Laughs]. Their weight was making it bulge. Now you don't have to be foolish to do that, but it helps [Laughs].

They had a couple of boys that went ahead, they saw the fish and started "skating the fish down," trying to tire 'em out, keep 'em from going out in deep water—keep 'em within eight to twelve feet of water. If you go through the ice, it is deep enough you can drink standing up. Then a couple of fellas with axes, they'd chop a hole in the ice and try to steer the fish toward the hole. Then they could spear 'em. It's quite a deal. It's been more than forty years—that was 1952.

People outside of our area have a hard time believing the "skating down fish" story. We stopped one night down in Alabama, fellow was cleaning a fish there. We said up north we "skate down fish" on ice. The fellow said, "Well, ya know, I've heard a lot of fish stories in my life, but that beats them all." [Laughs]

Hank Orschel, of Zupin-Orschel Oil Company of Elk Rapids, arranged to take the "skating down fish" movies to a Gulf Oil Company distributors meeting in Toledo, Ohio many years ago. Hank showed the picture; after the showing, one of the distributors came up to him and said, "I saw the picture, but I still don't believe it."

Skating down whitefish on Torch Lake, February 16, 1952. Left to right: Ivan Hoopfer, Vic Haller Sr., Vic Haller Jr., Elmer Ruffer, Walt Merillat, Don Merillat, Glen Hoopfer, Floyd Goodman, Carl Merillat. All were natives of south Milton except Ruffer. Photo by Walter Kirkpatrick.

Warren Studley

Warren Studley was born in Grass Lake, Michigan in Jackson County and attended Michigan State University where he earned his Bachelor's and Master's degrees in Natural Resources. For more than thirty-six years he was an employee with the Soil Conservation Service of the Department of Agriculture. In 1987, I met with Warren to talk about his many years as Soil Conservation Official with Antrim County and to discuss his views on major environmental issues of the day. Warren is an outspoken advocate of doing what is right; he is admired by his peers as a man of integrity and high ethical standards. He has been one of the prime movers in developing the Grass River Natural Area. This interview took place in Warren's home on Derenzy Road north of Bellaire. I conducted a second interview with Warren after his retirement in 1995, and updated both interviews with him in 1997. Today he lives with his wife, Lois, in Traverse City.

With this unusual Chain of Lakes we have in Antrim County, what do you see as the major problem as far as soil conservation is concerned?

The area is rather unique from a glacial or from a land form aspect. The glaciers left us with a varied landscape and what we call drumlins which are long cigar shaped formations that the ice formed. We have narrow ridge tops, steep side slopes that are subject to erosion, we have wetland areas in between. As farmers or developers come in and shift land use from woods and grass to more intensive uses, high potential erosion increases which will impact our wetlands and our water quality. What we're talking about is keeping our water clean and we can do that if we keep the uplands areas in grass or treated with an integrated soil and water conservation program.

Anytime you see intensive development or a change into a recreational resort where you try to capitalize on the views over the lake, there's a real danger unless you do adequate planning. You may move too fast and have erosion and sedimentation problems from the highland areas.

If you were to look at a United States Geological Survey map you would see Antrim County, with the Chain of Lakes with all the little feeder streams that come out from the base of every hillside—we have a large number of these. As we work in the uplands areas, if we're not careful to leave greenbelts and take adequate measures to prevent the sediment from entering the water, then this ends up in lakes or the streams. There has been a problem in the past with developers not realizing proper planning whereby sediment would get into the streams and lakes: Lake Bellaire, Grass River, or Clam River. It would seem that the developer and resort owner who ignores the water run-off from the hills here is biting off his nose to spite his face.

You mentioned that Lake Bellaire is already suffering some of these difficulties. Could you explain how that happened?

In the past, on the east side of Lake Bellaire—it's in a cove—creeks from the upland areas have carried considerable sediment to Lake Bellaire. These sediments are fine clays and silts and they stay suspended in the water during the summer months when there are waves. Then they settle in the winter when the lake freezes. But if we get a strong wind from the west—either southwest or northwest—waves will come in, pick up this sediment and keep it suspended. There'll be days in the summertime where the east shore of Lake Bellaire will be real brown; people who live there would have to take a shower after they go swimming.

Quite a few of the people who use Lake Bellaire, they may go down and swim once or twice. But they don't see the permanent damage. If you talk to the people on the east side of Lake Bellaire, they say, "Well, they've impacted the lake quite severely, we'll sell and move on." But this is not a solution. The next person to buy it, they have the same problem.

Aside from having to shower, does it do any other damage to the ecology of the lakes?

The fish biologists talk about the covering of fish habitat whereby spawning areas are affected. There is a tendency for the water to warm which can change fish species. If we do not protect it, it will convert from cold water lakes to warm water lakes—if we do that, our trout goes. We end up with a warm water fishery. I think this development pressure can happen in Traverse City; it can happen in Petoskey; it's happening in southern Michigan.

This is one of the things that makes the north so nice. People in southern Michigan, the Midwest, other parts of the state, just don't see crystal blue water. A real resource in the county is our water quality. Sixty per cent of the county is wooded, the remaining forty per cent is open, so it's the scenic part of it. Tourism is our key resource—I don't think people at the township, and possibly the county level, fully appreciate this.

Is there a sort of innocence on the part of people thinking "We're so far removed here, especially on the east side of Torch Lake, from the expressway or US 31, that it'll never happen, that the pollution and crowded conditions in the Traverse area just aren't going to hit this area?"

I think this is one case, but the American people look to some agency in Washington—FDA [Federal Drug Administration]—to set a standard of permissible residue and contamination as being acceptable for the human body. It wasn't here before our chemical age, so who can tell us what level is safe in the body. How much cancer can we live with? We have a false idea that we can allow a certain amount of this to happen each time somebody new comes on the scene, but we fail to realize this has a cumulative effect. This is where we fall short.

Let's talk about the associations, the organizations here in the Chain of Lakes that are trying to maintain water quality standards—the Elk-Skegemog Association and the Three Lakes Association.

There're three of 'em that are actively concerned about the environment, water quality and use—the nice things in life. They have done a good job of keeping the issues—clean water and green hillsides—before the people. Quite often they are professional people; they have retired. They sit on commissions, township boards, village councils; they have the money to put out their newsletters. This is the biggest thing they can do—the newsletters are first rate; they're issue-oriented. They monitor improperly functioning sewers and septic systems. They're real valuable and do a nice job.

Take a look at the northern part of the county—Ellsworth, in particular. There have been some problems. Morweld Steel Company was doing some things that weren't too desirable.

We have to be careful. Anytime we load our soil or our water with an impurity, something that the good Lord didn't put there to start with, we've created a problem. With this much water, this many people, and as many roads that we have, each person doing his own thing, if it isn't correct, it eventually is going to degrade the quality of life.

The Chain of Lakes originates at Beal Lake. Let's look at the Chain.

That's the first major lake. But if you would walk upstream, actually it would start east of Bellaire a little bit, probably by Herb Reilly's farm. Within a half a mile of where Herb lives, there's a little spring on the side of a hill that just trickles down, and it picks up another little spring. It starts off on Skinkle Road—this is where the headwaters of the Chain of

Lakes start. It goes through Pleasant Valley, under Dingman's Bridge, north into Charlevoix County and at Ellsworth, it comes back south, outletting at Elk River in Elk Rapids.

They talk about Minnesota being the land of lakes. Actually, we've got a land of water right here in Antrim County.

As a body of water, is it unique?

It is unique because it's naturally made. When the glaciers were here some 10,000 years ago, we had a warming period and all the melt water from the glacier would flow between the glacial front and the high hills to the east, and so this Chain of Lakes was carved out. It's an ancient water course that was formed. At one time though, at Eastport probably, Lake Michigan and Torch Lake would have been tied together. There would have been a peninsula from Elk Rapids north through Milton Township.

You know the county like the back of your hand. What's your favorite view?

Meggison's Point—west of Central Lake on the east side of Torch—you get a magnificent view. If I had a planning staff, I'd ask each county in the state of Michigan to select three view sites in each county, and we'd have a special fund to set these aside for the public. I don't think a view should belong to one or two people or a family. This is something that should be enjoyed by all people in the future.

How do we get people to be sensitive and aware of the environment and all these issues we've been talking about?

Maybe one of the ways is to consider the caring capacity of a resource base. If you have company in the home and children in the home, and in the morning the kids say, "We want French toast"—we have six kids and six adults and one frying pan. We can get six pieces of toast in there. We cannot feed all twelve people at once. So we have an agreement—we'll feed the kids first; get them outdoors; let them go swimming. Then the adults eat. We share the common resource with a limited capacity.

What we're talking about is each parcel of land, or each factory or each village, has a certain caring capacity—that's the ability to produce a certain element, a quality element over a period of time. I think until we start addressing our caring capacity and how we use it—until we do this, we will continue to have problems.

Any development—Grand Traverse Resort, Shanty Creek, Schuss Mountain—as long as the development fits the landscape and the natural resources, we will have no problems. But when we start to go beyond the capacity—whether it's our soils to [handle] drainfield effluent or if it's beyond our ability to accommodate our boaters or swimmers—when we have a conflict in use or competing uses, we have a problem.

269

Let's get a description of all the areas on the Chain that have been preserved—the way Grass River has been preserved.

Grass River Natural Area is about eleven hundred acres, starts on the southeast shore of Lake Bellaire. It encompasses all of Grass River and the south shore of Clam Lake. It's been set aside for nature lovers and other non-consumptive uses. The County commissioners have done a good job—using state and federal monies, local volunteers—it's a nice program, passive in nature. A fine educational program has developed.

June and Harry Janis in the Skegemog area have done the same thing. That property is owned and managed by the state. The area on the east side of Lake Skegemog is set aside. They worked with The Nature Conservancy, the State of Michigan. There are restricted activities, there is a boardwalk and observation platform. Again, people use it in a passive non-consumptive way. It's a real educational tool.

In Wandawood [Palmer-Wilcox-Gates Preserve], they are working with the Michigan Chapter of The Nature Conservancy, working with the people. There is over 1300 feet on Grand Traverse Bay north of Elk Rapids. The owners felt there was a need to keep some remnants of primitive sand dunes. They have set it aside in perpetuity.

Antrim County has over 4000 acres of publicly owned property, some are parks, some are wooded acreage—nice view spots. Where are the nicest views? There's one in Echo Township, it's called Murphy Park—it's eighty acres with trees. In the early morning you can see the sun rise over Beal Lake. The Eastport Park is done very nicely. There's a county park in Elk Rapids on the south side—1300 feet of frontage. Out of that 1300, we've created 300 feet of beach. The people living on the north and south need protection—a green belt. So we've got 500 feet on both ends that hasn't been impacted. We kept the parking lot small by design because it will fill up in the summer. The answer isn't to double the parking lot to put more people in there. Let's maintain the quality, let someone come back tomorrow to look at it.

In 1995, I met again with Warren Studley. Since our first interview, he had retired and is now living in Traverse City. His commitment to the land and water is still strong and he remains involved. His passion for the Chain of Lakes is seen in this second interview:

Warren, let's review a couple of topics that we discussed in '87. Looking back over the past decade, what changes have you seen in the lakes area of Antrim County? Were we prophesying correctly back in the '80s that there was going to be too much growth, too much pollution? What's your impression of the land and the water in the last ten years?

It's interesting to note: the environmental awareness that started fifteen years ago is still active and people are picking up on the issues and continuing. I feel good because some place along the line, some of the 4-H tours, the work that Karl Larson, Burt Stanley and others talked about is still being carried on in the whole Grand Traverse area. There's the Traverse Bay Watershed Initiative. With the Elk River/

Chain of Lakes Watershed from Elk Rapids going clear up to Ellsworth and back into Pleasant Valley—people are still aware of these environmental concerns.

The Friends of the Jordan River have become a non-profit group. It's a continuation of the work Dr. David Prey and O.D. Walker, Bryce Vance, Teddy Kotavich and others started. The seeds that these people had sown in the past have sprouted and another generation has come along and carried on this awareness. This is the most satisfying part. I'm satisfied and others should be too.

The growth comes in—Bellaire has a McDonalds, they're talking about one in Mancelona. Along with this growth, it's good as long as it fits the community and it is regulated.

So you're optimistic as far as the environmental awareness issue is concerned?

Oh, I think so. I think the best thing that happened was that the Lake Country Gazette came out—Mark Stone and Greg Reisig. Not only do they have the newspaper, but they have the Stewardship Quarterly. I think this group of people has done more than anybody else to put these issues in first-class editorial material in a number of homes on a regular basis. It's something that was needed and they've found a niche. They've done very well with it.

Is zoning the water a possibility?

Each lake has a certain area and depth—it's a physical body. Torch Lake has a lot more capacity than Lake Bellaire by virtue of its size and depth. You are going to see a time when condominiums will ring most of the Grand Traverse Bay area. If we don't take our septic effluent and properly treat it and take it back away from the water, we will be in trouble. A lot of these septic tanks are eventually gonna contaminate the groundwater. Water quality and both surface water and groundwater are our most precious resources. They're issues we ought to be looking at.

We've got the whole Chain of Lakes—we go through Bellaire, Central Lake, and Ellsworth—they are zoned. But as soon as we go a little east in Echo Township—that's where the headwaters of the Chain of Lakes are—they're unzoned. There's no zoning to the east. Warner and Star Townships do not have any zoning. You've got the Jordan Natural River zoning provisions with a setback, but you've got all the feeder streams, and people don't always protect those.

When we talk of zoning, we think of government restrictions and government regulation. Does government know best in all of these environmental issues?

My definition is different. Government is a group of people around a coffee table—whether it's in the Village Chalet in Bellaire, or in Elk Rapids, or in Mancelona. It's people from a wide range of ages, who can sit down and converse about an issue or topic in a friendly way, with a few barbs or an argument or two. Everybody gets a chance to offer their input. This is fundamental government; government closest to the people is the best.

I feel this is where the problem should be solved—at the village, city, and township level. The things we can't take care of—our roads and airports—then we have to move to a higher level.

Even though there's increased growth, are the environmental problems fewer?

I think so. I look at Kearney Township—other people have run for office, they've taken in a lot of seminars, they've asked a lot of questions. Tip of the Mitt Watershed [Council] has come in and filled a void; they assist townships with computer-generated maps. They can map all the steep slopes, all the wetlands, areas that are highly erodible. When you go to the township, you can no longer fool these people. There's more accountability.

The township people are better-educated; they have additional information that's available to them that wasn't before. They can do a much better job of planning that they couldn't do fifteen years ago. It's very positive.

Warren Studley, 1987.

Those with environmental concerns are often referred to as the "spotted owl crowd." With that in mind, is there enough room for everyone on this fragile Chain of Lakes; can real estate people continue to sell and sell the back lots, the view lots, the over-the-hill lots? Antrim County now has 18,000 people. Let's project that it's going to be doubled in X number of years. Is there enough room for everyone to come in here?

I have a concern. I do consulting on wetlands, soil erosion. There are definite limits as to what an area can hold or be developed. That's why we have zoning and land-use planning. As long as we don't create a problem for our neighbor or the natural resources we are okay. The county is a quality area.

Let's talk about the changing character of the area. We see a lot of artificial development taking place. Many folks are complaining that the visual character of the area is changing. What are your thoughts on the changing character and how do you think we could keep it more natural?

I suppose we can step back in time. When someone took up the old boardwalks and started pouring concrete, people were alarmed—it'll never be the same, it's the demise of the village. Before we venture too far, we have planning commissions, the

272

garden clubs—they do monitor the quality of life where they live. I don't think we're going to find too many extremes without some counterbalancing of this.

I think there is a changing character, but I think it's positive. We've been able to capitalize on our Chain of Lakes and we have a strong resort business. As a result, there's been a lot of money from outside the county—retirees—they bring along a lot of professional expertise and they also bring along some pensions and some money to spend. So they're willing to invest.

It's no longer an area of speculation like it was in the early '70s—it was uncontrolled growth. Now they realize that if they're going to protect this quality of life—the green hills and the blue water—they're going to have to say, "We cannot have uncontrolled growth, we have to regulate this within reason. We want to live in peace and harmony with what we have."

One final question, Warren. Let's go back to your early days. How did your interest in land and soil develop?

I was lucky. My scoutmaster and my Sunday school teacher, Frank Trull, was a soil conservation employee in southern Michigan. He was probably the one person, outside my family, who had the most influence in my life.

I was born and raised in a small community. Our home was at the outer edge of the village, a couple of cows, horse. My grandparents had a little acreage where we could take the cows down to the pasture. We could hunt and fish. I was fortunate. I thank my parents and their friends for guiding me right.

Whether gathering at Alden's dock for a reunion of Civil War veterans (top), or making a brief stop for ice cream at Anderson's Clam River Store (center) before entering Clam Lake, boat travel was the preferred method of travel in the early years of the twentieth century. Complementing public steamers such as the Ruth and Mabel were many smaller private launches (below).

274

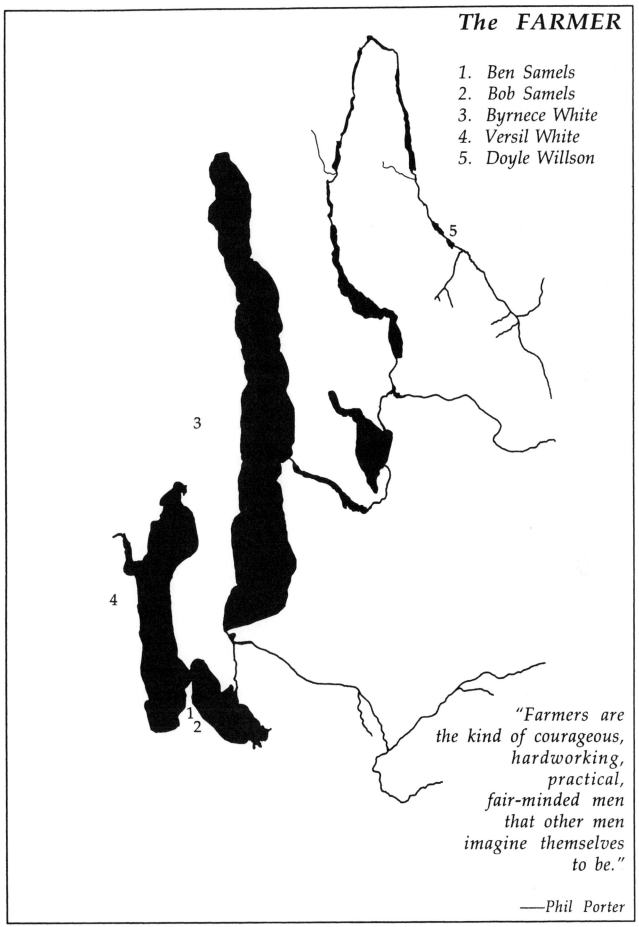

The FARMER

1. Ben Samels
2. Bob Samels
3. Byrnece White
4. Versil White
5. Doyle Willson

"Farmers are
the kind of courageous,
hardworking,
practical,
fair-minded men
that other men
imagine themselves
to be."

——Phil Porter

Ben and Bob Samels

Ben and Bob Samels were born on the farm their father, Frank Samels, bought in 1889. Frank married Mary Laubscher and together they tilled the soil of an eighty acre farm located on Skegemog Point. It reaches to the western shore of Lake Skegemog. Ben and Bob never left, living on the farm into their ninth decade. Their work ethic and simple lifestyle have made them, without exaggeration, legendary in the area. They represent the best of American values: modesty, integrity, and fine craftsmanship. I had the pleasure of interviewing them in 1987, and again in 1991, and 1993, with a final visit in 1998.

There are still quite a few farms operating on Skegemog Road, and yours looks to be a much more prosperous farm. It looks like you folks were more successful.

Ben: We always kept it up. At that time some people would plant crop after crop and never seed it back. Of course, we'd always seed it back into the clover and hay and let it build up to sod again and then work the fields up and crop them again. That kept it up.

Describe that seeding back. What do you mean by seeding back?

Ben: A lot of time we had a crop of corn or a crop of beans and we'd work it up and sow it to oats and seed it. Well, first there's clover and timothy and after we got

276

alfalfa, when we'd see it go back to sod, then we'd cut hay on it for three, four, five years maybe. Then we'd plow 'em up and start over again.

You go down about sixteen inches and you get clay and hardpan. The top is sandy loam and that clay under there held the moisture up and we raised pretty good crops.

If you were looking for a farm today, would you buy this kind of farm with this soil?

Ben: Yeah, because it's easier to work. You take these clay farms, you got to work them when they're right. With this, you have a good rain and in a day or two you can go out again. Some of those farms you have to wait for them to dry out. I like this kind of land.

Did your dad ever tell you why he bought this farm?

Ben: He liked it down here. 'Course this piece here was quite level, and when he was in his twenties he had a chance to buy it. The Elk Rapids Iron Company lumbered off this land, and then they let it go back for taxes.

When he was going to move down here, people thought he was crazy. "Down here ain't worth nothing, you'll starve to death." "Well," he said, "I think I know enough to move if I get hungry." [Laughter] He never moved. Now if he knew what we'd have to pay for taxes, he'd probably turn over in his grave.

Bob: He worked awful hard. 'Course when he got down here the timber'd all been taken off. All there was left was the pine stumps. He had to take them out.

The Samels' farmyard, 1992.

Mary and Frank Samels, 1892.

Your dad must have made a pretty good living off the farm because he did stay.

Ben: Yeah, we had everything. Of course, we couldn't have everything that everybody else wanted, but we were pretty much self-contained. They had their cattle and hogs and raised wheat and took it to Elk Rapids and had it ground for flour. We even had bees, had our honey.

Do you recall at about what age you actually put in a full day. What did your dad require of you?

Ben: As soon as we were big enough we would carry in the wood, feed the chickens and gather eggs. He always had something for us to do. We had work by the time we were fourteen or fifteen. In the morning, breakfast would be at six o'clock. Of course, we had to feed the horses before then. After breakfast we had to milk the cows and curry the horses and put the harness on. Be in the field by seven o'clock. Hour out at noon and work till six o'clock—ten hour days.

Of course, we didn't try to work like some people we knew. They worked their life out too soon, but we worked. They had too much and couldn't do it all and were behind all the time. We worked, but we didn't try to kill ourselves. The main thing was we figured we couldn't get rich anyhow. No use killing ourselves trying to [Laughter].

278

Bob: Our dad didn't require us to work any harder than we could. We'd have our time off.

Your dad bought this farm in 1889. Describe your dad. What kind of a man was he. Was he a happy-go-lucky person?

Ben: He was a pretty serious person. Of course, he lived to be eighty-seven years old and he had a pretty healthy life. He never was sick. When he was eighty he had a lot of his stomach closed up and he had to have an operation. They made a new opening and he lived six years just as nice as ever.

Describe your mom as you remember her. What kind of a person was she? Was she jovial or serious?

Ben: She was a little of both. She could be serious but she generally was pretty pleasant. She come from Meinisberg, Switzerland. She was eleven years old and her brother was thirteen.

She made the butter and baked bread twice a week—four loaves twice a week. Churned the butter and all that, cleaned the house and made the beds. She worked too hard. She never was hardly sick a day in her life. When she was sick, she never complained. She'd say, "I can work it off." I can only remember her being in bed sick once. That was three or four days—she got kind of congestion finally.

Were there medicines or formulas or home remedies that could be used to take care of an illness that you recall?

Bob: She used this castoria quite a lot when we were kids. If we needed a laxative, in the summertime she would pick sage leaves and dry 'em and catnip blossoms. If we got a cold, before we went to bed, she'd fix up a sage tea or catnip tea to go to bed on.

Your mother was orphaned in Switzerland and had to come across as a child by herself. Your dad's folks came as immigrants from Cornwall and then settled in the Bruce Mines in Canada and then bought a rather rugged farm on Skegemog Point. Did they think of it as being a rough life?

Ben: They never complained. In the wintertime sometimes you couldn't get out. I never heard our dad complain. My mother either. No, they would think that was awful. Our folks was never in debt. Some neighbors around seemed to always have a debt. Of course, if our dad wanted anything, he saved money first, then buy it. He'd never go in debt.

Let's talk about the Depression, paying taxes and low prices.

Ben: Well, we'd seen the Depression come on there. We had beef in the barn, hogs in the hog pen, chickens in the chicken coop and honey bees. At that time you could take a dozen eggs and you could buy a pound of coffee and sugar; I think we could

The Lodge at Skegemog Point, c.1900.

buy about a hundred pounds for six dollars—about six cents a pound. Of course, at that time, taxes were twenty-five dollars for several years there.

One fall there we had a bull and thought we better get rid of him. He had them damn horns and so we sent word to the cattle buyer, and he said, "Well, he weighs about fourteen hundred pounds, I can only give you two cents a pound." Dad said, "I guess we'll get rid of him."

Well, that made twenty-eight dollars. The tax was twenty-five dollars and we had three dollars left. About four years ago, when I started to get rid of cattle I sold four head and I got around twenty-eight hundred. That wasn't enough to pay our taxes.

Then the next year we sold four more at a pretty good price—for twenty-eight hundred and the tax was 'bout four thousand. A year ago, I sold the other two. I got my income tax, social security tax, state tax, that made it about a third of it—all go for tax. Hell, we had plenty to eat and enough to wear. Of course, farm wages then were a dollar a day and your dinner.

What does farming mean to you? Is it a special way of life?

Ben: Well, I think it's a good way of life. A lot of times a boy would go and work for a neighbor, you know, a year or two. He'd slowly get money and buy a team of horses and plow and drag and get maybe even forty acres. He'd get married and have a good place to raise a family. As they growed up, they'd help on the farm and they learned discipline. They learned how to work. As soon as you get big enough, you had your chores. Now, they call that child abuse—you mustn't do that.

One thing is you'd see them [young men] go down to Detroit and work the factory; they learned maybe one thing. But here we learned just about everything. We'd do

The Lumber Barons: "They're just like a bunch of grasshoppers in a wheat field." — Bob Samels

the plumbin'. I'd done quite a bit of cabinet work; we built cupboards. My brother, he'd do the plumbin' and some electric work too. We learned all of 'em that way.

See, we didn't have kids to play with when we got home, so we went to experiment with these other things. That's how we learned. If we had other kids to play with, maybe we wouldn't have developed these other things.

Let's talk about lake level and the myth that Lake Skegemog wasn't always there.

Bob: Part of our shoreline is swampy. According to archaeologists, after the glacier melted, we was right on the beach of this big lake—called it Lake Algonquin. Hell, one time they figured this was an ocean bottom. This stuff here that we call limestone which is flakes of stone, you break them apart and you find those fossilized limes and some of those Petoskey stones. They're supposed to be fossilized coral. They claim that was about sixty million years ago—just like the day before yesterday [Laughter].

We know it was a lake, ya see, because our grandfather came to Elk Rapids and he had a sailboat and put it over the rapids and sailed it up there to our landing. So there had to be a lake. Our grandfather—these narrows before the dam was in— would take his clothes off, hold 'em up over his head and he waded across that ridge across the narrows to the other side. Had to be four feet of water. Now there's six-seven feet.

They run tugs on the lake hauling logs down to Elk Rapids. They had that furnace in Elk Rapids. They cut cordwood all around the lakes and hauled it down there. Our uncle, William Samels, was captain on one of those tugs, the Albatross. Must've been fifteen years, I guess. Our mother's cousin, Fred Laubscher, was captain of the tug before Uncle Will took it.

281

Bob and Ben Samels resting at the end of the day.

Bob and Ben enjoying a view of their farm.

How do you feel about the lumbering? Do you see it as doing damage to the land? What do you think of the lumber barons of years ago?

Bob: They're just like a bunch of grasshoppers in a wheat field. They used to come over here and just slashed and fed. Of course, now I guess they wouldn't let them do that so much. They slashed that stuff off and wasted it; sometimes it made our dad sick. If they'd a had selective cuttin', you know, they coulda' done like the Weyerhausers—they can lumber all the time and we coulda' done that here.

As you walk around the farm, what is your favorite view?

Bob: Oh, I guess we like to look at the woods. We're gonna live here long as we're able. Always been a pretty healthy place. We got good water here.

282

Byrnece White

Byrnece White was born Byrnece Nelson as the horse and buggy era was coming to a close. Her father, Ralph Nelson, died when Byrnece was eight years old. The hard times of the Depression forced her mother, Ethel, to seek work away from home. She headed east to become a housemother at a girl's school. Byrnece and her brother, Ralph, lived with Aunt Anna and Uncle Oscar Swanson in Kewadin. As World War II began to take shape, Byrnece married Bob White and they bought the farm which she continues to operate fifty-seven years later. With Bob's untimely death, the failed crops, and the pressures of modern-day farming, Byrnece White is known to her friends as a survivor. In this 1997 interview, she reflects on the sad and happy times, and her love of the earth around her.

Mrs. White, let's go back to your childhood and describe your grandfather's sawmill in Kewadin and its final days.

We lived on the farm at that time below Maplehurst toward Torch Lake. My grandfather, Fred Stafford, invited me down to see the last of the sawmill. Of course, being little, he held on to me so I wouldn't get too close to that big blade. I was six years old. He had the blade down to the water to catch the sparks because it would catch the logs and sawdust on fire if it didn't have water. The logs would be drawn up from the water, pulled up on a platform, run on the elevator. It ran through and made slabs. It was run by steam. Stacked logs, I couldn't say how many huge logs were in these mountains of logs from grandfather's place to Osborn's mill. Grandfather made shingles and he sold the lumber. They'd bundle the shingles, haul them by wagon to Elk Rapids and ship them out by train. There were no more logs and lumber in the area. It had been harvested. It was finished.

Byrnece, 11 years old.

Describe your school days in Kewadin.

I was on the baseball team—we didn't have enough boys. Eight grades. We walked to the Roberts school and played against their team. We walked up to north Milton on Friday afternoon; we played baseball there. I was a tomboy. I could run faster than anyone.

When we went to school in the eighth grade, you had to take a county test to go to high school. You had a whole day of questions in order to pass.

If you didn't pass the test?

You stayed there. There was one boy that couldn't make it that year, but he did the next. He graduated from Elk Rapids. He was lost in the war, too.

We had eight grades in one room, and kindergarten. Kindergarten children would go home at two o'clock. The rest of the day would be real serious studying. Gerda Anderson was our teacher. She taught all the grades; she kept the fires, cleaned the building, filled the water tanks.

How do you personally recall Gerda Anderson?

She was the best teacher in the world. Not only did she take time for the slow children, encouraged them to just do their best, she broadened it. We had art classes, art appreciation—looking at famous artists. We had music— started the day with the pledge of allegiance, then we all sang "America." Then next was "Father, we thank thee for the night and the birth of the morning light." That was the important beginning of our day. She was the one who understood, wanted to see everyone do their best.

Let's talk about the social life on the shore of Elk Lake at Kewadin.

From the time I was growing up—I seemed to be the oldest of the group—no parent came with the children and we had all these little children—Powells and Beards, just many families. I didn't dare go swimming, I'd go along the shore and every once in a while I'd go, "Now, everybody stand up so I can count you." So it'd be up to me to look after all these little ones. It was tricky.

We had a stump called "spider stump" and if you got your foot in the limbs that were still left on the roots, you couldn't get out. Water was probably five foot deep. That was a very special thing: keep away from "spider stump." My cousin got caught in it.

Our families had picnics there. We all picnicked together. A man from across on the point came. He said," You'll never believe this, but someday this'll all be houses."

284

We laughed; we were little; why it couldn't be. Today it's all houses [Chuckles].

Aside from the sawmill, describe the shoreline on the north end of Elk Lake.

That was a bayou and all the stumps with moss between them [on the northeast corner]. The wild berries grew on them; you just don't see them anymore. Cranberries, wild flowers. In front of the mill around to the store, it was sandy, beautiful beach. Everybody came together, grown-ups as well as children, on Sundays. Oh, I miss the lapping of the water I would hear.

Since you spent so much time there, do you have a favorite view?

Oh, yes, the beautiful curve of the bayou and the lake where all the stumps were. I had a water ball that was unique. It was made with rubber tire material and it got away. I swam out to the stumps on the far side. Today, I look at that and wonder, "How in the world did I ever get that far?" Finally, I got it. Headed back, hanging on for dear life and rest. But the little waves had just put it beyond fingertips. I was tired when I got back.

In the wintertime, everybody skated. We had two inches of ice and there were one hundred people out there skating. It was the most beautiful sight. My old Uncle Clint Stafford came out, clamped his skates on his shoes, made the most beautiful figure eight and all the fancy things. Here we're struggling just to skate [Chuckles].

mary Sogod age 116

As a young girl, were you aware of the Chain of Lakes?

No, just that Elk Lake and Torch Lake were so long. We really just couldn't believe that Torch Lake was eighteen miles long and I don't remember how long Elk Lake is. I was real surprised when I heard and read about how big Torch Lake was.

You mentioned that your grandfather, when he had the mill, had an agreement or treaty with the Indians.

Yes, it was Mary Sogod. She lived to be 118. She had a treaty with grandfather not to pick his vegetables and walk across his property. There were only a few Indians at that time.

When Mrs. Sogod got ill and was going to die, she wouldn't stay in her house. There was an old dilapidated table by our house. This was in October, cold, windy. She was out there, black clothes on, blowing in the wind, tattered—my gracious.

Bob White and daughter, Gale, c.1950.

She was going to die, she told me. She wouldn't die in her house.

You graduated in 1938 and you met a young man named Bob White. Tell me about your first encounter with your future husband.

We went to school together. He had the most beautiful smile. He was in the eleventh grade and I was a freshman. He and I picked each other out real soon. He went to Detroit and then he went on to the boats. I didn't see him for several years. When I graduated, he came back north and gave me my engagement ring. Then I went to Ypsilanti State Normal [Eastern Michigan University] to college.

What was a young girl expected to do with her life after high school? What opportunities were presented?

Very little. Everybody left. When you graduated, you went some place else to work. There was nothing. The farmers farmed what little bit they had. There was work at the packing plant at harvest time, but there was no work for the young people. There was no one around my age. After the war [World War II], they started gradually coming back.

Why do you suppose that so many come back?

Everyone comes back to their home grounds. That's human nature. You always want to go home. No matter where you go, you meet wonderful friends, you make your home there, but you always seek where you came from.

Here we are today, sitting on the farm in Milton Township awfully close to where you got your start.

It's been fifty-seven years since Bob and I were first married. In 1940, we rented the farm from the Smith estate. Everything was included: the chickens, the pigs, the cows, and sheep. We had our own horses. It was crop farming; we raised potatoes and beans and corn. In 1944, when the war was on, we bought it. We had it paid for in ten years. To buy machinery, a tractor, we got a loan. We had four hundred acres. We bought Carl Erickson's farm which was one hundred and sixty; that added a beautiful part to ours. It gave us the hills to raise cattle on.

We started out with no electricity. Hired men, horse-drawn equipment, milked our cows by hand by lantern light, separated the milk to cream, and sold it to the co-op. We had threshers that were unbelievable—first of all, neighbors got together and buzzed wood; everybody helped one another. We had community help; that was a nice thing. There was Ed Sutter, George Hockin, Perry and Norm O'Dell, John Boals, Aaron and Charley Coleman, Carl Erickson, Harry Warner, William and Don McLachlan. I remember Bernie Powell, Charley Fox, Axel Hjelte, Claude and Harry Russell.

The threshers would come on that big old-fashioned threshing machine, pitched the bales into it, threshed the oats, the wheat—the beans would be the last ones in November. We would have silo fillers. Silo filling was really hard the first year. They had to cut the corn with a corn knife, load it on the wagons, bring it in, then put it in the silo. The next year we had a binder that would cut and bind it in bundles. Later on, we had better equipment. We would have sheep shearers and that beautiful golden fleece came off these sheep. It was a constant group of people you were feeding and I wasn't very old. I was only twenty-one—and all these things had to be done [Laughs].

How many different ways we farmed here. We started out with loose hay, picked up the hay and loaded it on to the wagon. Bob would mow it on, drawn by horses. We had hired men all the time.

What is your main crop today?

Cherries and beef cattle—we have one hundred and fifty beef cattle. The calves go in the barn in the winter, fed silage, sold the last week in April. They're corn-fed and ready to be sold at auction.

You're a farm family that is totally supporting itself from farming, no other income?

I had a choice when my husband died: would I keep the farm? Mark was only fourteen. I just couldn't leave; we'd built so many wonderful memories. This is the family farm. Everyone had contributed; everyone had lived here and been happy

Farm Field Day at the White farm to examine growing methods of cattle feed, c.1960.

here. Once Bob wanted to build a new house—I said "No, these are our memories."
I can always live in a house, but you can't replace the memories. So we didn't build
a new house [Chuckles].

Tell me who your children are and how the family grew from 1940?

Kay was born first. Gale was born here in Kewadin on the farm near Maplehurst.
Then we had Tom and then Margaret, then Janie. I raised my grandson, Mark, later—
that was more work than all five, but he was enjoyable [Laughs]. He's been a joy. We
had a wonderful time.

*Let's talk about the farm day. When the crops were in full bloom, the summer months were
coming, describe a farmwife's typical day.*

My sister said, "Write down what you do all day. We'll [Chuckles] see if we can't
arrange your time better."

Walter Kirkpatrick was our County Agent and he was a wonderful agent. He went
to all the farms. Cal Bargy up here, he started him in strip farming because he had
low land and high land, close to each other. He promoted the kids in 4-H. Kay won
her scholarship to Michigan State from sewing in 4-H. Janie and Margaret and Gale
—their sewing and their cooking. The most joyful time—one Christmas, each one
secretly was sewing something for their sister. One made robes, another made
blouses. It was terrific to see four girls each making something.

We had dairy cattle when Tom was growing up and he won trophies in 4-H with his
calf. The next year Margaret took her calf and she won. It was a great time in 4-H. I
was a leader in sewing and cooking for quite a few years.

The milking, by the time the kids were in school, was automatic. I would get my house in order, then I'd go to the barn and wash the milkers and the separator when we had cream, probably work in my garden—I had a beautiful garden. It had the biggest strawberries I ever saw; they were just giants.

Weather, it seems, plays such an important role for the farmer.

I went to the Cherry Festival with my grandchildren to see President Ford—it was bright, sunny. We came home, I went out to the garden for some lettuce—there wasn't any. I had cultivated it the day before and I thought, "Did I do that?" My tomatoes were ruined; everything was ruined. It had hailed two and a half inches while I was gone. Up in Traverse, beautiful—here a tornado had gone through. It took all our fruit, no apples; we had no cherries to sell that year. The corn came back, so we had feed, silage. It went through here and everything was ruined.

Wouldn't that be terribly discouraging?

Yes and no. We had our cattle; we had other crops. We got through it; we knew we would.

Why did you know that you would?

I could do anything with my husband. He and I together—go to the end of the world. In 1955 and '56, we had a drought—completely. It would rain north of us and it would rain south of us. The first year we'd had a lot of snow that winter; the soil was wet; the corn grew. So we had corn and silage, little bit of hay. The next year there was nothing, no hay, no corn—and we had a large number of dairy cattle.

Bob White with his team in an oil painting by his daughter, Gale.

289

We ran out of hay; we bought everybody's in the area. Bob's dad gave him a mow of what he had—we bought that.

The feed truck load was supposed to be in on Thursday. They called us, the truck had gone through the barn floor. It'd be another day before we could get feed. The cows in the barn bellowed. They bellowed more. Then they roared. It was the most terrible sound to hear—starving cattle. The next day we got hay and feed. But we bought feed that whole year and that was expensive. At first, we thought we should sell the cattle. But we stuck it out.

When it came to planting in the spring and harvesting in the fall, what role did the weather play in determining when you did what?

This is a wet farm—always so wet. It's heavy clay and the lowlands—that's where we have the cattle. The highlands are the fruit. One time we had beans up on the top, when we were first here. In the fall, we had to time it to get the corn off before it rained too much. We lost our potato crop one year to the wet. They were all spoiled in the ground.

Most people would think this was a pretty hard life. It was work and everybody worked. That's my family; they all took part. We picked cherries—the children helped. Janie, the youngest, can pick twenty-two lugs a day. Tom and Kay were the same.

Is it possible to compare farming with village or city life?

You entertain the children in town. You provide them with a show; you provide them with all the things they are involved in. On the farm, they're thinking for themselves, doing their own—they're skating, skiing, picking wild berries, picking mushrooms, fishing, going out on the ice. You're involved with your family and everybody's doing things. They've done things from the time they've been little people. We're a family that worked together.

Is that generally true of most farm families?

I think so. I think it's the responsibility they have to themselves. I really think it is a place to raise children.

From what I read, surviving on a farm today is quite difficult.

Very. A lot of farmers went out two years ago. The crops were worth nothing. Your spray material had risen so high. We used our savings to keep our farms—that is how we survived here. Last year was a good year; we hope this year will be a better year. But it takes a little planning. You never have a guarantee on the cattle prices—they've been very low on the market. Can you imagine selling a steer calf for twenty-five cents a pound? Should have been seventy-eight to ninety cents. The farmer goes home with nothing; he couldn't pay for the grain or the milk.

290

Bob and Byrnece White's farm on US 31, c.1950.

Of course, the cherries were only five cents two years ago. You just can't pay hired men, fuel oil, spray material. It took some maneuvering to keep things going.

What's the future of farming? Is the family farm something of the past?

Yes. 'Course in our area, they want it developed and I don't want my farm developed.

Have you had offers to sell?

Always. Always offers. I'm always asked. You go up on the top of that hill—Bob and I would drive up there almost every evening in the summer, in the pasture. You can count five lakes—you can see so far. You have the hills straight down—beautiful. Torch Lake, you see Elk Lake, Bass Lake, Birch Lake, Mud Lake. That means you can see forever, and the water—oh, the Bay, it's so beautiful up there, it's so blue. It's just a gorgeous sight.

Would a couple of bad years make you reconsider an offer to sell?

No. I would sell it to my grandson only. For outsiders, no. I don't want houses and people all over. This has been a farm. I'd like to keep it that way.

It seems that religion plays some kind of role in the lives of farmers.

It's very important. Religion is within you. I'm not one to tell anyone else, but God's presence is around us always. We go out in the field, He's with us, guiding us. We say prayers when it's cold—many times we've had crops when others froze out. God's blanket is there. God is with us always. He guides us. He gives you ideas of what you should be doing, what you should be feeling and thinking. It's very important.

291

Is there a spiritual quality to farming?

Absolutely. It's creation. You've got your little calves that are born; what a beautiful thing. Got the cherry blossoms and His breath and it comes out in fruit. You've got your crops that grow, and the bees are busy. You're out there cutting the hay—it's all so spiritually rewarding. He's at my right side all the time. That's why I've got the farm.

We've sat here for several hours talking about your history. Do you feel like you're part of history?

Oh, yes. I know I'm part of history [Chuckles]. I'm glad to be a farmer.

Farmers of Antrim county, c. 1915.

Versil White

Versil White was born on the family farm south of Elk Rapids in 1923. He graduated from Elk Rapids Rural Agricultural High School, served overseas in World War II, and returned to spend his life farming the soil of Elk Rapids Township. Believing that a man should serve his community, he has devoted twenty-seven years to the Elk Rapids Township Board of Trustees, fourteen years as Supervisor. Today, he and his wife, Jane, still live a half-mile south of the family farm on US 31. This interview was made in 1994 and updated in 1997. These are Versil's recollections:

My dad, Vernon P. White, was born in Grindstone City in the Thumb and moved to Elk Rapids in 1901. My mother, Edna Murray, was a farm girl from Brown City. My granddad had a harness shop in the back of Dockery's old store in Elk Rapids. A few years later, he bought the hardware store and he continued the harness shop in the hardware store, until he passed away in the early '20s.

My dad left here when he was seventeen, went workin' on the railroad. He was workin' out of Saginaw and that's where he met my mother. Maybe 1920 was when they moved back to Elk Rapids—my granddad was sick and they came back to run the store. They handled the International line of machinery, most of it horse-drawn. It was in '21 when my folks bought the farm where Jack [brother] lives, just a half a mile to the north of us. Then we continued to farm, raise potatoes, corn, small grain, beans, radishes.

I was born on the farm—1923. Spent all my early years there.

Tell me about your dad. What was his disposition—happy-go-lucky?

He was—happy-go-lucky. He was away from home through the day because he would buy and sell cattle and horses. This was part of the store business originally;

when you sold machinery, you would take in cattle. When they bought the farm, he continued buyin' and sellin' cattle. At that time, we'd say he was a horse jockey. Then he started buying horses outta Indiana, Illinois and bringing those in here. Sometimes North Dakota; from there they'd bring 'em on rail to Elk Rapids, Traverse City.

How did the farm operate with dad gone so long?

There were quite a few boys—six boys. Vern, Bob, Josephine was the first girl, then Bill, then myself, Betty Jane, then Richard, and Jack. We're all about two years apart. We had a hired man to help out too.

Who decided who did what; how was the division of labor determined with dad gone?

He'd be there in the morning; he'd say "We'll do this today"—whether it's cut hay, haul hay, hoe the beans, chop thistles. He would work with us too. It was pretty well understood that the older ones would drive the horses and if there was any hand work the younger ones did that.

My older brother, Vernon, had left home when he was sixteen. He went to work on the Great Lakes, but he would come back and work also. We all worked together—there were very few disputes on what was to do.

When did a young boy start doing a full day's work—or when did a boy become a man on a farm?

By the time he was fifteen, he was given the reins and sent out to cultivate. He always had a good horse, one that was well-mannered. He wasn't given something he couldn't drive.

Take me on a day on the farm; give us a brief description.

We'd be out to do chores before seven o'clock, taking care of the hogs or young cattle. Through the summer months, cultivate. You always had somebody comin' out, bringin' you a jug of water. My mother'd always send 'em out. At noon, we'd drive our horse in, unhitch, go in at noon. We'd stay in the field until six. Just back and forth across the field. Things have changed, ya know—the tractor. You still cultivate the same way, it doesn't do any better job. You're just going faster.

You cover a little more ground with a tractor, but is there anything you miss about the teams?

Not really [Chuckles]. I've got along quite awhile without 'em. You had to be out there and feed the horse at six o'clock in the morning and you would curry 'em and then harness 'em, you always watered 'em too. Then go have breakfast. After breakfast you go out 'n hitch 'em up and head for the field.

Sheaves of wheat being put in shocks.

That was a long day. Do you look back on it as drudgery?

No. When I look back on it, the only thing I can think of: what a waste of time it is for anybody to work just forty hours. Really, I do. When I was younger and worked one hundred hours a week—I don't feel everyone should—I feel if they want to get ahead they should—more than forty hours. This wasn't all through the season, but there were a lotta weeks you'd work sixteen hours a day. Harvesting. Corn you could harvest anytime, you weren't in a hurry. But the hay—you wanted to get the hay in soon's the dew was off in the morning—you were in the field. You'd work until the dew started to fall. Then Saturday and Sunday you'd take it a little easier. You wouldn't work quite as many hours.

Tell me about your mom. Where was she during the day—in the fields with you?

She was at times. Very hard worker, yes, she was a good farmer. She was one of a large family. She knew all about farming; she would pitch hay with anyone. When my dad wasn't home, she'd tell ya what had to be done.

Describe the kitchen of the farmhouse. What appliances did you or didn't you have?

We had the great big wood cookstove—always a fire going. We didn't have electricity; it wasn't like today. The electric line didn't come south out of Elk Rapids until 1932. The homeowners had to pay to have the line put in. This was gravel [US 31] until the asphalt was put in in 1929. We did have the icebox. As far as appliances, there was no need for one—no electricity.

295

We had a cistern with a pump in the kitchen and we had a tank from the well over the kitchen for water; we had a windmill that would fill the tank.

Were there ever bad years when the farm didn't do too well, where you'd get a little discouraged?

I suppose, but, ya know, there might have been a lotta short years. My mother, I would say, was very thrifty and could manage 'er.

You were about seven or eight when the Depression hit. Did it affect the farmers very much in this area?

Oh, certainly. We were raisin' cherries at that time. Ya know, when you're sellin' cherries for a cent and a half a pound and then don't get your money [Chuckles], it's kind of a let-down. Yes, there were ups and downs. When cows were four or five for $100—lotta times, $20 a head.

We always had beans and potatoes. We had our cows, so we always had milk. At that time, you had chickens, too, but you didn't have the feed for egg production. Now, you have chickens that produce year round, where we had lotsa eggs in the summer months, the winter very few.

You were close enough to Elk Rapids—did you notice a welfare problem? Were people destitute?

The WPA [Works Progress Administration] started then. You'd see the men working on the WPA year round. The village would have projects to do. There were programs where they gave out food.

Shovel snow. I remember the extension of one street—that was in the winter months—that these fellas out there with pick and shovel, diggin' off the top soil, putting in gravel. This ground was frozen, just gettin' their exercise really. Asa Maxwell was with the village at the time and he would oversee those jobs.

There seems to be quite an attachment to the land in your family. You have a lot of brothers, cousins, and sisters still farming. Why is that the case with the Whites?

I think it's the love of the land and bein' your own boss. Bob, he was the first that left home and bought his farm. My sister and her husband, they'd been in Detroit a short while, came back and went in to farming. Bill came back from Detroit, he went in to farming. They knew there was something else they really wanted. Myself, I'm only half a mile from the old home farm. Ya know, I've enjoyed it.

How many Whites are there still in farming?

Bob's wife, Byrnece, is still farming; her grandson is there helping her. Cal and Jo [Bargy], their two boys are still farming. Jack has the old home farm; he has two boys that help him full time and another one part of the time. Bill, he has quite a farm on Elk Lake Road; his grandson helps him. I haven't expanded from the original hundred acres that we have. Vernon, my son, is here with me. He helps.

We enjoyed it. As kids, we had a pony—we had three. As I grew older, I had a horse to ride. At that time, you could ride from Elk Rapids to Acme down the beach on Grand Traverse Bay. We would go for rides in the evening—throw a bridle on the horse and take off. My favorite spot, where now it's Sunset Shores, from there south to 'Tobego [Petobego Nature Preserve]. We'd go down to Yuba Park through the summer quite a bit. I was born and raised at a good time. There're very few that can tell you about going down along the beach. There wasn't one house between Sunset Shores and Yuba. Yuba was the first house.

We had a lot of times—even days when you were workin'—you always had enjoyment. At different times, I think: What are kids missing today?

Speaking of riding horses, tell me the story of coming through town on a dead run?

[Chuckles] We used to run the horses through town. You always need groceries at different times. My mother'd say "Run down to Crisp's Grocery." You'd take a sack, lot stronger than burlap, jump on the pony or horse, run down to the store, tie him to the light pole, get your groceries. Different times, you'd need kerosene for the lantern, you'd take a couple of jugs, go down to the gas station. Sure. There was only one speed [Chuckles]—wide open. Yes.

You're surrounded by the Chain of Lakes to the east and the Bay to the west. In what way has the water affected your life as a farmer? Let's discuss that.

Elk Rapids when Versil was a boy, c.1935.

297

It does hold back the growth of the trees in the spring because we do have frosts through May, late May. It holds back the bloom, so hopefully, it holds it back enough, we miss the frost. Some years we don't and we'll have a failure. But most the time, we have a crop.

The water—the ice in the water will hold the growth back. The temperatures are cooler in the spring—just naturally tends to hold that fruit back. You take in other areas, they're quite a little ahead of us. Up here where we get those cool breezes, keeps the blossoms from coming out too soon.

My dad was a strong believer in having us haul manure in the winter months and put that around the trees. Long after the ground would be bare, under that manure was a ring of snow and ice. That would hold those trees back.

You've been involved in township government for a long time. What is your philosophy on local government; what should local government do for the people?

I'm like Ben Franklin: the least government is the best government. I stand by that. Too much involvement by the government—somebody has to pay for these programs. Everybody sittin' back and wantin' a handout.

The area is under tremendous pressure. From Yuba north, what do you see happening?

Further development. Not that I like to see it, but that's the way it's leanin'. Ya know, everyone likes this area once they've been here. Today, we can't jump on a horse and ride through everybody's front yard. Eventually, even this land here will be split up and developed.

Is there no way to protect agricultural interests?

Buying development rights where the other taxpayers in the area do that; that is one way. If somebody wants to develop theirs, it would sell for a lot higher price. If the current owner would sell his development rights—say if they were to pay him $60-70,000 for the development rights, then it would stay in the present state. If it was agricultural, it would stay that way.

What's unique about this area?

Just the way the land lays. Jane and I were both raised here. I've been around the whole country, just a short distance from being around the world. I've seen some nice places, but none that I liked as well. Our air is cleaner. It isn't noisy; we can sleep nights.

Living here all your life, do you have a favorite spot or a favorite view of this area?

I've got two or three. In the spring of the year, it's close, right back here by the hardwoods. I've got a spot there, look toward the house here—whether the trees are in

298

bloom or whether the fruit's on the trees—beautiful time. When the fruit is on the trees and you see the sun hit that fruit first thing in the morning, that's out of this world. Another spot is on the Old Mission peninsula, on the shore road looking east over Grand Traverse Bay back here—very pretty spot. Same when you're east of Alden, toward Mancelona, looking over Torch Lake. Hard to beat.

Farm workers south of Elk Rapids, c. 1910.

Doyle Willson

Doyle Angus Willson was born in 1917 on the north edge of Beal Lake in Echo Township. His grandfather, Benjamin Willson, had emigrated from Canada in the late 1800s. Doyle's parents were Durward Willson and Clara Bradshaw and they had bought the farm—Doyle's birthplace—in 1905. Doyle enjoyed work and was a highly-respected farmer all his life. His sense of humor and his ability to poke fun at himself got him tagged by his friends as a "blue collar Will Rogers." He married Alice Batterbee and they raised five children. I interviewed Doyle in 1993, three years before his death.

Doyle, let's go back to your childhood. Describe your dad; what kind of a man was he?

He wasn't really stern. He looked stern; he acted stern, but he was really a pussycat. I can only describe him as I knew him; he helped me out; he was for whatever I decided to do. We'd talk about it and then he'd say, "Well, I don't see anything wrong with that—go ahead."

He bought a shingle mill. He set it up down at the edge of the swamp. There were a few old cars—I was interested in the electrical parts. I asked him, "Can I disassemble these cars and hook up to the line shaft that runs the shingle mill? Can I put a pulley on that line shaft and drive some generators and see if I can rig up some headlights on the cars?" He said, "We can't shut the mill down for any reason, but anytime the mill is down, you can work on it. Go ahead with your project in down time." I wasn't big enough to work in the mill; I was probably six or seven years old.

I could take these old cars apart, mount them wherever I wanted to. My mother made the belt for it out of straw ticking. I drove these things with that belt; they worked. When the shaft was turning, the lights would light up in the building. I thought, "Boy, that's really something—I'm a success!" He never tried to discourage me; he'd give me a little room.

Tell me about your mom; describe her for me.

She was like all moms—she was a wonderful person. She was born just two houses east of here and she was raised right there. Her name was Bradshaw.

Let's talk about the farm and its relation to Beal Lake.

It's on the north side of the lake—that is, the tillable parts are all on the north side. The section line came right down through along my father's forty; he was in Section 22. He purchased quite a strip of land from the East Jordan Lumber Company in Section 21 and gradually we cleared this up.

The fire went through which was in our favor. I'm sure it helped my father 'cause it got rid of a lot of rubbish. I don't know how it started but the Intermediate River didn't stop it—it crossed that easily—it was on both sides of the lake. 'Course I was only four years old when it went through; I can remember it at night especially. There were quite a few farms that burned out—Haywood's and Patterson's—anyone that wasn't home lost their buildings. There wasn't any communication in those days. You couldn't tell anybody; if they didn't see it, that was about it.

My father saved our buildings by backfiring around them—they burned everything that was burnable right close to the buildings, then let the fire go back and meet the other fire. They saw it coming; my older brother took part in this. It was nothing desirable, that's for sure. There was a high wind—it only lasted two or three days. It cleaned the area right off.

As we could, we cleared the stumps. We'd just work around them. The older fellas wanted to go straight; the corn rows were thirty-six inches apart. We'd carry our markers, marking the ground, we did it all by hand with a pole and some chain and we'd put 'em over these stumps. I hated some of those big pine and hemlock stumps—they were higher than my head—to get that marker over 'em was something else and try to keep the marker straight at the same time. If you're fighting too many objects like stumps or trees or fence posts—farmers didn't put many fences in because they were a nuisance.

When did you start doing a full day's work as a boy?

I really don't know. I was different than some of the other kids 'cause I wanted to work and I would do anything he would ask me to do.

It was my responsibility to keep the cattle rounded up because there weren't any fences. The cattle and livestock just ran loose. Everybody's cattle was all over everywhere. I had an old Indian pony. I'd keep track of the cattle and bring 'em in and stay with 'em even. That was my job, to live with 'em. I kinda fell in love with some of this land.

When they built the house in 1924—that made me seven years old—he said one day, "I want you to take the team and go to East Jordan to the cooperage and get a load

Doyle on his Indian pony.

of fire brick to build a chimney." People nowadays say, "Oh, c'mon." I went to East Jordan and got the load of brick and brought it back. I didn't even know there was such a place as East Jordan. He drew me a map on how to get there and I made the trip. It's about nine miles; it took me all day. I took a man's place that day.

The team was well broken—my father broke them himself. He would load logs with 'em all alone. They rolled up tremendous loads of logs—the horses on one side of the sleigh and him on the other. They would do what he said.

He had a set of values that meant a great deal. When I was thirteen, I wanted to buy some land from the East Jordan Lumber Company; there was seventy-six acres along the lake—I had researched this a little bit. I had a little bit of money in the East Jordan bank. I was just a kid so my father's name was on the bank papers with mine. I talked to my father and he said, "Why do you want that? It's just low, wet ground." I said, "Well, I kinda like it. I'd like to own it. I'd like to put in some crops along there." Finally, he consented, "Well, I guess you really wanna do it." I gave $150 for seventy-six acres. It was quite an investment; dollars were hard to come by. I sold that real estate just last March [1993]. I owned it since I was thirteen.

I was married at nineteen. It was between the time that I was thirteen and nineteen that I was doin' these things. My brother and I bought Sections 16 and 17. All that

302

the East Jordan Lumber Company owned, we bought. At one time, we had over two thousand acres. We bought it for a dollar an acre.

On one piece, I want to say, there's 220 acres in that block and I bought it for $220 and sold it for $4000 a few years later. The guy kept it for ten years and he sold it for $45,000. It sold just a year ago for $75,000—same piece of property. This is how crazy things have gotten [Laughs].

Some people stay on the farm, some people leave. What do you think it takes to be a farmer?

You have to like it. You have to love it, in fact, or you wouldn't do it. That's what's wrong today because people come in—they're not really farmers. They think they can make a buck. It takes 'em awhile to learn that they can't do this.

It's a lot of hard work, early frosts, late frosts in this area—they all enter in. You can't control the weather. For instance, I've seen years when you would get six, eight, ten, twelve inches of rain in the month of September. Well, in our area that was bad—you couldn't handle the water situation. We had a filtering system so the water couldn't go directly to the lake and that's important—you can't let the water go directly to the lake. It'll take all your top soil and deposit it in the lake. If you don't have a filtering system somewhere along the line, you lose all your top soil. Trees are the very best, a root system of trees that slows this down and practically stops it and makes it sit still.

When I was a little kid, we had a dock on Beal Lake and the lake was much larger than it is now—twenty feet out from the bank we had twelve feet of water. Now I don't think you can find twelve feet of water in Beal Lake; it's just a sediment basin. How much larger Beal Lake was I never will know, but when I was a kid I have plowed into bushels of clam shells in a place out in the fields, way up in the fields where we were farming. Now I don't know how those clam shells got there unless this was the lake at one time.

You mentioned that you've always been concerned about the quality of the water in Beal Lake. In what way have you shown a concern?

For one thing, we didn't clear-cut anything on the south side of the road. We tried to stop the water from rushing across and going into the lake. We never permitted any ditches to be put in all the way to the lake.

We went into a plan with the ASCS [Antrim Soil and Crop Service]. We put in a diversion ditch up at the north end of the farm. We put in 765 feet which cost about $3,000. It was designed to handle all the water for about a half a mile of the property across the base of the hill. Those hills on the north were all clay and they'd start to shed as soon as it started to rain, just like a roof. So this diversion ditch was really important to keep from trenching our field.

It seems as though you've been concerned about water quality and the environment all your life. Where did you develop this awareness that other people didn't seem to have?

Husking corn in Central Lake, c.1910.

I don't know, it just makes sense to me. If you have some plant food out on a certain part of your farm, you'd like to keep it there, ya know? I fought with this all my life: How do you keep it there?

What kind of plant food?

A lot of barnyard manure. In fact, our commercial fertilizer hasn't been around all that long. We would plow down green manure; we would plow down all the barnyard manure. But the idea was to keep it where you had it. This is quite a problem and water is really your enemy. It's gonna take it away if you don't do something about the water.

No farmer—and I really mean this—no farmer can afford to put out plant food and let the water take it into the lake. So he's not really the culprit. He can't afford it; he wouldn't do it, and yet, somehow or other, people think he is the real culprit. He might be to some extent, but that's not his plan.

Was there anything on the farm you couldn't do?

No, and I never let any task defeat me. I'm gonna whip it one way or another. If I can't do it one way, I'll do it another way.

Can you think of a situation that you couldn't whip?

It would have to be disease. We had a siege with brucellosis [a persistent and recurrent fever caused by bacteria, also known as "Bangs disease"]. We had it hit us twice; one time we lost thirteen cows. The next time brucellosis hit us, we lost forty

304

cows. But we didn't stop either time. Luckily for us, they had a program through the Extension office—brucellosis eradication program—right when this was happening. They helped us tremendously.

How does brucellosis first show itself in a cow?

Well, they abort. I had a little slaughterhouse. Evidently, someone brought in a brucellosis animal for me to slaughter. I'm sure this played a part. That was in 1950. It's a live virus and it's carried mostly from animals aborting. They'll always retain the placenta. Someone has to remove this. If you're not aware of it, proper sanitation isn't taken. It will stick to your clothing; it'll ride on your boots. There are a whole lot of things that are bad about it. We didn't really understand it. I got discouraged, but I didn't ever think of quitting.

Let's talk about Beal Lake. How big is it?

'Bout half the size of Scott Lake. Forty acres in Beal Lake and maybe a hundred in Scott Lake. The connecting river is Intermediate; I've heard some people call it a crik. It's a pretty good stream and it stays quite constant. It doesn't fluctuate with the weather much.

I enjoyed the lake. It was a good fishing lake. I didn't have time much in the summertime, but I'd fish through the ice in the winter. I got some nice fish there. They're gone pretty much now; it's over-fished. I like to go out there and spear fish.

I don't know if they had seasons in those days. I just fished when I wanted to fish and I think my dad did the same thing. One time he said, "Let's go fishing." It was a miserable day. You shouldn't oughta be outside because it was so nasty, so we went fishing. We had an old rowboat and we had a clothesline reel—handle on each side, you wind the rope up. We had a chalkline to fish with. He had a Junebug spinner and we dragged this line behind the boat. It was my job to hang onto the line; he rowed the boat. We had a galvanized washtub in the boat; everytime we'd catch one, he'd throw 'im in the tub. We just went once around the lake and came back—probably an hour and a half. We had twenty-one pike—some of 'em had their head 'n tail stickin' outta the tub—huge things, 'bout eight pounds, maybe some ten pounds—no little tiny ones. My father thought this was a real good day because we took 'em all home, cleaned 'em, salted 'em, put 'em in a barrel. So we didn't have to go fishin' for weeks, ya know. We had fish.

That's one thing my parents taught me: you don't waste anything, and today it's just a different story. Waste is just way outta control. Anyway, that didn't happen back in those days 'cause we didn't have it to waste.

Are the lakes as good today for fishing as they were then?

No, no. I think too many people filled too many washtubs. I don't know any other reason.

305

Doyle Willson, 1993.

Were you aware, as you were growing up, that Beal Lake was part of a chain that flowed all the way through Torch and Skegemog into Grand Traverse Bay at Elk Rapids?

Well, not very soon in my life. I was never aware of this. I did get acquainted with it because Dingman's had a dam between Scott Lake and Six Mile and there was a big mill pond down there. When I was a kid, in the summertime, that was a great place to fish because it backed out into these trees and willows—and that was good fishing.

I wasn't very big before I realized that this goes clear on around back to Central Lake. Everybody always said, "You live at the bottom of this country. You're right down in the bottom." I said, "The water runs from here away to wherever you guys are. I can't see how it could be the bottom if water runs away from here. Water doesn't run uphill."

I've gone all through there, clear down around. There's obstacles everywhere and I think maybe there ought to be obstacles because we don't need all this—the public. The beaver's quite a problem. They stop it up [the river] and they're a wonderful animal, the beaver, but he's a rascal also. He's an engineer and good one. They do things correctly for their own purpose. They gather and store food for year round. We had a group of 'em; they're still there on the east side of Beal Lake. They have a house on a little tiny crik that doesn't run more'n a hundred yards. They're workers, but they're dangerous and destructive. They cut some pretty good size trees.

Where does the water come from?

Well, springs, they're mostly springs. Up in Kearney Township, it just comes out of a hillside on the Company farm [East Jordan Lumber Company]. Up on Kladder Road there's another one comes out of the hill, goes down and joins this one and then all along these springs up in the hills comin' out on both sides and feeding this other stream. There's quite a number of 'em up there.

You've lived on Beal Lake most of your life. As you think back, what is your favorite view?

When colors come on—there's quite a big hill on the farm and you had a good view from the top of that hill. It was in my grandfather's sheep pasture; he ran sheep up there. If we wanted to really look around, we'd go up on grandpa's big hill. But again, when I was hunting cows, when I would lose track of the cows, I would head for the ridge which ran northwest and southeast on the north side of the valley there. Just ride the horse along that ridge and I would soon locate our cattle. I would get up on that ridge and I could see all over, see the lakes and streams. When the colors come on, it was beautiful. It was good.

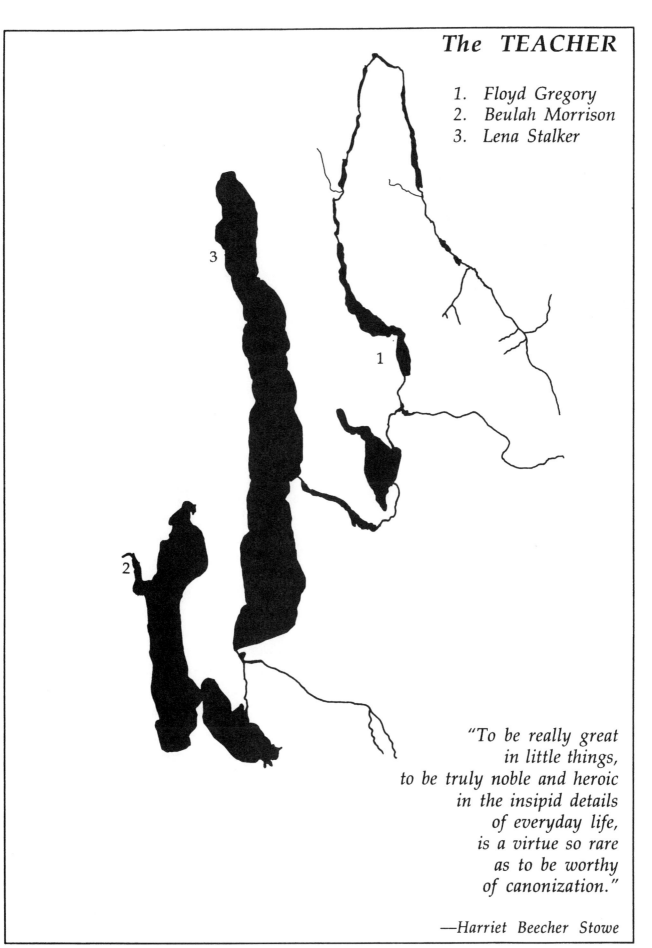

The TEACHER

1. Floyd Gregory
2. Beulah Morrison
3. Lena Stalker

"To be really great
in little things,
to be truly noble and heroic
in the insipid details
of everyday life,
is a virtue so rare
as to be worthy
of canonization."

—Harriet Beecher Stowe

Floyd Gregory

Floyd Gregory was born in a log cabin on the east side of Torch Lake in 1901, the son of Alva and Daisy Gregory. He was raised in lumber camps, taught in rural Antrim County schools for nineteen years, and was Forest Home Township supervisor for eighteen years (1938-1956). He and his wife, Lucile, raised a family of ten children. Though he held many jobs, he always considered himself to be a teacher and a farmer. Floyd died in 1993. In this 1988 interview, we are sitting on his farm near the western shore of Intermediate Lake as Floyd reflects on his life:

My dad was Alva Gregory. He was raised around Mancelona—the Antrim Iron Company. He knew the woods. He was general foreman for the camp. It was the first one we lived in after we left here—it was the Island Lake camp in Kalkaska County. We were there summers, and in the winters we were back here in Bellaire and he worked out of Rileyville camp over here [east of Bellaire] in the winter. We lived there one winter.

You see, the way they did it, they got cordwood—four-foot wood—where they could get it with wagons and horses—that was a short haul they called it. In the winter, the camp was farther away. He spent one winter down there.

Let's talk about the Island Lake Camp. Who owned the camp?

Elk Rapids Iron Company. They were cutting four-foot cordwood. It had to be hardwood—maple or beech, something that would make charcoal. That's what they used for stoking the iron furnace [in Elk Rapids]. After the cordwood was up—a cord was four feet high, eight-feet long, 'course it was four-foot wood—that made 128 cubic feet for a cord. That was a regular cord.

They had fifteen or twenty teams of horses in the camp. Of course, each team had a teamster and an outfit. When they put 'em in the barn, the barn boss did all the work, cleaning and feeding. Shem Pendock always drove team; I remember the name Art Cochran.

Was working in the woods dangerous?

Yes and no. I recall one time, where the tier of wood that he was sitting on in the front pitched down and killed him. His name was Paddy Webster. You probably don't realize how rough those woods roads were—they were just trails. He went down in between the team and the cordwood; the load run over him, killed him. He was from over around Alden. It was the same year that Polish man was killed at Dead Man's Hill. I can see 'em yet bringing him out of the woods. I'da been nine or ten.

Gee, we had a lot of fun. Play around the woods, we weren't close to any water. We did all sorts of boy tricks, building things. Very few chores. We'd get out and get the wood, pickin' up wood.

No indoor toilets—everything was outside. They weren't houses, they were shanties [Chuckles]. Our house that we had, it was three rooms—the kitchen, small living room, and a bedroom divided into two parts. We shared the bedroom. At that time there was just my two older sisters and myself; the boys came along afterwards. My older sister was three years older than me. We all had our friends; there was a family named Watkins, a family name of McGraw.

Facilities were very few. Cookstove. Pail of water. No facilities of any kind. Everything was outside. It was a community pump; carried it to the house.

There were probably around twenty houses––shanties. There was a barn for the horses—housed probably twenty to twenty-five horses, and a blacksmith shop.

The single men lived in a bunkhouse. All the bunks were two-bunk high, just lined up along the wall. Bench along the side where they could get dressed. They didn't have any

Alva Gregory, boss at the Island Lake camp.

Two lumberjacks take a break to pose for a photo, 1915.

At the Island Lake Camp. Art Cochran on top with reins, c.1910.

privacy at all. Always wore long underwear, ya know, usually summer and winter––wool. Lumberjacks got so they didn't know what a pair of shorts were.

How did they bathe?

Best they could. Some of 'em had a little bathhouse—had a little washbasin along one end.

There are a lot of legends and myths about lumberjacks. From what you recall as a young boy in that camp, what did these men seem like to you? Were they tough, rowdy?

On average, no. 'Course there'd always be some, just like nowadays. They were all very sociable fellas. Pastime in the evening was playing cards—especially in bad weather.

As I recall, very little drinking at that time—not in the camp. If they were gonna do much drinking, they usually went to town on week-ends. Very little rowdiness as I recall it.

The men got paid about twenty dollars a month and board—single men. They didn't have any insurance or benefits. They just did the best they could.

Some of these men were our best friends, especially a man who liked younger children—we always had a pal. Fella named Pendock. Did you ever know Walt Watson? He was a log foreman. Walt was a great friend of mine. I was just a little kid, but he took me fishing.

What did your mother do in the camp when there was an illness?

Get something wrapped around our finger for the finger. If we had a bellyache, we got castor oil or epsom salts [Laughs]. Did you ever have to take those? They didn't rush us to the hospital or doctor everytime we had a little upset. They'd get up in the cupboard and get a home remedy. They always had a salve—you remember the old Cloverine salve? It was a home remedy for sores.

Describe your mother and father. Who was the boss in the family?

Well, they both thought they were [Laughs]. 'Course my dad was a big man and my mother was smaller. Her name was Daisy. I've had some of 'em tell me, "Alva acted pretty gruff, but he usually did what Daisy said in the end." [Laughs] They got along very well.

He was quite strict, but a very easy-going man, too. He was the boss; he was the top one in the camp. Most of the men respected him; he never had much trouble.

You had to get an education. Where was the school?

The Gregory family in 1946. Front row (l to r): Arden, Retha, LeRoy, Lucile, Rhea, Marilyn, Donna (in front). Back (l to r): Emogean, Floyd, Phyllis, Gwen.

The school was almost to Barker Creek. It was about two and a half miles over there. We couldn't get there in the wintertime. There were no roads—couldn't walk—so we didn't go to school.

You finished high school in Bellaire in 1920, then you began teaching.

I went to County Normal in Mancelona—1921 and 2. I got a certificate for rural teaching. My first teaching job was six miles east of Mancelona—Bocook School. I stayed there one year. I got one hundred dollars a month; that was about the most I ever got. I had about twenty students, all ages, kindergarten—they called it chart class—through the eighth grade. They always come and go in those days—lumbering finishing up, people moving around.

The next year I taught in a camp school in Kalkaska County—when the camp was done, it was gone.

You've lived in Antrim County most of your life, born near the shore of Torch Lake. Of all the lakes that you've seen in the Chain, which is your favorite body of water?

Most everybody would say Torch Lake was about the most beautiful, but it's the most treacherous. It's cold and deep. More accidents. There've been more drownings in Torch Lake than there has any place else. They very seldom find a body if it goes down once. The water is so deep and so cold that they never come back up. When they go down in Torch Lake, they're usually down.

312

There's a lot of concern about the cleanliness of the water. Do you have any concerns about that?

Well, everybody has. They think they've controlled the pollution. When I was young, the sewage and everything went right in the [Intermediate] river down there; they thought that would take care of it—raw sewage. I can remember most anytime you go on down the river in Bellaire. When I was at the old school, there was a sewer pipe right down from the school—right straight down to the river.

You spent eighteen years as Supervisor (1938-1956) in this township. Let's talk about the lakes in Forest Home Township and problems that you had to deal with, policing the water.

Very few problems at that time because the county had taken over all the main projects. There's Clam Lake, Torch Lake, Lake Bellaire, and Intermediate Lake. The Chain starts almost directly east of here in those creeks over in the hills. I've been to the head of some of them. Beal Lake, Scott Lake, Six Mile Lake, and that's the same water that goes by here.

What do you think is the biggest problem with the Chain of Lakes today? Aside from pollution? Too many people up here?

Well, that has a lot to do with it, yeah. They'll eventually ruin the lakes, I think so—unless they find some remedy.

The people that've lived here all their lives would say, "Let 'em stay in the city"—but that won't happen, of course. In my own case, I couldn't say that 'cause I owned 225 acres along here. When we moved in this house, there wasn't anybody that lived down there [Intermediate Lake], but now I've increased the population. I've sold it off—there's about twenty-five people or so right on the land where we were all by ourselves at one time. I'm part of the cause.

Has the water affected the way you've lived your life?

Oh, yes. Us old people don't like to keep up with the Joneses—the ones that come in and buy now. They want to get away from the city, but they want to bring the city with 'em. They think we should do the same—their buildings, their habits.

I have never been a real water lover. I've always enjoyed the water; I'm close enough to it. I swim and I did some fishing, but it wasn't a hobby. I like to look at it.

Do you have a favorite spot?

I always enjoy going over on Torch Lake and looking out over the lake. I never got as well-acquainted around Grass Lake—it's Lake Bellaire now. I've lived more of my time here and on Torch.

After I got to be Supervisor, these small resorts like Miley's Lodge, Fisherman's Paradise, they were pretty well done. There was the Pere Marquette on Torch—that was the biggest hotel out there. Lone Tree Point south of Clam Lake.

When we lived over on Torch, my dad's property went right to the lake; he had 1320 feet on the lake. The next place—we used to call it Larson's Point—that's the yacht club property. North of there, a man by the name of Oliver, he moved in there as a farmer and just pastured the land along the lake. All that land on the lake was pasture land. When he sold out, he owned three-fourths of a mile. My dad sold his on a land contract for ten dollars a foot.

You were born in a log cabin on the east side of Torch Lake. You lived in lumber camps, taught in rural school houses, spent eighteen years as supervisor, and you've lived in the heart of the Chain of Lakes all your life. If you had to do it all over again, would you live your life differently?

Well, you'd have to, you couldn't live it the way we did—no [Chuckles]. But your decisions would be pretty much the same. I would be the oldest resident of Forest Home Township that was born and raised here. This was always my home.

Lumber camps throughout the Chain were Floyd Gregory's childhood playgrounds.

Beulah Morrison

Beulah Morrison was born Beulah Myers in 1900. Born of German parents, she was one of eight children. Her father was a farmer and carpenter near Lacota, Michigan. As the lumber era was ending, Beulah came to Antrim County at the age of nineteen to teach school in Elk Rapids. Cherry orchards and tourism had yet to dominate most northern Michigan towns. In 1921, she left teaching to marry Glenn Morrison and raise a family. This 1993 interview was updated with Beulah in 1997. At the age of ninety-seven, she still resides in Elk Rapids. She speaks here of her love for her adopted hometown and the water around it.

When did you first come to Elk Rapids?

I came here as a high school teacher from Western Michigan College—it was not a university then. Mr. Lane was the Superintendent and he came down to interview us. Lucille LaCore, from Elk Rapids, was also down there that year. He decided to hire me as one of the teachers in high school. So I came here in September, 1919.

Did you know where Elk Rapids was at the time?

My history professor was Mr. Hickey and he and his family came up every summer over on Old Mission. I happened to be staying in their home at the time. He said, "You know, Elk Rapids is a nice little town. It has two really good drug stores. I think you'll be happy up there. I think you would like that better than going to Detroit." I thought well, maybe it would be a good place. I had never been north at all.

It was just after World War I and the blast furnace had closed. Could you describe the town as you came into it on that first trip?

We came into Williamsburg and changed trains there and came into Elk Rapids on the spur. I stayed with Lucille LaCore. She took me all around town and I thought it was quite a nice little village. I was surprised that there was an east and west side, which was a little confusing to me at the time. You had to get used to it. If you didn't get used to it, you didn't know where you were half the time. We went across two bridges always—the one on Dexter Street and the one across [the power plant].

I was impressed with the Town Hall and I was impressed with the fact that they had a sewer system and city water in a town as small as this.

There wasn't too much going on here at that time. The town was small; there weren't even a thousand people—maybe seven hundred. It has always been a resort town. A lot of these houses around here were vacant. I wasn't that much interested. School was important.

Was there a noticeable difference between the east side and the west side?

There weren't many homes over there. The old kilns were still there—remnants of them. The Bee Hive [boarding house] in the sand hill was about half covered. There wasn't much over on the east side. That [Longfellow] school was over there, however.

Has the east side been considered the poorer part of town?

Yes, the least desirable. I don't know why. People just liked the west side of town better—maybe because we were on the Bay, where the east side was on the lake and the river. People still prefer the west side of town.

The old school house is gone now. Give me a picture of the school as you recall it.

I lived within a block of the school. I can remember wading the snowdrifts in that block that I walked to school. The streets were not cleaned. Of course, we had no busses. People either brought their children to school or they walked; it was mostly town, you know. A few country people came in and the east-siders all walked over.

Elk Rapids Public School. "I came here for eighty-five a month." —Beulah Morrison

They'd come in sometimes pretty wet. But they soon got dried out and they were used to it.

The school was quite nice. It was an old building. We used the third floor then; we had a chemistry lab up there and there were other classes up there too. Of course, we had all twelve grades. The high school wasn't large; it was very small. I remember the senior class—about ten students.

Tell me what a teacher's day was like in 1919, and your duties.

I can't remember how many subjects I taught. I maybe had five subjects and maybe six. I taught eighth grade history. We had five high school teachers and the Superintendent—Mr. Lane; he taught too. There was Olive Day who was the principal; there was a girl from Ohio. The second year I was here, I was Principal and I was twenty years old. Can you imagine? No one knew how old I was. I always looked old for my age; now people think I'm young for my age.

The second year, we had a new Superintendent, Mr. Street. He was from the Upper Peninsula. We had to hire a Latin and English teacher. That was the year Miss Langstaff came from Ohio. Because they had to pay her more than they paid me, they raised my salary ten dollars a month. I came here for eighty-five a month. That seemed to be what they were paying.

I boarded at the hotel downtown and I walked downtown for my meals—the LakeView House. Good food. Big dining room; not many people ate there either. It was just what I would consider a country hotel.

What did you do that made you a good teacher?

I was born on a farm in Lacota, Michigan. My mother died when I was two years old. My father, a farmer and carpenter, moved to Kalamazoo when he married my step-mother. I'm very tolerant of people. I am very independent. I have a great sense of right and wrong. I like people, but I am quite reserved.

Your husband, Glenn, started a lumber company during the last days of the Depression. Wasn't that a risky time to start a business?

Yes, it was. I would say about 1938 or 39—along in there. Brown Lumber in Traverse City backed us. They were part of our partnership; they were nice men.

Tell me how the Depression affected your life in this small town?

Well, I'll tell you—it was bad. Glenn was a carpenter, so he had work in the summer, but when winter came, there was nothing to do unless you had a house you were finishing on the inside or maybe people wanted something done during the winter. So you ran bills—you ran a grocery bill, you ran a meat bill, you ran a fuel bill. If you didn't have credit, I don't know what you did. I can remember when we didn't even have a postage stamp in the house. We didn't have any money.

Beulah and Glenn, 1920.

At Christmas time, I can remember telling my husband I was going to get him the *Country Gentleman* for Christmas and I never had money to send for the subscription. We always seemed to have something for the kids, but very little. We always had a Christmas tree. We had food because our credit was good.

These were just hard times. But everybody was having a hard time, so we weren't the only ones. You didn't think much about it; you got along with what you had.

We were buying this house. It had no plumbing, a little blue sink where the water came in at the back of the house. We had a little barn in the alley and an outdoor toilet.

What did you do to cut corners or make do in tough times?

I did some teaching once in awhile and ten dollars a day was wonderful. I can remember substituting at the drug store one time. Around Christmas time, I worked at the post office because it was a busy time. At that time, Natalie Marker was postmaster.

We had nine cabins on the Bay [Bay Beach Cabins] and we rented them overnight and by the week and by the month. I went over in the summertime and took care of the cabins and rented my house. We were over there ten years— starting about 1938. They were one-room cottages with cooking facilities and bathroom. We stayed in a double one all summer. I think we charged five dollars a night for the single ones, probably fifteen dollars for the double ones. They lasted for quite awhile.

We haven't been rich, but I don't think the poor years hurt us. Sometimes it's good if you have poor years. I think it was good for our children; our children are all independent. They have all turned out to be the right kind of people.

What do you see as the biggest change in Elk Rapids?

I can see quite a few changes—some of them good, some of them not so good. My husband always said, "Yes, they want to put in a harbor out there, but they will always have to dredge that harbor."—and that's exactly what they have to do—purt near every year. I don't think the harbor has been such a gold mine that Elk Rapids thought it was going to be. I think the rates are too high for local people to keep their boats there. I don't think the people are shopping in Elk Rapids like they thought they were going to. Perhaps it is a wonderful harbor, but Elk Rapids is growing too fast to suit me.

We're too close to Traverse City. Everybody goes to Traverse City—they even go over there to grocery shop; they go there to buy things they could get right here in this town. If you live in a town, you should buy your things in the town. Having

318

been in the lumber company, I know. It doesn't help to buy stuff out of Traverse City; it doesn't help your town.

Let's discuss the lakes. Did you ever get out on Elk Lake?

I did. I had a girl friend who had friends on Elk Lake. This farm was across from the Samels Brothers. We would go out to Skegemog Road on Elk Lake. There were very few houses out there—maybe a half dozen. We used to swim, take picnics. The Skegemog resort was there—the hotel. We didn't go out to eat at places like that like we do now.

What influence do you think water has on people's lives?

I think it has a lot more today than it did back then. I can remember as a young person, we would take food and go to the lake and stay all day. We would fish and cook our fish on the beach at night. We would spend the whole day; it meant a lot to us. The water to me was wonderful. It was pretty anytime—a beautiful blue. I was used to the water, but not as much water as there was up here and I thought it was a gorgeous place. I hope it never changes. I've been here ever since. I've never been sorry I came to Elk Rapids.

Do you think water influences the way people live?

Lots of times we drive around the bayshore at night and say "we don't half appreciate this beautiful Bay." You look across, you can see cars on Old Mission. That view out there I think is beautiful. We're so used to it—and last night, did you see the sunset? It was gorgeous!

Let me ask you a philosophical question. Why do you think we're here?

I think we are all here for a purpose. I think we should do as much good to our fellow man as we can. I don't know that I have any good answer for it. I think we need to live as near like Christ as we can, as we understand the Bible. I think we're either all going to heaven or hell. Anybody that doesn't believe in God is out of his mind. There are too many miracles going on in the world to not believe in a Supreme Being. This world is too wonderful not to believe that there is somebody directing things.

Beulah (left front) with friends for breakfast on Torch Lake, 7:30 am, May 20, 1920.

Lena Stalker

Lena was born 1899 to Dessie Smith and Charlie Anderson on her grandmother's farm on the Manistee River. She returned, after her birth, to Torch Lake Village where her father worked in Cameron Brothers Lumber Company. Retiring with honors after forty-five years of teaching in Flint schools, Lena returns each summer to her childhood community. This interview was conducted in 1994, and a second visit updated it in 1995. At ninety-six, her laughter and optimism belie her age and brighten the entire household.

Lena, describe your earliest childhood memories of your parents.

When my mother and father got married they settled in this little house in Torch Lake Village. When she became pregnant, there were no hospital facilities, so they decided to take me down to grandmother's. When I was born, grandma wrapped me up and put me in her brick oven to keep me warm. I was there for about ten days. The doctor charged five dollars to drive out in horse and buggy to take care of me and to weigh me and to find out I was five pounds.

My mother was not able to nurse me so my father went out and bought a Jersey cow. The Jersey cow got homesick and would go home all the time. My dad was always chasing it back and forth to the farm. But I certainly did thrive on that Jersey milk 'cause I've lived to be ninety-six years old.

My grandmother got a job working on the scow that travelled all around Torch Lake here. She cooked up the meals and fed 'em. When my mother got married, she couldn't even come to the wedding—she was busy on the scow. It was like a house-boat; I got to see that.

When children got sick, were there any home remedies?

My little sister Jenny—she died of cerebral meningitis. She was beautiful. If I had an earache, we called Mr. Sandy Dean who smoked a pipe. He'd come over and blow smoke in my ear 'n that cured it [Laughs]. We had anti-phlegestine patches we'd put on when I couldn't walk. They'd heat 'em up real hot. The doctor prescribed that. He thought it was tuberculosis of the bone. We all had the whooping cough—I remember all three of us—kept my mother busy. We fixed up a tent—she called it the croup tent.

Let's go back to your childhood days as a young girl in Eastport and Torch Lake. Can you describe those days?

We practically lived out there in that lake. We rode logs 'cause when the lumber company got through with the logs they just let them float. We used those for rafts. I learned to swim—nobody ever taught me. We taught ourselves. All the kids in school—Eva Wilkinson, Ladema Dawson, we were always playing around the lake.

Eva and I would sneak down to the Bay and take all our clothes off, go skinny-dippin'. Women weren't supposed to do that. Hang our clothes on the bushes. She had a cousin, George Hopkins, that used to follow us down there and peek through and watch us and laugh. He must've got a thrill out of it or something [Laughs].

We did have a lot of good swims. The Bay would be warmer and we could jump over the big waves. That was the part we liked to do. Torch Lake could get pretty cold, ya know.

Weekends our families—there were two families of us, my Aunt Ethel and my Uncle Charlie. We put all our food together and all come down here to Aunt Nora's. She lived in that place that's now Brownwood. We'd have corn roasts, pies 'n cakes 'n buns. We'd do that so many weekends at Eastport.

My uncle gave me a puppy—a St. Bernard dog. I had a chicken that I named S.T. and I used to carry that down to the factory to meet my father when he came home for lunch. The Cameron Lumber Company is where my father worked.

There was no fire alarm. They had a great big bell on the outside of the school house. No one was ever supposed to touch that bell because when that bell would ring everyone would come to put out the fire. I went down there one day and I rang the bell. Well, I never forgot that because I got the hardest spanking I ever got.

Compare your childhood with life today. Do people have more fun?

Many people think that we oldsters missed so much fun and had no recreation. Not so! My father had twin bikes with a basket fastened on for me and my mother in her new split bicycle skirts. They travelled the bicycle paths to church, square dances, picnics, and ball games, and I was never left alone. It was a good life.

321

We didn't have to worry so much. I was happy. I don't hear the kids singin' any more. Do you think people are happier if they sing more?

Down here was the Grange hall and once a year all the old soldiers and their wives gathered there. My mother use to sing—she sang all those old songs, "Tenting Tonight on the Old Camp Ground." I'd come down here as a little girl and I could remember all those older people and I thought, "Well, they just don't have any fun at all." They always had homemade ice cream. My Uncle Wendell—he got his ice from Torch Lake and he said he was always glad when they had a real cold winter because the ice would get big and thick. The ice cream was made with real cream.

Describe the beach parties you had as a child.

I was always making potato salad. They'd have frankfurters—just make a big fire and cook a lot of marshmallows. I had a little ice cream freezer, I used to freeze that all up and take it along. Boys and girls, we all went together after we got in high school. We always had a chaperon that went along with us, of course. The parents chose her. I can remember her, Mrs. Gokee. She'd say, "C'mon now, it's just about time to go home." We didn't want to go home. Sometimes we used to take Mrs. Gokee home and turn around and go back. I don't think things have changed much.

We usually took our bathing suits, we went swimming a lot in Torch. If you changed your clothes, you put 'em in the bushes 'cause they didn't have any houses for dressing. We used to ride on those logs. This used to be a lumbering district and all those logs that they cut, they would throw 'em out. Torch Lake was fulla logs. We never bothered that it was cold—we went in anyway. It is the most beautiful place. That was our fun. We'd sit on those logs and ride all over the place—we'd float on 'em.

There was none of that that goes on today. You'd never hear of a girl that was pregnant. If it happened at all, the parents would move 'er outta town to some relative. There was no sex down at the beach with all those parties. They kept track of the kids. All of our neighbors did the same thing. We had to be home.

That year that it froze over like glass. They built boats—they called 'em sail boats. Aunt Nora let 'em borrow her sheets for sails. They'd get on and sail all over the lake. Very seldom does it freeze like that.

You've lived in Flint, East Jordan, many places. Why do you keep coming back to Torch Lake?

I don't know what there is about it. I always come up to Torch Lake. I think a whole lot of it's family. We're real close. The taxes were going up and up and up. I don't know how I can pay all those taxes. But I just like this place. I don't know what there is about it ... always loved it.

Back to family again. I always took care of the cemetery. My grandmother—her

The men at the Cameron Brothers Sawmill in Torch Lake Village where Lena's dad worked, c.1900.

The Grass Lake tug at Torch Lake Village. Sixty to sixty-five feet long, these steam-powered tugs were the "work horses" for the lumber companies on the Chain,

A houseboat (Wanigan) similar to the one where Lena's grandmother cooked meals. The tug boats pulled the scows, loaded with cord wood, to the blast furnace in Elk Rapids.

grave is up there and my father and mother and my little sister. They're all up here at the cemetery. So, you see, it's mostly family.

Are there too many people moving on to the lakes?

You can't blame 'em, what a beautiful place this is. My neighbor's been to Lake Lucerne in Switzerland and he says it doesn't stand a chance with Torch Lake. I think Torch is first.

What is your favorite view?

It's the sunsets. I come up here for the sunsets. Last night, full moon came up and it reflected down into the water—like daylight.

The joy of being up here. We have lots of wild animals. We've always had flocks and flocks of ducks—but they've been building up houses, they took away all the nests up here, so we don't have many anymore.

You can't go back, but the greatest gift that God ever gave us was the gift of memory.

The HISTORIAN

1. Mary Kay McDuffie

*"Local history is not a microscope
that narrows our vision,
but a telescope
that allows a clearer view
of man's place
in the universe of time."*

——Ray Allen Billington

Mary Kay McDuffie

*Mary Kay McDuffie is descended from the founding families of Bellaire. Born in Detroit, she has spent her childhood summers on Torch Lake and most of her adult life year round in the area. Her paternal great-grandparents were Frederick and Maxi Bechtold who arrived in 1880; her maternal great-grandparents, Charles and Chloe McCutcheon, arrived soon after. Mary Kay is a well-qualified historian having published **The Courthouse** in 1974, and **Our First Fifty Years on the Point** in 1978. Her love for Torch Lake is clearly visible in this 1987 interview; it was revised and updated with another visit in 1997.*

Describe your childhood on Torch Lake.

The day school was out, my father would bring us all up here to the cottage and drop us off and we would spend all summer on the lake with our grandparents. We would spend every day on the beach.

At that time there really were very few residents, summer or otherwise. We usually didn't have a car, or else didn't have gas—one or the other. If we wanted to go to visit friends we would walk down the road to get there.

We always had a big garden. My grandfather would hire me to be in charge of picking potato bugs and tomato worms. I was supposed to get paid a penny a hundred for all the potato bugs I caught, but my profits were eaten up because my brother would eat my potato bugs so I didn't make much money [Laughter].

Evenings we made our own family entertainment together. Whittling, reading, playing games or singing by lantern light.

The pets we had were young crows, a robin, a bunny, but never a dog or cat. The crows were best since we could teach them to talk.

I've spent more than sixty years on the water. The biggest activity was swimming and building sand castles. During the '40s we didn't have a boat—we had a rowboat that my grandfather made.

Who were your closest neighbors?

Our closest neighbors—in my earliest memory, there was one house between our house and the yacht club a mile away. That was a little farm house. We didn't really have close neighbors.

When I can first remember there was only one light across the lake at night. There just weren't any other people. On our side, there were very few people. There was a small group of people who went to the yacht club, but it was not a large group.

When did it start to change?

After the Second World War. People started buying and building. Probably the biggest change has been in the last twenty-five years. The population grew after World War II. There was a tapering off, then it started picking up.

Were those summers in the '40s so memorable simply because you were young and had nothing to do but swim?

Summers in the '40s were memorable because of just being at the lake. It seemed like a peaceful life with lots of freedom for me as a child. I wasn't aware of all the difficulties of just surviving. Everyone staying at the cottage was involved in everything we did. Canning, baking our own bread, churning butter, or walking the mile to the blackberry patch with our little lard pails attached to our belts to pick berries. What I thought was family fun was actually our family working at being self-sufficient.

I did have my potato bug business. We did have running water, but we didn't have anything like a washing machine. I remember washing day with the old laundry tub out in the yard, especially during the war. At one point we had several little cousins at the cottage when all the husbands were off at war—we would wash the things in the laundry tub and then carry them down to the lake to rinse. I thought it was wonderful. There would be diapers floating all along the lake shore and it was a great game chasing them down.

When I think about it today, the number of us living in the cottage and the work that the women would have had to have done, it doesn't sound like so much fun, but I used to think it was great.

I remember when they first put electricity in the cottage and my memories—for many years there was just a little dirt road out in back here, and if even one car came by during the day, we'd all run out to look 'cause it was so exciting.

No pavement, no electricity, no telephone. The running water was our one luxury, you could say. But we only had cold water. We had to heat the water in the tea kettle.

In the 1940s, would most cottages be in the same position—a lack of modern facilities?

I think so. I wasn't in a lot of cottages. Probably we all had indoor plumbing and I know there was not electricity along here. I can remember the day they planted the electrical pole. It was a big event. To me, electricity wasn't an improvement. That meant the excitement of the ice man coming to deliver ice each week was gone. Worse yet, it meant we had to sit quietly and listen to every Gabriel Heatter news report.

My father and mother fished. When daddy would be here on week-ends, my mother would row the boat and my father would troll and they would catch one or two fish.

One of our occupations during the '40s—during the war—was finding old tires to sell. At some point, people use to dump old tires in the lake. We would walk along the lakeshore in the water and find old tires to haul back. I think we took them to Claude Kauffman's gas station. I think they were melted down and sent to war.

Going to Kauffman's in Bellaire was very special because on the rare occasions Claude and my grandfather agreed I had been well-behaved and I got to sit in the ice house while they talked. Another occupation we had was collecting milkweed pods for the life jackets as stuffing.

Who were your closest friends?

Early on we were just here and I don't remember there being any friends. There wasn't anybody near enough geographically to have friends. At some point, about '41 or '42 maybe, some friends of ours from Birmingham started coming up here in the summer. So we could play together and walk back and forth.

Do you think of yourself as living on Torch or living on the Chain of Lakes?

Oh, no—I think of myself as living on Torch Lake. I think of it as my lake. It's very much a part of my life and I enjoy it every day—summer and winter.

Why do you think it is so much a part of your life?

My fondest memories of my childhood going back as far as I can remember were always things here at the lake. It sounds like we didn't do much of anything as children growing up on the lake. The lake was—I couldn't wait for school to get out to come up here to be on the lake. I always cried every Labor Day when we were driving back to Birmingham. I'd cry at least as far as Mancelona because I had to

Bellaire in 1953.

leave the lake. It's just always been very important to me.

You've travelled a lot and you've had a chance to make some comparisons. You keep coming back to Torch. Is it still because of those childhood roots?

I certainly think it's more beautiful than any of the other lakes I've seen. I don't know—I guess I can't give you a very good reason why it's so important to me, but it is.

I don't know whether it's the memories, but I'm very comfortable being here. There's something soothing about water to me and I just really enjoy my blue water out here.

You've been writing and researching the history of the area for years. Why do you do that?

I really didn't start paying enough attention to the history soon enough. All of my relatives who could have given me information were gone by the time I really got interested. Maybe in the beginning I was trying to make some connection for myself. I think my ancestors were important because they were some of the founding citizens of the area and had a lot do with the beginning of Bellaire and the directions it took.

When did the concern for pollution and other types of problems begin to develop? When did you begin to notice this question of water quality?

Mary Kay McDuffie at her home on Torch Lake.

It would have been in the '70s that it became more obvious that there was a problem. We were involved with the Three Lakes Association. It had to do with preserving the quality of Torch, Clam and Lake Bellaire. It was started by Hartley Comfort for the purpose of preserving the water quality. Central Michigan University got involved because of Doc Curry being head of the biology department and being a summer resident here. Doc would bring a graduate student each summer to do water quality studies on the lakes.

I think there is potential over-use of the lake. While it seems like a big lake, as the population grows, there's more boating, more swimming. I think most people have quit bathing in the lake, although that was something everybody did. You took your bar of soap when you went to the beach.

A lot of people claim that Torch is so large it's foolish to think that it would be endangered; that because of the activities of the Three Lakes Association and others, there's nothing to worry about. How would you respond to that?

I think that we have some things to worry about. I have seen so many changes in the lake since I was a child that I think that there are things to worry about. I don't think you can have wall-to-wall people around the lake without it taking a toll.

We have so many motor boats that I really feel that all that churning from the propellers has to make a difference in the water quality over the years. I have great concern about houseboats on the lakes. One, as a taxpayer I highly object to someone else having a tax-free vacation on my lake. I'm not convinced that the sewage on those boats is going to be kept where it belongs. It's just a hunch I have.

330

In many ways things have improved sanitation-wise. They're more careful where the septic tanks go, and the health department has to issue permits.

How do we resolve this dilemma of appearing to be so provincial that we don't want anyone else in, and yet solving these problems of all the development? What's the answer?

Well, I admit I liked it thirty and forty and fifty years ago when there were considerably fewer people and more wild. I think that we have to be very careful to have zoning and organizations like Three Lakes, Skegemog and the Upper Chain Association—people who watch over the lakes and plan ahead for some kind of controlled growth.

I'm sure that people coming in resent being told what they can and can't do, but if you come to an area because you like the clean, clear water and then you don't treat it properly, it's not going to stay clean and clear for very long.

My feeling for a long time has been if we have the no-holds-barred open door policy, people will come here and the lakes will not stay clean and clear and people will move on and we will be left with an area that is not as desirable.

What if someone accused you of being snobbish or elitist? How would you respond to that?

It's happened before. They probably would be right. That doesn't bother me. If I have to be snobbish or elitist to protect the lake, so be it.

There are many faces and voices of men, women, and children that have become lost in time. The unidentified man and woman (above) and the farm children of Milton Township (below) are as much a part of our history as those whose stories have been told.

Epilogue

The oral histories here give lie
to the belief that history is something old
and dead and distant.
Our children should know that local history,
through the technique of
the tape-recorded interview,
is alive and current and vibrant.
It gives meaning and direction
far more clearly than the ancient myths
or political meanderings of traditional texts.

Lewis Mumford,
nationally known city planner
and historian,
puts the value of local history
in perspective when he states:

"All of us feel, at bottom, with Walt Whitman,
that there is no sweeter meat
than that which clings to our own bones.
It is this conviction that gives value
to local history:
we feel that our own lives,
the lives of our ancestors and neighbors,
the events that have taken place
in the particular locality where we have settled,
are every bit as important as the lives of people
who are more remote from us,
no matter how numerous these others may be;
or how insignificant we may seem
alongside of them."

Consequently, we celebrate our lives
and the lives of our friends and neighbors
by recording their voices.
They are the voices on the water.
They are memorialized here in print;
it is a testament to their affection
for the earth around them.

Acknowledgements

There are claims that no one reads acknowledgements and, therefore, they need not be included in a book. What a conceit to think that I could have done this by myself and so, whether or not it is read, I must acknowledge these wonderful people. The immeasurable support offered by them is difficult to describe. But without the moral and material support of so many, this book would not exist.

My heartfelt thanks are due the thirty-eight interviewees who allowed me into the privacy of their homes, their lives, and their innermost thoughts. They are the heart of the book. I have taken great care to respect their privacy. The ethics of an oral historian requires judicious editing. Thus the interviews have been edited in their content, but not altered in their intent.

I shall always be indebted to a special few whose warm hospitality, lengthy conversations, and cheerful advice often included breakfast, lunch, dinner, libations, and a roof over my head The cordial settings made it easier to borrow their photos, maps, and great ideas: Susan and Jim Galbraith, Greg and Terri Reisig, Betty Beeby, Glenn Neumann, and Burt and Winnifred Marsh Weyhing. They are unforgettable.

I am especially thankful for the love and support of my family who put up with my incessant babbling about the Chain and who aided in research, editing, grammar, questions of propriety and questions of good taste: to my wife, Margee, whose grasp of the English language solved many knotty questions and to my children, Scott, Julie, Tim, Suzy, and Angela, whose encouragement and proofreading were so essential. A special thanks goes to my daughter, Marissa, whose talents in diligent proofreading and graphic layout on the computer were surpassed only by her gumption and fearlessness to correct me when I was dead wrong.

Many thanks to my wonderfully talented brother, Eugene, for his memorable poems of our childhood.

I am grateful to those whose generosity and enthusiasm allowed me to dip into their archives for old photographs and documents found only at a local level: Mary Watson and Glenn Neumann of the Elk Rapids Area Historical Society, Dorothy and Phil Walter of Alden's Helena Township Historical Society, Carol Boros of the Bellaire Area Historical Society, Dave Wolfe, Jan and Gary Raymond, Jean Howard and Anna Patterson, Donna Booth, Mike Huntly, Carolyn Shah, Sally Malatinsky, James Aenis, and Fen's Rim Publications.

A special note of gratitude must go to photographers Phil Ohmer and Rose and Bud Bechtold. Their marvelous scenes of the Chain, both in the air and on the ground, have added enormously to this book.

My thanks goes to the staffs of the Grand Traverse Regional Land Conservancy especially Ty Ratliff, Glen Chown, Anne Marie Fleming, and to the Tip of the Mitt

Watershed Council especially Doug Fuller, Wil Cwikiel, and Scott McEwen. Their openness and generosity in sharing their resources far exeeded my expectations.

I am indebted to Charlie Meyers for his time and talent in exploring the history of the American Indians and their language. His suggestions and his extensive knowledge were vital additions.

A hearty thank you to all my friends and acquaintances (in alphabetical order) whose thoughtful suggestions, research, and guidance eased my task: Loyd and Martha Aemisegger, Leon and Shirley Beal, Ann Bretz, Tom Chandler, Vic Cole, Walter Cowles, Guy Dean, Jerry Daenzer, Bud and Erma Deater, Nancy Dunn, Gary Fraser, Mary Frey, Roger Fulkerson, Christa Gaugler, Warren Goodell, Vic Haller Jr., Peggy Hamminga, Victor Hayes, Prince Hillman, Lenore Hiscoe, Kristen Jacksa, Howard and Marilyn Kessel, Marge Kinery, Leslie Lee, Ed McDuffie, Joe and Nancy Malonis, Frank Marra, Carl and Dorothy Merillat, Art Mlujeak, Tim Moller, Sid Morkert, Richard Morscheck, Charles Murphy, Mitch and Marjorie Paradis, Lavonne Penoza, Jeff Penrod, Mike Petoskey, Fred Procissi, Jerry Roe, Mark Randolph, Lou Sanford, Valerie Santoro, Ed Scherrer, Adam Schuler, Laura Sexton, Brian Shefferly, Ken Smith, John Spitzley, Burton Stanley, Ryan Starr, Roger Strauss, John Tobias, Marie Veliquette, Fred and Kay Vermeersch, Claude Watson, Sally Weatherholt, Jackie Weber, Mary Weborg, Retha White, Amy Whitaker, Fitch and Louise Williams, Geneva Kebler Wiskemann, and Terry and Wendi Wooten.

And, finally, my gratitude goes to those nineteenth and early twentieth century photographers who wandered the shores of the Chain recording many of the memorable scenes you see here. Most of their names have been lost or forgotten, but two – –Frank Adams of Bellaire, and E.L. Beebe of Kalkaska—stand out. We are indebted to them for their good sense and impeccable timing. Without them, our visual sense of the past would be missing.

Bibliography

Breathnach, Sarah Ban. *Simple Abundance, A Daybook of Comfort and Joy.* New York: Warner Books, Inc., 1995.

Cleland, Charles. *The Environmental Adaptations of the Prehistoric Cultures of the Grand Traverse Bay Area of Michigan.* East Lansing: The Museum, Michigan State University, 1967.

Community Profile for Antrim County, Michigan. Boyne City, MI: Report by Northern Lakes Economic Alliance, 1990.

Cowles, Walter C. *Antrim Steamers.* Published Privately, 1997.

Dennis, Jerry; drawings by Glenn Wolff. *The Bird in the Waterfall.* New York: HarperCollinsPublishers, 1996.

Dodge, Roy L. *Michigan Ghost Towns of the Lower Peninsula.* Las Vegas: Glendon Publications, 1971.

Fitting, James E. *The Archeology of Michigan.* Garden City, N.Y.: The Natural History Press, 1970.

Galbraith, D. James and Susan Scott Galbraith. *Hartland: Change in the Heart of America.* Hartland, MI: Galbraith-Scott Publications, 1985.

Gray, John. "Sundown on the Marsh," *Michigan Conservation,* September-October, 1956.

Hartley, Rachel Brett and Betty MacDowell. *Michigan Women: Firsts and Founders, Volume II.* East Lansing: Michigan Women's Studies Association, 1995.

Hathaway, Richard, ed. *Michigan: Visions of Our Past.* East Lansing: Michigan State University Press, 1989.

Hinsdale, Wilber B. *The Archaeological Atlas of Michigan.* Ann Arbor: University of Michigan Press, 1931.

Jensen, Oliver, ed. *Bruce Catton's America.* New York: American Heritage Publishing Co. Inc., 1979.

Kammen, Carol, ed. *The Pursuit of Local History.* Nashville: The American Association of State and Local History, 1996.

Lee, Leslie, ed. *Backcountry Ranger in Glacier National Park (1910-1913). The Diaries and Photographs of Norton Pearl.* Elk Rapids, MI: Leslie Lee, Publisher, 1994.

336

Leopold, Aldo. *A Sand County Almanac.* New York and London: Oxford University Press, 1949.

Michigan Gazetteer. Wilmington, DE: American Historical Publications, Inc., 1991.

Neumann, Glenn. *Bay Breezes: Local History Unfolding, Volume I.* Elk Rapids, MI: The Elk Rapids Area Historical Society, 1996.

Neumann, Glenn. *Bay Breezes: Local History Unfolding, Volume II.* Elk Rapids, MI: The Elk Rapids Area Historical Society, 1997.

Nichols, John D. and Earl Nyholm. *A Concise Dictionary of Minnesota Ojibwe.* Minneapolis: University of Minnesota, 1995.

Noble, Percy. *Noble Memories, A Firsthand Recollection of Northern Michigan's Lumber Boom Days.* Nancy Niblack Baxter, ed. Traverse City, MI: Pioneer Study Center Press, 1981.

Orvis, Charles F. and A. Nelson Cheney. *Fishing with the Fly.* Secaucus, NJ: The Wellfleet Press, 1989.

Romig, Walter. *Michigan Place Names.* Detroit: Wayne State University Press, 1986.

Ruggles, Eugene. *The Lifeguard in the Snow.* Pittsburgh: University of Pittsburgh Press, 1977.

Stone, Nancy. Designed and illustrated by Betty Beeby. *Whistle Up The Bay.* Grand Rapids: Wm. B. Eerdman Publishing, 1966.

Tanner, Helen Hornbeck, ed. *Atlas of Great Lakes Indian History.* Norman, OK: University of Oklahoma Press, 1987.

Traverse Region, The. Chicago: H. R. Page & Company, 1884.

Vogel, Virgil J. *Indian Names in Michigan.* Ann Arbor: University of Michigan Press, 1986.

Wakefield, Larry. *Ghost Towns of Michigan.* West Bloomfield, MI: Northmont Publications, 1994.

Wilbur, C. Keith. *The Woodland Indians.* Old Saybrook, CT: Globe Pequot Press, 1995.

Wissler, Clark. *Indians of the United States.* New York: Anchor Books, 1966.

Appendix

Protecting the Chain

**Grand Traverse Regional
Land Conservancy**
3869 North Long Lake Road
Traverse City, MI 49684
(231) 929-7911

Tip of the Mitt Watershed Council
P.O. Box 300
Conway, MI 49722
(231) 347-1181

Grass River Natural Area
P.O. Box 231
Bellaire, MI 49615
(231) 533-8818

Elk/Skegemog Association
P.O. Box 8
Elk Rapids, MI 49629

Three Lakes Association
P.O. Box 353
Alden, MI 49612-0353

Michigan State University Extension
P.O. Box 427
Bellaire, MI 49615
(231) 533-8818

**St. Clair Lake-Six Mile Lake
Natural Area**
3869 North Long Lake Road
Traverse City, MI 49684
(231) 929-7911

Skegemog Wildlife Area
c/o The Nature Conservancy
2840 E. Grand River, #5
East Lansing, MI 48823

Friends of the Cedar River Watershed
P.O. Box 652
Bellaire, MI 49615
(231) 347-1519

**Antrim Soil & Water
Conservation District**
4770 Stover Road
Bellaire, MI 49615
(231) 533-8363

Conservation Resource Alliance
Grandview Plaza Building
10850 Traverse Highway
Suite 2204
Traverse City, MI 49684
(231) 946-6817

**Michigan Department of
Environmental Quality**
Surface Water Quality Division
120 W. Chapin Street
Cadillac, MI 49601
(231) 775-3960

Michigan Land Institute
1200 W. 11th Street
Traverse City, MI 49684
(231) 941-6584

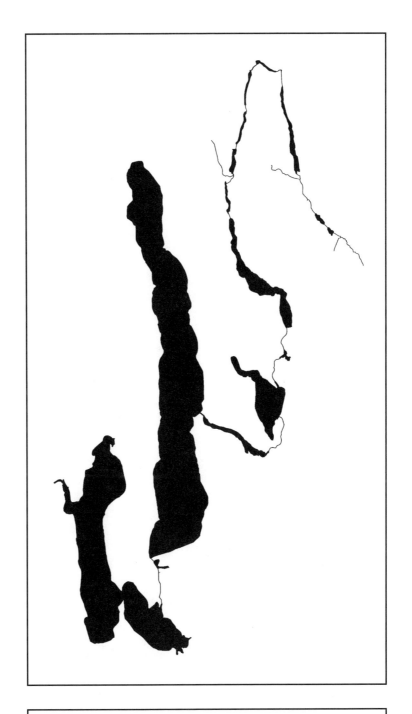

To order additional copies of **Voices on the Water**
send $29.95 plus $5.00 shipping and handling to :

Blue Heron Press
2531 Watonga Drive
Commerce Township, MI 48382

Please include name, address, and daytime phone number.